New Rules for Global Justice

*To Jo Marie
For inspiring the title
and much more!*

Zan Clair

New Rules for Global Justice

Structural Redistribution in the Global Economy

Edited by
Jan Aart Scholte,
Lorenzo Fioramonti and
Alfred G. Nhema

ROWMAN &
LITTLEFIELD
─── INTERNATIONAL ───
London • New York

Published by Rowman & Littlefield International Ltd
Unit A, Whitacre Mews, 26-34 Stannary Street, London SE11 4AB
www.rowmaninternational.com

Rowman & Littlefield International Ltd.is an affiliate of Rowman & Littlefield
4501 Forbes Boulevard, Suite 200, Lanham, Maryland 20706, USA
With additional offices in Boulder, New York, Toronto (Canada), and Plymouth (UK)
www.rowman.com

Selection and editorial matter © Jan Aart Scholte, Lorenzo Fioramonti and Alfred G. Nhema 2016. Copyright in individual chapters is held by the respective chapter authors.

All rights reserved. No part of this book may be reproduced in any form or by any electronic or mechanical means, including information storage and retrieval systems, without written permission from the publisher, except by a reviewer who may quote passages in a review.

British Library Cataloguing in Publication Data
A catalogue record for this book is available from the British Library

ISBN: HB 978-1-78348-774-5
        PB 978-1-78348-775-2

Library of Congress Cataloging-in-Publication Data
Names: Scholte, Jan Aart, editor. | Fioramonti, Lorenzo, editor. | Nhema, Alfred G., editor.
Title: New rules for global justice : structural redistribution in the global economy/ edited by Jan Aart Scholte, Lorenzo Fioramonti and Alfred G. Nhema.
Description: London ; New York : Rowman & Littlefield International, [2016] | Includes bibliographical references and index.
Identifiers: LCCN 2015043511 (print) | LCCN 2015047922 (ebook) |
  ISBN 9781783487745 (cloth : alk. paper) | ISBN 9781783487752 (pbk. : alk. paper) | ISBN 9781783487769 (Electronic)
Subjects: LCSH: Poverty. | Globalization—Economic aspects. | Distributive justice. | Equality. | Democracy. | Political participation.
Classification: LCC HC79.P6 N485 2016 (print) | LCC HC79.P6 (ebook) |
  DDC 339.2—dc23 LC record available at http://lccn.loc.gov/2015043511

∞™ The paper used in this publication meets the minimum requirements of American National Standard for Information Sciences—Permanence of Paper for Printed Library Materials, ANSI/NISO Z39.48-1992.

Printed in the United States of America

Contents

Acknowledgements   vii

List of Abbreviations   ix

1   Why Global Redistribution Is Needed   1
Jan Aart Scholte

2   Structural Redistribution through Global Social Democracy   17
Valentina Fedotova

3   Rethinking Global Investment   31
Yash Tandon

4   Engaging the Diasporas: An Alternative Paradigm from the Caribbean   43
Beverley Mullings and Alissa Trotz

5   Corruption of Anti-Corruption: Deconstructing Neo-liberal Good Governance   57
Pınar Bedirhanoğlu

6   An Alternative Global Money: Special Drawing Rights or Bitcoin?   71
Taoxiong Liu with Mendang Huang

7   Financing Global Public Goods: The Case for a Currency Transaction Levy   85
Nina Hall and Inge Kaul

8   Copyfight: Global Redistribution in the Digital Age   93
Blayne Haggart

9	From Land Grabs to Food Sovereignty *Heloise Weber*	109
10	Global Redistribution through Climate Justice *Dorothy Grace Guerrero*	125
11	Governance Innovation: Enabling Collective Action for Structural Redistribution *Lorenzo Fioramonti and Alfred G. Nhema*	139

Bibliography	151
Index	171
List of Contributors	181

Acknowledgements

We, all authors, are grateful for a very special collaboration. We assembled in June 2014 in South Africa as a diverse group. We were all concerned with global economic inequality, but we came at the issue from different world regions, different social positions, different mother tongues, different academic disciplines, and different ideological perspectives. Most of us had no prior personal acquaintance with each other either. Yet fifteen months later, we have completed a book together. It is testimony that global dialogues of diversity have enormous intellectual and political possibilities for knowledge production.

The book project has been a joint endeavour of Building Global Democracy (BGD) and the Centre for the Study of Governance Innovation (GovInn) at the University of Pretoria. BGD is thankful for generous core funding from the Ford Foundation and the accompanying vision of former Ford officers Michael Edwards, Lisa Jordan, and Leonardo Burlamaqui. GovInn is grateful for funding support from the European Commission through the Jean Monnet Research and Information Activities programme (Project N°. 538192-LLP-1-2013-1-ZA-AJM-IC). The workshop that laid the ground for this book was also made possible by an additional grant from the Gothenburg Centre for Globalization and Development at the University of Gothenburg.

The broader BGD vision and methodology has been developed through a programme convening group comprised of Diana Brydon, Jessica Byron, Alla Glinchikova, Sitiveni Halapua, Anand Kumar, Alfred Nhema, Moema de Miranda, Peng Zongchao, Heba Raouf Ezzat, and Jan Aart Scholte.

For the workshop organization, we owe a special debt to GovInn's staff, namely, Camilla Adelle, Amy Giliam, Stephanie Minou, and Sonja Theron. Colleagues John Boik, Patrick Bond, Susan George, Vito Laterza, Booker Magure, Angela McIntyre, Chris Nshimbi, and Mandeep Tiwana gave invaluable discussant input to the workshop. We also thank Amy Giliam for preparing the book's composite bibliography.

For subsequent feedback on draft chapters, the authors are grateful not only to each other, but also to Arne Bigsten, Antonio Martínez, Martin Weber, and the publisher's anonymous reviewers of our manuscript. Jan Aart Scholte acknowledges the inspiration of indefatigable activist Jo Marie Griesgraber, whose 'New Rules for Global Finance' network substantially prompted the title of the book.

Finally, we greatly appreciate the energy, encouragement, and belief of our commissioning editor, Anna Reeve.

List of Abbreviations

A2K	access to knowledge
ACTA	Anti-Counterfeiting Trade Agreement
AGM	anti-globalization movement
AGRA	Alliance for a Green Revolution in Africa
AIDS	Acquired Immune Deficiency Syndrome
AKP	Adalet ve Kalkınma Partisi [Justice and Development Party]
AR5	Fifth Assessment Report
ASEAN	Association of Southeast Asian Nations
ATTAC	Association pour la taxation des transactions financières et pour l'action citoyenne [Association for the Taxation of Financial Transactions and Citizen Action]
BEE	Black Economic Empowerment
BGD	Building Global Democracy
BIS	Bank for International Settlements
BRICS	Brazil, Russia, India, China, South Africa
CARICOM	Caribbean Community
CDM	Clean Development Mechanism
CEO	chief executive officer
CJN	Climate Justice Now
CLS	Continuous Linked Settlement
COP	Conference of the Parties
CTL	currency transaction levy
EPA	Economic Partnership Agreement
EU	European Union
FAO	Food and Agriculture Organization
FDI	foreign direct investment
FOE	Friends of the Earth

FOSS	free and open source software
FTT	financial transaction tax
G7	Group of Seven
G8	Group of Eight
GDP	gross domestic product
GFC	global financial crisis
GHG	greenhouse gas
GPG	global public good
GVC	global value chain
hinwi	high net-worth individual
HIV	Human Immunodeficiency Virus
ICT	information and communications technology
IEA	International Energy Agency
IFI	international financial institution
IIED	International Institute for Environment and Development
IMF	International Monetary Fund
IOM	International Organization for Migration
IP	intellectual property
IPCC	Intergovernmental Panel on Climate Change
ISP	Internet service provider
LDC	least developed country
LIC	low-income country
LTC	Litecoin
MDGs	Millennium Development Goals
NASA	National Aeronautics and Space Administration
NEPAD	New Partnership for Africa's Development
NGO	non-governmental organization
NIEO	New International Economic Order
ODA	official development assistance
OECD	Organisation for Economic Co-operation and Development
OPEC	Organization of the Petroleum Exporting Countries
P2P	peer-to-peer
PIPA	Protect Intellectual Property Act
PPC	Peercoin
REDD	Reducing Emissions from Deforestation and Forest Degradation
RMB	renminbi
SDGs	Sustainable Development Goals
SDR	Special Drawing Right
SOPA	Stop Online Piracy Act
SRGD	Structural Redistribution for Global Democracy
TI	Transparency International

TNC	transnational corporation
TPP	Trans-Pacific Partnership
TRIPS	Trade-Related Aspects of Intellectual Property Rights
UAE	United Arab Emirates
UK	United Kingdom
UN	United Nations
UNCTAD	United Nations Conference on Trade and Development
UNDP	United Nations Development Programme
UNEP	United Nations Environment Programme
UNECA	United Nations Economic Commission for Africa
UNFCCC	United Nations Framework Convention on Climate Change
US	United States
USA	United States of America
USAID	United States Agency for International Development
USTR	United States Trade Representative
VAT	value-added tax
WEF	World Economic Forum
WHO	World Health Organization
WIPO	World Intellectual Property Organization
WSF	World Social Forum
WTO	World Trade Organization

Chapter 1

Why Global Redistribution Is Needed

Jan Aart Scholte

Readers who open this book are presumably troubled (maybe also outraged) by global economic inequality. Today's globalized world means offshore finance, airport boutiques, and high-speed Internet for some people, as against dollar-a-day wages, used t-shirts, and illiteracy for others. Latest research suggests that the richest 1 per cent of world population own 48.2 per cent of all assets, while the bottom half own less than 1 per cent of economic wealth (Credit Suisse 2014, 11). As this book goes to press, hundreds are drowning in the Mediterranean in desperate attempts to migrate across global inequalities. How do these highly skewed distributions happen, and what can be done to counter them? That is the concern of this volume.

The book engages with widespread public disquiet. Bank bailouts, Occupy protests, Greek plebiscites, and more have all put a spotlight on global inequality. In this situation, a 700-page analysis of economic inequality that would otherwise gather academic dust becomes a runaway bestseller (Piketty 2014). Antiglobalization icon Naomi Klein likewise returns to the headlines with a critique of capitalism and climate change (Klein 2014). Others bemoan that social justice has got lost amidst obsessions with growth (Fioramonti 2013). A debate is on.

This volume's special contribution to this debate is twofold. First, the chapters collectively offer a veritably global exploration of global economic inequality; authors bring age, gender, race, and regional diversity from Australia, Canada, the Caribbean, China, Germany, New Zealand, Russia, South Africa, Sweden, Thailand, Turkey, and Zimbabwe. Second, the book is action-oriented and empowering, presenting concrete proposals that could reduce the global inequalities which most people deplore.

New Rules for Global Justice develops these proposals through three steps of diagnosis, prescription, and process. Diagnosis asks how current circumstances of global political economy generate highly skewed distributions of world resources. Prescription asks how alternative principles and rules of global governance could yield progressive redistributions of world resources. Process asks what opportunities and obstacles for implementation face these proposals for change. In short: how did we get here; where do we want to go instead; and how do we get there?

The following chapters relate these three core questions to specific suggestions in respect of various areas of activity. Chapters 2–4 address long-standing issues of the so-called 'real' economy, such as foreign direct investment and migration. Chapters 5–7 shift the focus of redistributive strategies to globalized money and finance. Chapters 8–10 put the spotlight on newly emergent issues of redistribution connected with the Internet and global ecology. The aim in each chapter is to offer novel workable ideas for resource redistribution in today's global political economy.

Ahead of the elaboration of detailed proposals, this introductory chapter discusses the general problem of huge resource gaps in the contemporary global world. This opening overview has five steps. The first section below presents the project that has generated this book, thereby putting the analysis in a context. The second section describes the nature and extent of material inequalities in today's global economy, thereby summarizing the problem under investigation. The third section identifies broad circumstances that give rise to these resource gaps, noting in particular the role of rules and policies. The fourth section reviews general types of prescriptions for global redistribution that are developed through specific proposals in later chapters of the book. The fifth section surveys process, assessing key possibilities and challenges in the politics of global redistribution.

STRUCTURAL REDISTRIBUTION FOR GLOBAL DEMOCRACY

All knowledge emerges from a context, so it helps to say something at the outset about the development of this volume. The book is part of a broad programme on Building Global Democracy (BGD). Since 2008, this initiative has pursued action-oriented research on the nature of democracy in today's more global world (BGD 2015b; Scholte forthcoming). BGD has explored how to achieve people's power (*demos kratos*) in relation to the global-scale issues that figure so strongly in contemporary society. For example, how can affected publics have due say and control on problems around global ecology, global trade, global health, global media, global conflict, and so on?

BGD has approached the question of global democracy in a holistic fashion from five interrelated angles: conceptual, pedagogical, institutional, economic, and cultural. Thus, a first project examined concepts of global democracy: that is, what the very idea of 'global democracy' could mean. A second project considered learning for global democracy: that is, how affected people could gain the information and knowledge required to be empowered actors in global politics. A third project investigated institutional processes: in particular, how marginalized (and usually silenced) groups could gain access to and impact on global policymaking. A fourth project (the one behind this book) explored economics of global democracy: that is, the material conditions for effective people's power in global politics. A fifth project enquired how global democracy could respect, answer to, and benefit from cultural diversity across the world. BGD has therefore handled global democracy as a multifaceted issue that is at once philosophical, educational, procedural, material, and anthropological.

Structural Redistribution for Global Democracy (SRGD) is the fourth and economically focused BGD project. The starting premise of this investigation is that meaningful public participation and control in global politics requires that all affected people have sufficient resources to make their voices heard and their influence felt. In other words, achieving global democracy requires more than clear concepts, educated citizens, open processes, and cultural sensitivity. Global democracy that is worth its name also demands that everyone has adequate – and equitably shared – material means for effective political involvement. If those economic preconditions are not met, then – if one wants the global world to be democratic – measures are needed to achieve a more level resource distribution.

As the next section details, today's global world is very far from that more even and just distribution. Hence, a key question for contemporary democracy becomes to understand how current huge global inequalities are produced and what could be done to reverse them. That has been the challenge for the 'structural redistribution' project and the essays collected in this book.

This volume on structural redistribution for global democracy involves, suitably, a global conversation. The contributors herald from diverse world regions, diverse cultural frames, diverse academic disciplines, diverse social groups, and diverse ideological outlooks. The project has assembled participants from the Caribbean, East Asia, Europe, Latin America, Middle East, North America, Pacific, Russia/Central Asia, South East Asia, and Sub-Saharan Africa. The group includes researchers from the fields of economics, gender studies, international relations, philosophy, politics, and sociology. Social diversity figures across age, gender, language, and race – albeit less so across class and faith. Ideological outlooks range from reformism to radicalism. Thus, while the authors in this volume are united by a broad goal to promote an economically and politically more equitable global world, they hold divergent perspectives on that objective and how to achieve it.

Indeed, the BGD programme has deliberately fostered dialogues of difference. Other thinking on global democracy has tended to come mainly from narrow and privileged geographical, social, and ideological locations. To put the point somewhat crudely, past research on global democracy has largely been a preserve of middle-aged professional liberal white heterosexual men (and some women) in the global north. (See the extensive bibliography at BGD 2015a.) The BGD premise – implemented also in the SRGD project – is that exchanges which better encompass the world's diversities can generate ideas and practices of global democracy that could be more meaningful for more people in actual global politics, including marginalized people in particular.

Together with the benefits of diversity, most contributors to the SRGD project are action researchers who combine academic enquiry with substantial engagement of governance institutions and/or social movements. Whereas much mainstream research on global democracy and global justice more generally has focused on theory (cf. Brooks 2008; Pogge and Moellendorf 2008), the writers in this volume integrate academic knowledge and non-academic practice. Alongside their intellectual labours, many of the authors have held public office, advised policymakers, and interacted with civil society and resistance struggles. This praxis orientation, too, hopefully helps this book speak effectively to the concrete circumstances of global politics.

The SRGD researchers came together for a workshop at the University of Pretoria in South Africa on 4–6 June 2014. The deliberations examined the three aspects already highlighted: namely, diagnosis, prescription, and process. The workshop explored these questions across a range of issue-areas, including climate, corruption, finance, investment, knowledge, land, migration, and money. Importantly, the transregional, transcultural, transdisciplinary, transsocial, and transideological character of the meeting generated especially searching, dynamic, and creative discussions.

With so much diversity around the table, it could hardly be expected that the SRGD workshop – and this book that follows from it – would produce a consensus on how to achieve a democracy-enhancing redistribution of global resources. That said, the three framing questions of diagnosis, prescription, and process gave the proceedings considerable coherence. The rest of this introduction examines these themes in general terms.

PROBLEM: GLOBAL INEQUALITIES

Recent research indicates that, as of 2008, the top 5 per cent of households worldwide obtained two hundred and forty-five times more income than the bottom 25 per cent (Milanovic 2013). Yes, that is an astounding ratio of

245:1. Moreover, this calculation only covers income and excludes assets. How much higher the ratio could rise if the value of private property were also brought into the equation (Davies 2008)?

Economic inequality across today's global population is larger than inequality within just about every country in the world. The global-scale Gini coefficient, a statistical measure of the distribution of household incomes, is reckoned to be as high as 70 (Milanovic 2012; also Nissanke and Thorbecke 2007). This number is equivalent to the highest country-based Gini coefficient (namely, for South Africa). A global Gini of 70 makes Brazil at 55 and United States at 48 look egalitarian by comparison, not to mention Slovakia at 26 and Sweden at 25 (Gini 2014).

The focus here is deliberately on *global* material inequality. Researchers have typically calculated resource distributions in relation to country units (cf. Wilkinson and Pickett 2010; Ostry *et al.* 2014; Piketty 2014). Yet with heightened globalization over the past half-century, it increasingly makes sense to assess economic inequality also on a planetary basis. Of course world-scale inequality is not particular to recent decades, with economic disparities between continents growing particularly after the early nineteenth century (Maddison 2001; Bourguignon and Morrison 2002). However, contemporary globalization has hugely increased the amounts, types, frequencies, speeds, intensities, and impacts of transplanetary transactions and interdependencies (Scholte 2005: Chapters 2 and 3). Thus, material inequalities are now more deeply entwined in global relations (Weiss 2005; Therborn 2006). Resource gaps have become that much more a function of the ways that people are connected on a planetary scale – and by implication, those gaps could be reduced if global relations were organized differently.

Today's global world lives with huge material inequalities. Gated settlements of the rich exist alongside a sprawling 'planet of slums' (Davis 2006). Major gendered economic gaps pervade across the globe (WEF 2013). Indigenous peoples constitute 5 per cent of current global population, but around a third of the world's extremely poor (UN 2009). Persons living with disability, an often invisible 15 per cent of humanity, likewise face comprehensive socio-economic disadvantage (WHO 2011). Other global resource divides on lines of age, caste, faith, race, and sexual orientation go uncalculated, but the structural discriminations are plain for those who will look.

Global inequality is therefore complex (Holton 2014). It is not merely, or even primarily, a question of rich countries and poor countries. Nor is it simply a question of wealthy classes and deprived classes. Nor are the cleavages only between Western and non-Western cultures, or between men and women, or between whites and coloureds, or between middle-aged and youth. These various axes of inequality intersect with each other in intricate ways (Grzanka 2014). Global economic gaps tend to become particularly large and entrenched when several structures of privilege intersect (e.g. rich country and wealthy class) and when several structural disadvantages converge (e.g. female gender and black race).

Enormously skewed distributions in today's global economy fail pretty well every test of equity. Hundreds of millions lack access to resources which could substantially improve their life chances (Collier 2008). Oases of concentrated plenty amidst sweeping deserts of deprivation offend most moral sensibilities (Caney 2005; Pogge 2008). Huge resource inequalities easily subvert democracy as the wealthy capture regulatory processes. Consequent feelings of injustice can weaken social solidarity and fuel (violent) social conflict. In addition, overconsumption by the very rich and resource exhaustion by the desperately poor inflict major environmental damage. In sum, large inequalities undermine a good society: economically, morally, politically, and ecologically (Wilkinson and Pickett 2010; Therborn 2013).

And yet, so little is done to reverse global economic inequality with proactive progressive global redistribution. 'Aid' and 'development cooperation' have a redistributive motivation, but their flows are paltry relative to global resource gaps. 'Fair trade' constitutes but a tiny fraction of overall world commerce. Transactions in alternative currencies amount to seconds of turnover on global financial markets. Global justice campaigns for *inter alia* debt cancellation and access to essential medicines usually take years to achieve limited results. Meanwhile, a more comprehensive systematic programme of global redistribution to take the world away from 254:1 and 70 is not in sight.

Certainly, there has been periodic collective resistance against global inequality. Already 150 years ago, labour movements urged international action to counter class inequalities (van Holthoorn and van der Linden 1988). In the 1970s, governments of the so-called 'Third World' jointly campaigned for a New International Economic Order (NIEO) that would reduce resource inequalities between rich and poor countries (Murphy 1984). Around the turn of the millennium, a so-called 'antiglobalization movement' (AGM) attacked neo-liberal capitalism for producing unacceptable material inequalities worldwide (Starr 2001). Similar arguments were revived during 2011–12 in Occupy and related protests on behalf of 'the 99%' (Sitrin and Azzellini 2014).

Class-based mobilizations of the late nineteenth and early twentieth century achieved some significant progressive redistribution of resources on a national scale. Welfare states developed in certain countries, and anti-capitalist regimes emerged in others. On the whole, intra-national inequalities came down considerably during this period, particularly in the first and second worlds, albeit they have widened again in many countries since the 1980s (Roine and Waldenström 2014).

Thus far, initiatives of the late twentieth and early twenty-first centuries have not achieved similar progressive redistribution on a global scale.

The NIEO, the AGM, and Occupy have each subsided without advancing a global welfare state or other significant global redistributive policies. However, experience from the era of nationalized capitalism suggests that such outcomes take time. The current moment in the mid-2010s may be a waystation in a long-term struggle for global reallocation. On this reading, the need for fresh creative proposals (as developed in this book) remains great.

DIAGNOSIS: GOVERNANCE MATTERS

Struggles for global redistribution can be greatly strengthened when actors understand the dynamics which generate the large inequalities. Strivings for change can be more effective when the sources of the problem are clearly identified, so that campaigners know what to target. To be sure, multiple and at some points conflicting explanations for global inequality are available, as is reflected in the varying approaches that are taken in the chapters of this book. Nevertheless, the authors in this volume concur on several broad points regarding the causes of global resource gaps.

One such point of general agreement is that today's global inequalities have not developed purely by accident. To be sure, accidents of birth substantially determine whether individual persons land in one or the other household, country, class, gender, race, etc. – and have their life chances affected accordingly. However, the material inequalities into which people are born have not come from thin air, but are a product of particular historically located social forces. Global economic gaps are not random, but result from certain kinds of social relations.

A second point of broad consensus in this book regarding causes of global inequality is that the huge scale of current gaps is not required in order to incentivize economic innovation and effort. Wealthy people do not need to earn several hundred times as much as poor people before they will work energetically and creatively. Conversely, impoverished people arguably would increase outputs if they obtained more than tiny fractions of overall wealth. Indeed, countries with lower Gini coefficients do not ipso facto have lower efficiency and reduced standards of living. The opposite can as well be the case, as comparisons between low-Gini Europe and high-Gini Africa indicate. Perhaps deeper egalitarianism can somewhat weaken personal work incentive, as certain evidence from the most progressively redistributive social democracies suggests (Lundberg 1985; Andersen 2008). However, global-scale egalitarianism is hardly on the horizon, and lowering the global Gini coefficient from 70 would, one could safely surmise, sooner raise economic productivity than reduce it.

A third general point of explanation is that large global inequalities can be encouraged when capitalism combines with individualism. Capitalism gears economic activity towards the accumulation of surplus, so that people produce ever greater resources beyond their subsistence needs. The question then arises how to divide those surpluses across society. Approaching allocation in a collectivist fashion – where surplus is seen to belong to the population as a whole – tends to yield more even distributions. Approaching allocation in an individualist fashion – where surplus is assigned to personal ownership – tends to produce more skewed distributions. To this extent, liberal capitalism – with its emphasis on competition among utility-maximizing individuals – can be a major force driving (global) material inequalities.

A fourth agreed broad point on causes of global inequality is that positions along the collectivist–individualist spectrum are substantially influenced by policy choice. Neither capitalism nor the way that resulting surpluses are distributed is a 'natural' process. So-called 'market forces' do not exist outside of society and politics. Instead, it is socially constructed rules that bring order and direction to an economy, and these rules substantially shape distributional outcomes. This principle – that governance matters – is as valid for a global economy as it is for any national or local economy.

To take some concrete examples, it matters hugely for the nature and scale of global inequalities when rules governing money determine that certain currencies such as the euro will circulate across the planet, while others such as the kwacha will not. Likewise, it matters substantially for the distribution of global resources when intellectual property regimes divide benefits between inventors and users in particular ways rather than others. It also matters enormously for the division of global wealth when rules of taxation determine who pays how much to which public authority. It furthermore greatly matters how rules of social policy set minimum wages, pension arrangements, access to health care, etc. And it matters considerably for global resource distribution when migration rules allow some people to move with relative ease across the planet, while others are locked into (usually highly disadvantaged) places.

Hence, huge global inequalities prevail in good part because existing governance arrangements create and sustain those gaps. By the same token, alternative rules and regulatory institutions for the global economy could significantly reallocate resources more evenly across humanity. Indeed, major progressive redistribution of global resources *requires* major changes in global economic governance.

PRESCRIPTION: NEW RULES

This book explores what such alternative governance arrangements could entail. How could rules and regulatory institutions of the global economy be reshaped to generate a more even and equitable distribution of resources? The various chapters propose changes in relation to specific regulatory measures as well as transformations in underlying principles of political–economic organization. Thus, the 'new rules' for progressive global redistribution can involve specific institutional policies (e.g., a new law or a new tax) and deeper structures (e.g. a reconfiguration or transcendence of capitalism).

The proposals in this volume are very much geared to the present-day global economy. To be sure, several of the issues covered in the following chapters were already prominent in the NIEO debates forty years ago. Ideas about decolonizing global investment (addressed in Chapter 3) and different forms of global money (considered in Chapter 6) remain relevant now as they were then. Likewise, advocacy for a currency transaction levy (Chapter 7) dates back to the Tobin tax proposal of the early 1970s, although the proposition gained broader political traction after the large financial collapses of 2008. Meanwhile, other issues addressed in this book did not appear on the NIEO agenda. These more recent concerns and possibilities include diaspora networks (Chapter 4), corruption (Chapter 5), digital resources (Chapter 8), food sovereignty (Chapter 9), and climate change (Chapter 10).

This collection of suggestions for new global economic rules is far from exhaustive, of course. For instance, further ways to promote global redistribution could be advanced in respect of arms trade, commodity prices, digital access, health care, other global taxes, and voting arrangements in global economic institutions. However, the proposals assembled in this book cover a broad range of possibilities in terms of issue-area as well as type and degree of change.

In terms of general policy orientation, prescriptions for global redistribution can be distinguished along conformist, reformist, and transformist lines. Of course, like any analytical distinction, this three-way division is overly neat. In practice, there is much diversity within each category and some overlap between them. Nevertheless, it is conceptually useful and politically important to highlight broad qualitative differences regarding the degree of change in governance that various proposals seek.

Conformist perspectives hold that existing governance arrangements of the global economy are generally adequate to deliver a suitable distribution of resources (Wolf 2004; Bhagwati 2007). Such analyses suggest that, to achieve sufficient global equity, nothing is needed beyond fine-tuning of established rules and regulatory institutions of neo-liberal market capitalism (on neo-liberalism, see Harvey 2005). Possibly, certain philanthropic interventions (à la Gates Foundation) are wanted to alleviate the deepest poverty. Several neo-liberal economists have also made equity (alongside efficiency) arguments for the removal of immigration restrictions (Caplan 2012). However, conformist perspectives generally hold that no substantial policy reconstruction is required to obtain a just global distribution.

As will be apparent from the discussion so far, this book does not adopt a conformist position. None of the following chapters suggests that minor tinkering within prevailing governance frameworks will suffice to attain equitable global distribution. On the contrary, current policies and structures are regarded as a large part of the problem. Perhaps 'balance' would urge the inclusion of conformist arguments in this volume; however, the book opts to argue strongly for change and invites its critics to make the case for continuity.

In contrast to conformism, reformist perspectives regard existing policies as a major force behind unacceptable global inequalities. Reformists argue that altered rules and regulatory institutions within global capitalism can generate more even and equitable resource distributions. The phrase '*within* global capitalism' is key here. For reformists, unacceptable global inequality is not intrinsic to capitalism itself, but a function of the kind of capitalism that policy choices produce.

A number of the contributors in this volume develop proposals in a broadly reformist vein. For example, in Chapter 2, Valentina Fedotova advocates redistribution through global social democracy. In Chapter 6, Liu Taoxiong and Huang Mendang suggest the development of a supranational global reserve system as a path towards more equitable global capitalism. In Chapter 7, Nina Hall and Inge Kaul elaborate ideas for a levy on international currency transactions to fund global public goods – in this case seeking greater equity through a reform in capitalist financial markets that could mobilize resources needed for investments in more sustainable and inclusive growth.

Several other chapters straddle a reformist–transformist line. For these contributors, global capitalism can be part of the solution to fair resource distribution, but also is not enough. For example, Blayne Haggart argues for a different kind of intellectual property regulation on digital technology, one that puts less emphasis on individual profit and more on social good. Beverley Mullings and Alissa Trotz explore how democratic deliberations in a virtual Caribbean diaspora space could generate an alternative development path in which grassroots remittances work against inequalities of class, gender, race, and sexuality.

Other proposals in this book target the very heart of global capitalism. In contrast to reformism, these transformist perspectives maintain that unacceptable global material inequalities are inherent to contemporary surplus accumulation. On this premise, governance alterations which remain within a deeper structure of global capitalism can never generate a sufficiently even and equitable distribution of resources. For transformists, maldistribution can only be overcome by abandoning globalization or capitalism, or both.

In a transformist vein, Yash Tandon argues that imperialist inequalities can be countered when peripheral countries decouple from global capitalism and local communities resist commodification. Pınar Bedirhanoğlu affirms that reformist anti-corruption discourses distract attention from deeper abuses of global capitalism which generate the larger economic injustices of today's world. Heloise Weber suggests countering the maldistribution of capitalist land grabs with food sovereignty, where localized agriculture is coupled with participatory democracy and ecological integrity. Dorothy Guerrero identifies politics of climate change as an opportunity to generate post-capitalist reconstruction for deeper social and ecological justice.

In addition to variation along the reformism–transformism spectrum, prescriptions of new rules for global redistribution also hold different views on the suitable spatial scale for the pursuit of positive change. For instance, the food sovereignty movement (discussed by both Guerrero and Weber) takes a localist position that distributive justice is best achieved through small communities living within restricted territorial places. Other 'de-globalization' strategies for equitable redistribution, as illustrated by Tandon, suggest combining local action with a reassertion of the nation-state. In contrast, other proposals (e.g. by Liu/Huang and Hall/Kaul in this volume) emphasize global-scale interventions to counter global inequalities. Meanwhile, others suggest a local-to-global transscalar approach. In this latter vein, the Mullings/Trotz proposal blends grassroots mobilization, state policy, regional vision, and global transactions.

Related to the issue of geographical scale, contemporary prescriptions for global distributive justice need to reflect carefully on the role of the territorial nation-state. For some, the state remains as vital for global redistribution today as it was for national redistribution a century ago. Certainly, the state is in most parts of the world still the best resourced and most powerful governance institution. However, other strategies of redistribution place more emphasis on suprastate (regional and global) agencies and policies. These approaches maintain that a capitalism which has substantially escaped country confines needs to be met with considerable regulation beyond the state. Then again, localists argue that even the state is too distant from the everyday lives of marginalized people, so that progressive redistribution in today's more global world is most effectively achieved through local action (Hines 2000).

Finally, it is striking that several prescriptions for global redistribution advanced in this book have an explicit ecological aspect. Links between social justice and ecological integrity were generally missing in the NIEO movement of the 1970s. They were also generally more subdued in the anti-globalization movement at the turn of the millennium. However, in this volume, Fedotova, Guerrero, and Weber all underline that redistribution needs to respect the limits of the Earth's carrying capacities. Thus, it may not be ecologically possible to achieve a more equitable global resource allocation through additional 'green growth'. Instead, structural redistribution for global democracy in the twenty-first century may require a reallocation of existing levels of output, or possibly even lower levels of overall world production (Elliott *et al.* 2008; Jackson 2009).

PROCESS: GETTING THERE

So far, this introduction has: (a) described the problem of contemporary global maldistribution; (b) identified the role of governance in generating that problem; and (c) surveyed proposals for new rules as a way to counter the problem. It remains to discuss process, namely, the politics of turning prescriptions into practice. After all, alternative ideas which are not implemented accomplish little for actually lived lives.

As stressed before, this book and its authors have an action orientation: the aim is to make a difference. Hence, the proposals for new rules need to be coupled with an astute assessment of prevailing conditions that favour and/or hinder the realization of change. Later chapters discuss the circumstances which are particularly relevant to the implementation of their specific proposals. Here, the following paragraphs note several general strategic considerations that apply to the overall struggle for global redistribution.

A first point in this regard is not to underestimate the strength of resistance against attempts at progressive redistribution of global resources. When reading a book such as this, filled with optimistic energies for change, it can be easy to forget the weight of the counterforces. Large global corporations, G7 governments, and high net-worth individuals (hinwis) are generally not waiting to cede their entrenched material advantages. Moreover, this opposition to new rules for global redistribution has enormous lobbying capacities and media influence, as well as privileged access to important regulatory institutions. Elites can go far to preserve their economic and political advantages. This was witnessed at the SRGD workshop itself when agents from global agribusiness attempted to disrupt a plenary talk by the veteran global justice campaigner Vandana Shiva.

On a more optimistic note, the current rise of new actors in global political economy could improve the prospects for new rules with redistributive effects. However, the role of so-called 'emerging powers' and 'BRICS' (Brazil, Russia, India, China, South Africa) warrants careful consideration. On the one hand, forces in Brazil have been key drivers of the World Social Forum as a major site for deliberations on global change (Sen and Waterman 2012), and the post-apartheid government in South Africa has strongly promoted Black Economic Empowerment (BEE). On the other hand, Brazil and India have often aligned with the European Union and the United States in the World

Trade Organization (WTO), and reallocation of votes towards the BRICS at the International Monetary Fund (IMF) has not (so far) generated substantial policy alteration. Is capital investment in Africa any less imperialistic for coming from China rather than Europe? It remains to be seen whether 'emerging powers' will enlarge opportunities for major progressive global redistribution (among social groups as well as among countries) or whether BRICS will simply be new sites for the perpetuation of old structures of global inequality.

Actors involved in the politics of global redistribution have also changed over recent decades with major increases in civil society mobilization. Relatively few citizen associations rallied to support the NIEO in the 1970s, but today thousands of advocacy groups around the world back a global justice agenda. They include movements for consumer protection, democracy promotion, environmentalism, health access, human rights, indigenous peoples, labour standards, peace, religious faiths, women, youth, etc. Occasions such as the AGM and Occupy have demonstrated the potential breadth of popular support for global economic redistribution.

The challenge is to convert such passing moments of generalized resistance into large, sustained, impactful campaigns that attain substantial lasting global political–economic change. In particular, a successful contemporary struggle for structural redistribution of global resources arguably requires a coalition across multiple movements (consumer, environment, women, etc.). Old strategies to achieve intra-country redistribution focused on labour unions, but this approach is too narrow today. However, forging wider combinations of a 'multitude' can be challenging (Hardt and Negri 2004), as Guerrero's discussion of the Climate Justice Network in Chapter 10 illustrates.

Also key to forging significant energies for global redistribution is to combine the forces of professional NGOs and grassroots social movements. Such alliances regrettably have remained largely underdeveloped to date. Part of the problem may be that most NGO activists (and indeed academic researchers) are privileged in the established distribution of global resources. Self-critical reflection is therefore required to think through how NGOs use their positions of advantage to unravel those very advantages. For example, how far will middle-class activists (of the kind who blocked the Anti-Counterfeiting Trade Agreement in 2012) go to a deeper reconstruction of economic governance? Relatedly, careful negotiation is needed around collaboration of elites with the subordinated circles who help make elite privilege possible. In this regard, for example, the global peasant movement La Vía Campesina has required that all of its leadership positions are filled by farmers, with elite participants restricted to support roles (Desmarais 2007).

Campaigns for global economic redistribution also face important tactical choices regarding the use of official and/or unofficial channels (Fogarty 2011; Dür and Mateo 2013). Sometimes movements may find it advantageous to engage with formal governance arrangements in efforts to refashion rules of the global economy. That means collaborating with local governments, national states, regional institutions, and/or global governance agencies. Going the formal route, change agents might run for office, participate in official task forces, and so on. However, on other occasions mobilizations for global economic change may perceive more advantage in subversive resistance to established rules and regulatory bodies. In this case, campaigners could pursue, for example, illicit trade, boycotts, barricades, and occupations. Alternatively, strivings to achieve new rules for the global economy may combine above-ground and under-ground tactics.

Another issue of particular concern to contemporary political struggles for global economic change is the role of new social media (Aday et al. 2010; Fuchs 2014). Digital communications such as the Internet and mobile telephony provide today's campaigners with significant new possibilities of virtual mobilization as well as additional tools for face-to-face advocacy. However, these new technologies may of course also be used to powerful effect by status quo forces. Moreover, service providers and governments have considerable means to disrupt activists' access to digital networks. For some people, the new information and communication technologies (ICTs) can also invite a casual 'slacktivism', where preference clicks, Facebook 'likes', and online petitions displace sustained commitment for change. Thus, like the rise of BRICS, the spread of digital communications cannot be automatically and uncritically embraced.

Whatever proponents of global redistribution make of new social media, the content of campaign communications itself needs to be carefully formulated. In particular, activists must ponder their relationship to prevailing neo-liberal talk about 'markets', 'efficiency', 'productivity', 'growth', 'development', and so on. Couching arguments for global justice in such 'commonsense' terms can have the advantage of appeasing elites or perhaps even winning over elements of established power to the cause of redistribution. However, discourse concerning 'equal opportunity' for 'individual performance' in 'open markets' is arguably also an ideological underpinning of current global maldistributions, so that any appeal to such language could compromise a campaign for change.

An alternative strategy is insistently to invoke counter-discourses which disrupt established conversations, on the argument that a fundamental re-imagination of social reality is crucial to the actual reconstruction of that reality. Thus, for example, Guerrero introduces ideas of 'climate justice' rather than 'sustainability', and Weber talks of 'food sovereignty' rather than 'agricultural development'. For their part, Mullings and Trotz invite politics to adopt alternative notions of citizenship. The challenge is to make such alternative language accessible and appealing to large publics.

Another form of re-imagination that could facilitate global redistribution relates to consciousness of global solidarity. Progressive resource reallocations within countries became politically more possible following the consolidation in the late nineteenth century of national consciousness. Ideas of national identity, community, and solidarity – however mythical – provided a mindset that disposed citizens to share resources more evenly with 'their people'. Humanitarian thinking ('we are all human beings') has provided some mental underpinning for global redistribution, particularly in disaster situations. However, more comprehensive and lasting measures against 48.2%-for-1%, 254:1, and Gini-70 require deeper consciousness of global connections and global solidarities than generally prevails today.

In sum, this book in its modest way aims to equip advocates of global economic change with novel, concrete, feasible suggestions for a progressive redistribution of global resources. As the final section of this introduction has indicated, the challenges facing structural redistribution for global democracy are many and deep. However, history also teaches that structural change which initially may seem impracticable can unfold, sometimes with surprising rapidity. For example, the welfare state was hardly imagined in 1914, but it was extensively operational several decades later. Proposals for reconstructed financial markets were dismissed as fanciful only a few years ago, but now lie at the heart of policy debates.

Hence, the possibilities for structural redistribution in the global economy can be greater than sceptics presume. The historical juncture for change may suddenly ripen tomorrow, and at that point it will be vital to have viable ideas ready. Hopefully, this book contributes to that store of knowledge-for-action – and by its formulation and promotion of new ideas also helps create those conditions for change.

Chapter 2

Structural Redistribution through Global Social Democracy

Valentina Fedotova

The opening chapter of this book has explored general questions about global inequality, laying the ground for the development of proposals to counter these highly skewed distributions. Now this and the following chapters elaborate ideas to reduce global gaps. My contribution takes a broad approach by examining how principles of social democracy that are traditionally pursued within individual countries could be scaled up to the global political economy.

Global social democracy has to date been developed only fragmentally in both theory and practice. A major problem is that global social democracy has been conceived as an extension of the post-war European welfare state and national social democracy. However, by linking global social democracy primarily with globalizing capitalism, we come to a different perspective. The chapter argues that West European notions of social democracy are inadequate for the global sphere, such that a refashioned 'global social democracy 2.0' is required.

The first part of the chapter describes globalization and considers its implications for inequality. It is noted that certain countries such as China have thrived under globalization, but many other parts of the world have struggled. For example, old-style national social democracy has weakened in Europe, Russia has faced ostracism from the West, and migrants across the world have faced very precarious circumstances.

The second part of the chapter examines several possible responses to increased inequalities under globalization. They include Christopher Chase-Dunn's notion of a transition to socialism and (especially) Anthony Giddens' prescription of a 'global third way' ('global social democracy 1.0'). From a Russian perspective, attention is given to Mikhail Gorbachev's attempts to further social democracy in a global world. Each of these approaches is found to have significant limitations.

The third part of the chapter then outlines an alternative that I call 'global social democracy 2.0'. This approach suggests that social equality on a global scale is better promoted by thinking of classes of countries rather than classes of people. Thus, new rules for global justice should be designed that redistribute resources from rich countries to poor countries, coupled with regulations at the level of national governments and international organizations that ensure equitable distribution within countries.

GLOBALIZATION AND INEQUALITY

Redistribution on a global scale has become more pressing today because of globalization. Trends of globalization are not completely new. They were also quite prevalent in the late nineteenth century, until the disruption of the First World War. The current phase of globalization began in the late twentieth century with the collapse of communist regimes and the opening of all areas of the world to global trade and communications.

'Global' refers to the geographical realm of planet Earth. The essence of globalization lies in the reduced influence of boundaries in the planetary sphere. National frontiers remain important, of course, as visa regimes and migration controls demonstrate. However, with contemporary globalization, production, tourism, and the dissemination of scientific knowledge and technology can connect most of the world. Globalization can take modernization to all corners of the planet.

This is not to say that globalization is able to remove cultural differences and overcomes the disunity of humanity. There is not a single global capitalist modernization, as suggested by some (Friedman 2005). On the contrary, this vision of planetary uniformity is a utopian illusion. Globalization has not removed social contradictions (Fedotova *et al.* 2008; Ritzer 2011). Instead, specific features are retained as the global and the local combine in what Roland Robertson has termed 'glocalization' (Robertson 1995; also Scholte 2005). The entry of non-Western countries into global modernity is shaped by cultural specificity. Samuel Huntington and Lawrence Harrison have summarized this point in the formula 'culture matters' (Harrison *et al.* 2000). Indeed, globalization has increased the importance and influence of local expressions of religious and other meanings. Globalization has sharpened differences, fears, and confrontations between cultures. For example, global migration has in many cases undermined multiculturalism and solidarity in the European Union.

Yet across all of this diversity is a unity of capitalism. With globalization, the range of capitalism has extended to all of humanity. Capitalism has evolved into a global system. After the defeat of the socialist system, capitalism has become the single dominant form of economic life in the world. History has passed the stage of liberal capitalism in the nineteenth century and the stage of organized capitalism in the twentieth century to reach the present stage of global capitalism in the twenty-first century (Fedotova *et al.* 2008). Some pre-capitalistic features remain in many countries, but these local forms of production tend still to be entwined with, and subordinated to, global capitalism.

Like any stage of capitalism, global capitalism tends to create material inequalities. Dominant forces in society generally use their power to draw disproportionate shares of capital to themselves. This trend is observed not only when capitalism operates within a country, but also when it extends on a global scale. Indeed, as indicated in Chapter 1, economic inequalities within the global sphere are today larger than inequalities in just about every national sphere.

Arguably the worst off in today's global capitalism are poor and undocumented migrants. These vulnerable workers are found all over the world, moving from Africa to Europe, from Latin America to North America, from Central and southern Africa to South Africa, from South East Asia to Australia, from Central Asia to Russia, and so on. Often these migrants lack social protections in the receiving country. Often they live in isolated enclaves, detached from the established population, its language, manners, and civil identity. Poor migrants lie at the heart of what Guy Standing has evocatively called 'the precariat' (Standing 2011).

More generally, too, recent globalization has mainly seen Western countries gain over non-Western countries. Western-dominated global capitalism has triumphed over the national capitalism of non-Western countries. There have been some exceptions, of course. For example, China has in the context of globalization successfully pursued modernization of both an industrial and a post-industrial character (He 2013). China has used global markets to achieve unprecedented rises in output of agriculture, textiles, furniture, electronics, cars, etc. That said, material inequalities among people within China have increased in the process also.

Russia has not had this happier experience of globalization. For Russia, contemporary globalization has gone hand in hand with the collapse of communism and the dissolution of the Soviet Union. While globalization opened Russia to world communication, exposure to Western-dominated global capital resulted in a significant loss of national economic capacity. US Senator John McCain exaggerates when he says 'Russia is a gas station masquerading as a country' (*The Week*, 16 March 2014), as there are substantial exports also of chemicals, manufactures, metals, and wood products. However, globalization has brought Russia major struggles with industrial development and financial instability.

Gone is the Gorbachev dream of a Europe 'from Lisbon to the Urals' or a Euro-Atlantic space 'from Vancouver to Vladivostok'. Instead, 'Europe' has been usurped by the European Union, to the exclusion of Russia. It is a return to the kind of 'Middle Europe' to which Friedrich Naumann appealed one hundred years ago (Naumann 1917). At best, Russia and Eastern Europe are considered 'the other Europe', the non-Western Europe (Fedotova 1997). Yet the European Union is only a European organization; it is not Europe itself. One must remember that much of Russia is closely linked with Europe: for example, through Christianity (albeit in its orthodox guise); industrialization; bourgeois revolutions of 1905, 1917, and the 1990s; and – of particular interest for this book – the vision of social democracy.

As an antidote to capitalist inequalities, social democracy within national states developed after the First World War and after the Second World War in Western countries. This vision was largely a reformist response to the Bolshevik challenge to capitalism, centred in Russia. National social democracy involved a social contract between workers, employers, and the state. On the one side, workers pledged to support market capitalism: they would not normally demand large wage increases or go on strike. On the other side, the bourgeoisie (employers) pledged to uphold decent wages and working conditions: they would not normally fire workers or reduce wages. The state was the arbiter in these relations, making sure that the class bargain was kept. National social democracy was a part of national capitalism.

National social democracy continues today in many countries. However, it has been weakened by globalization, which allows capital to flee to other countries where higher profits are available. This global mobility of capital, as against the territorial fixedness of the state and most labour, has shifted the power balance very much in capital's favour. So does social democracy have a future in the more global world of the twenty-first century?

THE STANDARD PRESCRIPTION: GLOBAL SOCIAL DEMOCRACY 1.0 AND ITS LIMITS

Global capitalism is subject to serious criticisms. Today's inequitable distributions of global resources result from the way that the capitalist global economy is organized and governed. Existing rules and policies contribute to the problems of maldistribution, injustice, poverty, and social inequality. Global capitalism should move towards more equitable distribution, greater environmental care, and deeper humanitarian responsibility. The question is how to achieve these goals.

Some scholars holding a Marxist or other left orientation consider the globalization of capitalism to augur a transition to a socialist society. For example,

Christopher Chase-Dunn anticipates that the capitalist 'globalization from above' will prompt a reactive 'globalization from below' that transforms the world system into a global socialist commonwealth (Chase-Dunn 2003: 201). The proposition is that a contradiction between the global capitalist system and anti-systemic movements will generate a new post-capitalist mode of production with an equitable distribution of resources.

However, this scenario looks unlikely. The past twenty-five years of contemporary globalization as well as the previous experience of nineteenth-century globalization give cause for scepticism. Both periods have seen bottom-up resistance, including communism in the first case and anti-capitalist protests more recently. However, capitalism has in each case had more power.

A more possible prospect is a convergence of capitalism and socialism in social democracy. However, this would be a social democracy which is recast for a global era. Historically, social democracy has involved many national initiatives. These country-based movements (usually consisting of an alliance between trade unions and a political party) have interacted with each other, including through the Socialist International since 1889. Yet the various national movements have not formed a single movement for *global* social democracy that addresses global issues and takes global responsibilities. The question is how this globalization of social democracy could be done.

One idea is to move 'halfway' between the national and the global level through redistributive regional regimes. Some Western social democrats have looked to the European Union in this light. During the crisis of 2008, they saw the European Union 'as the most important mechanism of cohesion in the era of globalization, giving European countries a big advantage in solving global problems' (Velikaya 2013). Yet, social democratic hopes for the European project have not been realized. This failure is most starkly demonstrated by the current plight of Greece. Also Portugal, Italy, and Spain have recently experienced materially worsening positions within the European Union.

Another vision to revive social democracy in a global world is found in the notion of a 'global third way'. This conception was developed in the 1990s and 2000s by academics such as Anthony Giddens and David Held (Giddens 2001; Held 2003, 2005). Giddens, a sociologist at Cambridge and the London School of Economics, argued that social policies could still improve the quality of life under globalized conditions and thereby ensure peace between classes. In 2001, he published a collection, under the title of *The Global Third Way Debate*, in which authors from different world regions explored how social democracy could be adapted to globalization (Giddens 2001). At the heart of the project is a principle of social democracy with global responsibility. The 'third way' is an alternative to the old right of capitalism and the old left of socialism. These ideas were also taken up by politicians such as Tony

Blair in Britain and Gerhard Schroeder in Germany. Here I term this project 'global social democracy 1.0'.

The 'third way' encompasses a wide range of proposals for reforming globalized capitalism at the level of the nation-state. In general, the perspective seeks to reinstate concepts such as public goods and social equality that were largely lost in the hyper-liberalist globalization of the late twentieth century. 'Third way' ideas include a more social state, new approaches to welfare and employment, environmentally sustainable development, socially and ecologically responsible corporations, and an active civil society – as part of a broader promotion of social capital. The overall objective is to create conditions for the maximization of human potential in a global world.

Giddens' 'global' third way is not global in the sense of regulating capital at the global level. The project proposes reforms of national social democracies that will help to spread the model of the social-democratic state to many other countries beyond Western Europe (Fedotova 2002). After all, problems of economic breakdown, social polarization, environmental crisis, and moral decay worsen as many non-Western countries join the ranks of 'development'. Thus, although the 'third way' programme was primarily designed for European countries, it is suggested to be increasingly relevant for non-Western countries as well.

Critics argue that global social democracy 1.0 does not go far enough to tame or transcend capitalism. They see 'third way' social democracy as a weak reform on the lines of Tony Blair's New Labour. Whether or not one accepts this objection, it is clear that a revival of social democracy at the national level is not on its own sufficient to meet the inequitable inequalities of globalizing capitalism that were described in the preceding chapter of this book.

Concurrently with Giddens in the West, Mikhail Gorbachev in Russia has attempted to promote social democracy for a global world. The former leader of the Soviet Union (1985–1991) has been prominent in the Social Democratic Party of Russia (2001–2007) and the Union of Social Democrats (since 2007). His Gorbachev Foundation, operating since 1992, has also explored social democracy for globalized times.

In the late 1980s, I discussed with Gorbachev why he did not implement a national social democratic project in the Soviet Union to ensure a smooth transition out of communism. After all, it was the period when he declared 'more democracy, more socialism'. In his opinion at the time, however, people did not want to hear anything about socialism. Social democracy could have happened only with the help of international social democracy. Without such help, we would get a liberal social order, which is what happened. The wider world did not support Gorbachev as a possible social democrat, and post-communist Russia instead embraced a neo-liberal course. (For Russian analyses of social democracy, see Velikaya 2013; Myslivchenko 1998, 2000, 2001, 2004; Orlov 2012; Peregudov 2000; Rabotyazhev 2012, 2013.)

After his fall from power, Gorbachev had contacts with international socialists, including former prime ministers Felipe Gonzalez of Spain and Michel Rocard of France. Gorbachev has written, 'We social democrats must understand . . . the world context . . . From this comes our responsibility for the situation not only in Europe, but all over the world. It is necessary to make a new world order, a new global world more human, to work together to solve problems and challenges of the twenty-first century' (Gorbachev 2002). But he did not propose a more specific project.

AN ALTERNATIVE PRESCRIPTION: GLOBAL SOCIAL DEMOCRACY 2.0

So do the limitations of the 'third way' project mean 'the death of social democracy' (Lavelle 2008; Cramme and Diamond 2012)? Or can one envision an alternative policy programme – a 'global social democracy 2.0' – that develops a fuller and more distinctive global character of a kind that befits the more global world of the twenty-first century? That is the task of the rest of this chapter.

Democracy

Global social democracy is a form of democracy, so it is well to begin by focusing on that core. Modern democracy is primarily a structure of the state with a system of checks and balances and an active citizenship. Democracy recognizes the objective interests of various social groups within countries and achieves compromises among them (Almond and Verba 1963: 337–74). Modern democracy has been about a *nation* living in a *country* ruled by a *state*.

Yet, *global* democracy is about people living across the planet without a world state. The cultural community, the geographical unit, and the form of governance are not the same as in contemporary society with its nation–country–state framework. Like modern democracy, global democracy needs to recognize and achieve compromises among diverse interests; however, now the groups and the processes of compromise need to operate on a planetary scale. It is not obvious how such a system can be organized to the satisfaction of all who would be ruled by it.

After all, democracy has spread around the world not only in the forms found in the United States and Western Europe. There are many other ways, often associated with the culture of the society in which democracy unfolds.

Non-Western countries are not simply borrowing the Western model; they also keep the specific character of their own identity. For example, in Bolivia the *Movimiento al Socialismo* (MAS, Movement for Socialism) government draws on indigenous cultures. In South Africa, post-apartheid democracy has emphasized truth and reconciliation processes.

Even Singapore and Malaysia – which are not usually celebrated in the West for their democracy – have found balance between three ethnic groups: Chinese, Indians, and Malays. Lee Kuan Yew in Singapore and Mahathir Mohamad in Malaysia put an end to hostility among these groups by recognizing their interests and forging policies to meet those interests through compromise. Perhaps another type of democracy in these countries cannot be built at this time.

Likewise, it should be noted that democracy is not the same as activism. Protest mobilization can be part of a democratic process of balancing inequalities among social groups, as occurred in the United States in the 1960s. However, mass activism is not always a sign of democracy. For example, many people in Russia have been concerned that recent mass activism in Ukraine was suppressing the interests of ethnic Russians, although many observers in the West have had difficulty in appreciating this interpretation of what they see as democratic developments.

What these examples clearly demonstrate is that global democracy cannot merely be a transplantation of the Western model of democracy from the national to the global level. For many people around the world – including perhaps also many people in the West itself – this approach would look abstract and unattractive. Likewise, global *social* democracy cannot merely transplant social democracy as practised in the West to a global scale.

Social Democracy Globalized

As noted earlier, the Giddens–Blair project of global social democracy 1.0 involves spreading the European model of national social democracy to countries all over the world. But this is not enough. A different way to globalize social democracy would be to make social-democratic principles the basis not only of national governments, but also of international governance institutions at regional and global levels. In global social democracy 2.0, processes of redistribution would occur not only among social classes within a country, but also among countries in the international sphere. This is the sort of social democracy which is suitable for the global world of the twenty-first century. With major globalization today, redistribution cannot stop at the national level, but needs to occur internationally as well.

In the international arena, one can think of the 'bourgeoisie' in terms of rich countries, the 'proletariat' in terms of poor countries, while the role of the mediating state is played by regional and global governance institutions. The global social-democratic contract is secured through internationally implemented redistributive measures from rich countries to poor countries. Some of these redistributive policies could be pursued through a reform of existing international institutions (such as the Food and Agriculture Organization and the World Health Organization). Other redistributive measures might involve the creation of new international organizations (such as a World Environmental Agency and a Global Tax Authority).

To take one example of such international redistribution, we can examine climate change, as also discussed in Chapter 10 of this book. Global warming is occurring mainly due to an earlier history of industrial development which has made today's rich countries rich. Now measures to counter climate change could – if they are applied equally to rich and poor countries – deny poor countries opportunities of development that rich countries have already had. Such climate policies would increase global inequalities (and concomitant conflicts) between rich and poor countries. In contrast, a global social–democratic policy would place greater burden for climate change adjustments on rich countries and allow poor countries to pursue the development that rich countries have already undertaken. Such an approach could involve emission of harmful substances into the atmosphere by poor countries, although environmental pollution could be reduced if global redistribution also extended to the transfer of new less polluting technologies and resources for enhanced education from rich to poor countries. This is what Giddens has called the 'development imperative' (Giddens 2009).

Many other globally implemented redistributive measures could be considered. Some of them are explored in other chapters of this book. For instance, in Chapter 6, Liu Taoxiong and Huang Mendang explore how different forms of global money could redistribute resources in favour of poor countries. In Chapter 7, Nina Hall and Inge Kaul propose that a tax on international currency markets could generate significant funds to improve the economic conditions of poor countries. In Chapter 9, Blayne Haggart suggests that changes to international copyright laws could redistribute wealth towards the world's poor.

Global social democracy 2.0 need not look only to the West for its inspiration. For example, Chinese policies towards Africa may offer new ideas for redistribution. China is investing in Africa with tremendous activity, including major infrastructure development which benefits the African economies as well as the Chinese industries. In addition, China is enabling large numbers of students from Africa to attend its universities. The students learn Chinese and on return are prepared to work together with Chinese companies in Africa. Of course, one must take care that these relationships do not become a new form of colonization. However, the potential for a new kind of more equitable global distribution is there.

Global redistributive measures would also discourage unsustainable large-scale migration from poor to rich countries. Neither rich countries nor poor countries are interested in huge migration flows, which are destabilizing for everyone economically and culturally. Yet, people who currently feel compelled by poverty to migrate will not do so if they see that material conditions are improving in their home countries and that inequalities with rich countries are diminishing. It might even be suggested to have a redistributive global tax which pays prospective migrants for staying in their countries of origin.

Global redistributive policies need to be pursued with care. For example, a seeming humanitarian gesture such as sending free clothing from rich to poor countries could have the adverse effect of encouraging costly production and transport in the rich country while discouraging clothing manufacture within the poor country. Such 'assistance' would not promote equitable development in the long run.

Moreover, it is important to stress that international redistribution from rich to poor countries does not replace the need for continuing redistribution from rich people to poor people within countries. After all, the poor in developing countries are often put in deprivation by their own elites as well as by developed countries. In global social democracy 2.0, international redistributive regimes are introduced as an addition to – and not a substitute for – national social democracy. Otherwise unwanted situations could arise where resources were redistributed from poor people in rich countries to rich people in poor countries. Such a process would increase rather than decrease global inequalities. Thus, global social democracy 2.0 combines international redistribution between countries and national redistribution within countries.

Global social democracy 2.0 involves a planetary contract between rich and poor groups of countries. Rich countries accept that future global development gains will be distributed in favour of poor countries. Poor countries accept to contribute their share towards challenges such as global disease control, global environmental sustainability, and global migration management. Global social democracy of this kind encourages mutual commitments and mutual trust.

PROCESS: GETTING TO GLOBAL SOCIAL DEMOCRACY 2.0

The model of global social democracy 2.0 described above may seem rather abstract and utopian. Some critics might argue that global-scale rules and policies can never work in favour of poor countries. Thus, Yash Tandon in the next chapter proposes that poor countries should delink from global capitalism, on the premise that this system will always involve imperialist exploitation. My position is more optimistic. Certainly global social democracy 2.0 faces significant challenges – as discussed in the next paragraphs – but the project also offers important possibilities.

One major challenge for a programme of redistribution among countries through the use of international institutions is to build up those institutions. Existing international organizations are generally small and lacking in resources. Moreover, other international organizations that would be needed to achieve global social democracy 2.0 still need to be created from scratch. It took a number of decades to construct the policy ideas for global social democracy, and it could take at least as long to build up the global institutions. For sure, regional institutions are already quite developed in some parts of the world and could be used to advance social democracy beyond the state while global agencies are established and expanded. Nevertheless, the task of broadening global governance must not be underestimated.

Another large challenge for global social democracy 2.0 is monopoly capitalism. Monopoly is the ultimate expression of 'free-market' capitalist accumulation. Liberal globalization of the past thirty years has led to considerable centralization of corporate power in the world. Limited numbers of mega-companies dominate in most economic sectors: agribusiness, finance, media, pharmaceuticals, and so on. Monopoly capital is not interested to see its dominant position reduced through global redistribution, and global corporations have large power at their disposal to oppose global social democracy.

Perhaps it could be hoped that monopoly capitalists would see global social democracy 2.0 as a way to avoid anti-capitalist revolution. After all, fear of revolution led monopoly capital within countries to agree to national social democracy in the West during the last century. Yet, for the time being, socialist forces remain weak in the world, and monopoly capital successfully prevents a lot of potential opposition with modest measures of 'corporate social responsibility'.

Alternatively, maybe fears of terrorism and mass migration could provide a spur to global social democracy today, in the way that the spectre of socialist revolution motivated the development of national social democracy in the last century. Global inequality is a major source of migrant crises that are set to worsen still further if structural corrections to the global economy are not made. Likewise, angers born of global inequality are a major fuel for terrorism.

A further significant challenge to the implementation of global social democracy 2.0 is the rise of the middle class globally. The middle class is not super-rich, but its economic interests (savings, pensions, children's education, and so on) are considerably tied up with the existing system of global capitalism. The middle class has expanded in the West, also in much of Asia and Latin America, and to a lesser extent in Africa as well. These circles in general do not have major motivation to support redistributions which would lower their relative and perhaps also absolute wealth. However, prevention of terrorism and migration with the help of global redistribution would strengthen their feeling of future stability and security.

Another major hindrance to the development of global social democracy 2.0 is the continued strength of national-interest mentalities. Redistribution from rich countries to poor countries is more possible when people think in terms of collective global interests (the idea that everyone will benefit) and global solidarity (the sense of a duty to support all of humanity). However, mindsets in today's global politics are still often dominated by habitual thinking in terms of national interests, where people link their destiny to that of their own nation alone. We see this inward-looking defensive approach in many current 'fortress' approaches to migration and terrorism. Again, therefore, the challenge is to turn the prevention of terrorism and mass migration into drivers for global social democracy 2.0.

Finally, as mentioned already in relation to China's expanded involvement in Africa, care must be taken to ensure that global social democracy 2.0 does not become a new 'friendly' colonialism. Redistribution from rich countries to poor countries needs to occur in a context where poor countries determine their own destiny. That is a key part of the democracy in global social democracy.

CONCLUSION

This chapter has explored how social democracy can be reworked to counter economic inequalities in the context of globalization. Earlier forms of social democracy are not adequate in today's world of global capitalism. Arising from class struggles and fears of social revolution in Western countries, national social democracy has previously provided productive cooperation and prevented extremely unfair distribution between classes. Now this older model is being tested by globalization, particularly through the greater abilities of capital to leave one country and move to more profitable sites across the planet.

However, globalization of social democracy requires more than a spread of Western institutions of national social democracy to countries all over the planet. This global social democracy 1.0 ('the global third way') does not adequately address the global mobility of capital. Instead, an alternative of global social democracy 2.0 would embed principles and policies of global social democracy in redistributive global regimes.

The proposed model of global social democracy 2.0 has great potential for theoretical development, institutionalization, and implementation. Of course, we must not be utopian and must recognize the considerable challenges that were identified in the preceding section. Yet we can also be optimistic, remembering that national social democracy also seemed utopian until the threat of revolution and class struggles turned it into reality. Today, wishes in rich countries to avoid floods of migration from poor countries and to reduce threats of terrorism can provide a strong motivation to make global social democracy 2.0 a reality in the years ahead.

Chapter 3

Rethinking Global Investment
Yash Tandon

In the introduction to this volume, Jan Scholte distinguishes between conformist, reformist, and transformist responses to global inequality. Thus, there are those who believe the current world economic order can deliver a just distribution of resources; there are those who argue that adjustments to existing institutions can bring an equitable global economy; and there are those who affirm that a systemic change is required to reach this goal. Whereas the preceding chapter by Valentina Fedotova illustrates a reformist perspective, my contribution takes a firmly transformational line. I argue that only a full-scale reorganization of economy – changing its fundamental assumptions and basic practices – can effectively counter the intolerable material inequalities that mark today's world.

The underlying structural source of global maldistribution is capitalism. A system of surplus accumulation – where the economy is geared towards acquiring ever greater material wealth – is inherently bound to generate the sorts of large inequalities that were starkly summarized in Scholte's opening chapter. When capitalism operates globally, it will inevitably produce stark economic gaps between countries and people on a world scale.

Reformist and regulatory policies are not an answer to this situation, because its roots are historical and systemic. This is not to dismiss attempts at regulating capital and its many economic and social manifestations. Proposals such as Piketty's global wealth tax are not wrong per se (Piketty 2014). The problem is that reformative attempts – such as regulating capital – are only palliatives. They have reinforced the asymmetric growth of society, the polarization between the rich and poor within and between nations, as well as between humanity and nature. And so I advance the thesis that veritable development requires resistance to the capitalist roots of modern maldevelopment (see also Tandon 2009, 2015).

My chapter focuses on the role of capital investments in creating global maldistribution of wealth and welfare, and what role investments can play in an alternative development model. The discussion is in three parts. In the first part, I analyse the concept of investment capital, including its historical and systemic roots. The second part outlines two alternative development models for investments: the 'value addition' mode and the 'resistance model'. Part three teases out the core strategic issues that need to be addressed in both the immediate and the long run in relation to the two alternative models for investments.

THE HISTORICAL AND SYSTEMIC ROOTS OF GLOBAL MALDISTRIBUTION

Misconception about the Role of Investments

There is a widely shared belief that foreign direct investment (FDI) will get poor countries out of their development crisis. All they have to do is to improve the conditions to attract investments. An interesting example of this strategy is the New Partnership for Africa's Development (NEPAD), adopted by the African Union in 2001 (Nyong'o *et al.* 2002). It says:

> Political events in a number of African countries have for a long time discouraged foreign direct investors. [What is needed is] . . . improved environment, trade liberalization, strengthening of the rule of law, improved legal and support institutions, better governance, improved transparency. On their TV screens, company executives have seen civil unrest, starvation, epidemic diseases and economic disorder. Investment conditions until the early 1990s discouraged many companies from setting up shop in African States, especially as some companies found themselves subjected to expropriation when political winds changed.

On similar lines, at the World Trade Organization (WTO), the developed countries of the West highlighted the promotion of investment and free flow of capital as one of the WTO objectives under the so-called 'Singapore Issues', introduced at the First Ministerial Conference in 1996.

However, the case for FDI is not as simple as mainstream economic literature and much popular perception makes it out to be. Even a first-year basic university course in Economics treats investment capital as only one 'factor of production', the other two being land (a catchphrase to cover all natural resources) and labour. While capital is an important factor, the underlying cause of asymmetrical distribution of wealth and welfare is the undervaluation of labour and natural resources and the overvaluation (gigantic overvaluation) of money capital. This is true in both the North and the South.

(The 'North' and the 'South' refer here to the approximate division between the Western imperialist countries and the rest of the world.)

Misconception about the Capitalist–Imperialist Dystopia

There are misconceptions about capitalism as a world system even in mainstream Marxist literature. Marx's analysis of the fundamental laws of motion of capitalism in *Capital: Critique of Political Economy* is impeccable. It has stood the test of time since it was first published in 1867. However, Marx, along with his peers, was caught up in his own Eurocentric worldview. He presented capitalism as a 'progressive force' in its times. Yes, but it was 'progressive' only in a technical sense. To be sure, under capitalism what Marx called 'the productive forces' did grow colossally; the industrial revolution beginning approximately in late eighteenth century was an epochal game changer.

But before capitalism reached its industrial maturity, it passed through five centuries of pre-capitalist birth and gestation. Marx provided a vivid picture of 'primitive accumulation' that provided the basis of capitalism in England: the massive dispossession of the lands and property of the English and Irish peasantry (the so-called 'Enclosure Movement') and the appropriation of 'the commons' by a rising landed gentry. Well before that, however, the most colossal primitive accumulation took place during three interrelated historical developments: the Crusades, the slave trade, and colonialism. These fuelled the birth of *capitalist–imperialist dystopia*. The Eurocentric narrative of capitalist development glosses over this existential reality about our epoch. We must challenge this narrative.

The Crusades as Source of Capitalist Primitive Accumulation

Following the rise of Islam in the seventh century, the Ottoman conquest of Eastern Europe had shaken the Christians. Then, for nearly 200 years – from 1030 onwards – the West advanced with much passion and rage to reverse the Islamic supremacy. Arguably the Crusades were the first 'world war'. Driven by Papal ambitions to encounter the 'infidels', by princely greed for gold and silver, and by popular zeal, the Crusaders fought nine wars between 1095 and 1291. In the First Crusade (1095–99), the Crusaders seized Jerusalem, ending in a bloodbath of Jews and Muslims. In the Fourth Crusade (1202–04), Constantinople was attacked and its riches expropriated. This was the time of the Knights Templar financial innovations that tapped into the East's gold and silver. The Fourth Crusade was significant, for it transferred the monetary centre of the world from Byzantium and the Arab world to the West. Thus, well before Columbus set sail to discover 'the East' in 1492, the West had established control over the emerging global money system with the goldsmiths of Venice and the Italian and Catalonia banking houses. Eventually, one saw the creation in 1668 of the Bank of Sweden and in 1694 of the Bank of England (Zarlenga 2001).

The Slave Trade as a Source of Capitalist Primitive Accumulation

Then came the slave trade, the second source of capitalism's 'primitive accumulation'. As summarized in *History Man* (2001):

> At the heart of the institution of slavery was the Triangular Trade. This trade started with ships being loaded in Bristol or Liverpool with goods such as salt, cloth, weapons, hardware, beads and rum. These ships, known as slavers, would then sail south to the west coast of Africa, to modern day Sierra Leone, Senegal and Nigeria. When they landed in Africa, the captains traded these goods with African chiefs who gave the slavers able bodied men and women in return. The slaves were loaded into the holds of the ships and transported across the Atlantic to America. This part of the trade was known as the middle passage and about 25% of the slaves died during the voyage . . . those who died were hastily thrown over the side into the sea. The voyage ended in the slaves being sold to the plantation owners of the West Indies, and the southern states of the USA. When the slavers had emptied their holds of slaves were then filled with sugar, molasses, tobacco, rum and cotton. The ships now sailed back to Bristol and Liverpool where the whole process began again. . . . It has been estimated that perhaps as many as 10 million Africans were supplied to America from Africa over period of 400 years.

The transatlantic slave trade must be one of the most savage episodes in human history. It also contradicts the contemporary dominant narrative that trade is a benign enterprise. It is not. Trade is war – in particular during the pre-capitalist period and in the present Empire-(mis)led accumulation of capital (Tandon 2015).

European Colonization as Source of Capitalist Primitive Accumulation

European colonization of the rest of the world was the third source of capitalism's 'primitive accumulation'. In 1492, Columbus 'discovered' what he thought was 'the East'. This was followed by extensive colonization of the Americas by Europeans. Spain, Portugal, the Netherlands, France, and England colonized the Americas, in the process destroying the ancient Meso-American civilizations, cultures, and populations. In the nineteenth century alone, over 50 million people left Europe for the Americas (Eltis 1987).

Meanwhile, trade also became a weapon of war against people of the East. In the late seventeenth and early eighteenth centuries, English 'trade' with India ended up with England colonizing India. The East India Company initially came to trade in commodities such as cotton, silk, dye, salt, tea, and opium. Over time, and skillfully playing the game of 'divide and rule', the company created its own administration and military force to rule over India. When the natives revolted in 1857 (which the British called 'rebellion'), the uprising was brutally crushed, and in 1858 the British Crown assumed direct control of a vast country approximately 13.5 times the size of England.

By this time, the English had already established a monopoly of opium production and trade in India. From the mid-seventeenth century, England (along with other European countries) was also trading with China. China was more or less self-sufficient and had no particular urge to trade with Europe, but the latter needed Chinese tea, silk, porcelain, etc., for which the Chinese demanded payment in silver. England did not have enough silver to finance this trade, and so during the eighteenth century it forced China to accept opium from India instead of silver to finance the trade. The Chinese were not keen on opium, and this led to the so-called 'Opium Wars', also known as the Anglo-Chinese Wars, from 1839 to 1860, eventually ending in the European colonization of the coastal cities of China under forced unequal treaties.

Why Not Let the Past be the Past?

One might ask: why am I relating the above story? Why not leave the past where it belongs? I should say that I am partial to the general wisdom of letting the past be buried with the past, except where the past lives in the present and continues to determine the future.

This is a key point: capitalist imperialism is still with us today. The 'triangular trade' of the slave trade era persists, though in a different form. Like during the slave trade, contemporary commerce starts from Western capitals (with the USA now in the lead). Instead of carrying beads and slaves, modern ships are loaded with capital-intensive products (e.g. machinery) and guns (like in earlier centuries) from the North to the South. In return, the South provides primary commodities (e.g. oil, cotton, coffee, minerals). These commodities go through a process of 'value addition' in the North and are then exported globally in a competitive search for 'markets' in the so-called 'free market'– a system that is neither 'free' nor a 'market'. The market – such as it is – is controlled by global corporate cartels, fuelled by money and credit ('finance capital') provided by the globalized banking system. Finance capital is still largely controlled by Western banks and finance houses located in New York, London, Frankfurt, Paris and their outposts in Singapore, Hong Kong, Buenos Aires, Johannesburg, etc.

The difference between the 'triangular slave trade' of the sixteenth century and the 'triangular commodity trade' of the twenty-first century is only in form, not in substance. A good illustration of this continuity is the so-called Economic Partnership Agreement (EPA) signed between the European Union and East Africa. Under this arrangement, East Africa supplies raw materials to industries in Europe, which then exports 'value-added' products to East Africa.

Besides, the memory and pain of the slave trade is lived and relived through generations. Thus, Caribbean nations are today seeking reparations from Europe for the enduring suffering inflicted by the Atlantic slave trade (Guardian 2014). Meanwhile, the film *12 Years a Slave*, made from a memoir written in 1853, won the 2014 Oscar for Best Picture.

ROLE OF INVESTMENT IN TWO CONTENDING DEVELOPMENT MODELS

The 'Global Value Chain' Model

This 'model' (GVC model) has acquired increased currency in recent years. It has been underscored by various national, regional, and global institutions, as well as by academics and non-governmental organizations. The model is based on the following five premises:

1. Globalization is a reality of contemporary world; there is no alternative other than integrating into the globalizing world economy.
2. In doing so, each country, and each region, must seek to specialize in the production of goods and services in which it is most competitive.
3. A country must aim to add value beyond the first stages of production, and climb to higher levels of the production cycle.
4. Accordingly, beyond the labour-intensive agricultural activities, a country must seek to industrialize and provide value-added secondary and tertiary services, such as in tourism, banking, and health.
5. For the less developed countries, this strategy entails providing incentives to attract significant FDI, investments in infrastructure and technology, skill building, and specialization.

A recent study that embellishes the concept of GVC comes from the United Nations Economic Commission for Africa (UNECA). Its *Economic Report on Africa 2013* argues

> that the question is not whether Africa can industrialize by ignoring its commodities, but rather how it can use them to add value, new services and

technological capabilities.... Making the most of Africa's commodities requires appropriate development planning frameworks and effective industrial policies that are evidence based and take into account what influences linkage breadth and depth, as well as the structural and country-specific linkage drivers. (UNECA 2013)

At first sight, the above prescription is so self-evident that it would take some nerve to deny its validity. Who would want to opt out of the globalization process? Does anyone want to join the ranks of North Korea? Or Cuba? Do you not want to make the best use of your natural resource endowments? Do you not want to upgrade your abilities and skills? Do you want to remain permanently caught in low-level agricultural activities and primary commodity exports?

All this is fine ... until one begins to locate these common sense principles in the context of hard realities on the ground. And these realities are austere and unrelenting. Yes, you want to go up the value-added spiral, but don't expect foreign capital to do this for you. And if it does, don't think that you will get the benefits of 'value addition'. It is not that simple.

For example, I carried out a survey of the flower industry in Kenya in 2009. Kenya is Europe's major source of cut flowers. The country exported 137,000 tons of flowers in 2014, up from 41,000 tons in 2001 (KFC 2015). However, I found that the flowers which ten years before had been produced by hundreds of small producers were now produced by a handful of multinationals. I also found that the industry drew water out of Lake Naivasha at unsustainable rates (Awange *et al.* 2013). The papyrus swamps that were the breeding grounds for fish had almost dried up. Thousands of peasant producers and fisher folks had been alienated from their means of survival. People were facing severe problems of food and water insecurity. Into this already very fragile socio-ecological condition, the Alliance for a Green Revolution in Africa (AGRA) has made massive investments. AGRA is funded by the Rockefeller and Gates Foundations. It claimed that it was helping Africa to 'grow' high standard exportable food crops and flowers to promote Kenya's 'development'. AGRA employed certified agro-chemical crops under multi-genome patents. The end result was plain to see: the control (in the name of 'growth') over Africa's plant biomass to generate super profits for mega-chemical and seed corporations.

What kind of 'global value-added' metamorphosis is this? Who gains, who loses? The cost-benefit analysis of this industry is evidence-based. But the story does not end here. This one 'value-added' industry – the flower industry – was the main reason why Kenya concluded an EPA with the European Unionin September 2014. Kenya also managed to get other countries of the East African Community – namely Burundi, Rwanda, Tanzania, and Uganda – to join the EPA. In fact, as least developing countries (LDCs), these four need not have done so, since they did not stand to lose preferential access to the EU market. So why did they sign up? Among other reasons was the lure of investments: 'sign and Europe will bring investments into our countries'. But at what cost? The political class in Africa – who have their hands (and pockets) wrapped up in the profit-making foreign-funded 'value-added' enterprises – do not care if the price is paid by the fisher folk, small-scale farmers, and nature. That, in the convoluted language of mainstream economics, is called 'value-added growth' brought by 'much needed' foreign investment.

But one might say that one example does not make a 'proof'. I agree. I can give literally hundreds more examples from Africa. When examples multiply by the hundreds, they cease to be 'examples'. They draw attention to something structurally embedded in the system of production encouraged by FDI.

Of course, you might argue that the answer is to negotiate better terms of engagement with the owners of foreign capital. Indeed. But that takes us into another realm – that of political economy and geopolitics. Why were South Korea, Taiwan, Hong Kong, and Singapore (the four Asian 'tigers') able to attract foreign investments into their countries during the peak of the Cold War, whereas Ghana, Tanzania, Senegal, and Zambia were not? One thing is clear: the answer does not lie in economics of 'value-added production', democratic deficits, or corruption. It lies in understanding the geopolitics of East Asia in the 1950s and 1960s as compared with the geopolitics of post-independence Africa (though, as elaborated below, the 'four tigers' met their own fate in the financial crisis of 1997–98).

I return to the question of value addition when I propose (in the concluding section) that this process should begin first at the local level, then at the national level, then at the regional level, and only finally at the global level. But this prescription also is too simplistic, since the politics of value addition are related to national and class struggles before they become a matter of state economic policy.

An Alternative Model: Resistance to Imperial Control

There are important lessons economists can learn from the American War of Independence in 1775–83 and subsequent history. The United States and Europe are today demanding of Africa and the rest of the third world that they go by Western rules. From a historian's perspective, an obvious question is: did the Americans follow the rules of their past imperial masters?

At independence, the thirteen colonies were still producing merchandise for British industries. After independence, they embarked on a 'national project' to produce for themselves and not for imperial England. Alexander Hamilton, the first US Secretary of the Treasury, advanced the 'infant industries' argument. He challenged the British, who thought that the American economic future was best served by specializing in agriculture, where they had, following David Ricardo's theory, a 'comparative advantage'. The United States defied this Anglo-centric division-of-labour argument and went on the path of industrialization. By the middle of the nineteenth century, Americans put an embargo on the export of cotton (among other commodities) to England. They needed cotton to develop their own textile industry. This is what I mean by the phrase, 'the politics of value addition are related to national and class struggles before they become a matter of state economic policy'. First comes politics, then economics.

I will relate another experience, this one more contemporary. In 1997–98, East Asia faced a major crisis triggered by foreign exchange manipulations by speculators who played the Thai Baht against other currencies. In rapid succession, several countries in the region were affected. The International Monetary Fund (IMF) moved in. It advocated, among other measures, further relaxation of exchange rates and the raising of interest rates in order to attract foreign capital to 'save' these economies. Thailand, Indonesia, and South Korea religiously did so, and they suffered the worst as a result. South Korea was burdened with FDI-dependent non-performing loans. Many of the deeply indebted chaebols (South Korean conglomerates) were forced to 'fire sale' at giveaway prices to American and Japanese companies. Samsung Motors' $5 billion venture was dissolved, and Daewoo Motors was sold to the American company General Motors (Woo-Cumings 2003). The only cuckoo that flew over the nest was Mahathir Mohamed, Prime Minister of Malaysia. He resisted. He ignored the IMF advice and imposed capital and exchange controls. Malaysia came off the crisis much better than the others. Some commentators have dubbed this the 'Mahathir Doctrine' (Pesek 2015).

Those who believe that FDI is an answer to development might want to rethink. *National resistance against imperial imposition is the first law of motion of development.* You might be forced to accept defeat in resisting the will of the Empire, but the Empire cannot suppress your national will forever. Some may argue that nationalism is an outdated ideology, that globalization is the new reality. However, this view is an ideological position. Even as the European Union strives for regional integration and a diminution of sovereignty, nations such as the Scots and the Catalonians are still aspiring towards self-determination.

Economics is an abstraction from a concrete geopolitical reality. And economic theory – outside of certain basic propositions – is an ideology of the hegemonic powers. There is no such thing as 'the free market'. It does not exist even within a national economy (including that of the United States), let alone regionally or globally.

The main movement of our time is not globalization, but decoupling from it. Globalization demands following the rules created by the hegemons. Decoupling does not mean you do not participate in the global economy, but it means that you do so on your terms, and not on terms imposed by the IMF, the World Bank, the WTO, or the so-called 'donors'. How do we pursue this resistance against oppression and exploitation? I suggest a seven-point strategy.

Clearly, our first obligation is to obliterate from our psyche the widely (wildly) held misconceptions about the role of FDI as pushed by the World Bank–IMF ideologists, the so-called 'donors', and mainstream economists. Capital is of course important, but the other two factors of production – natural resources and labour – are far more important, because at the end of the day they are the ones that create value. Capital, as Marx clearly explained, is simply appropriation of value after workers are paid wages and nature is replenished. FDI is simply the accumulated wealth of the West as a result of over five hundred years of exploitation of the labour and natural resources of the South.

Second, *we need to understand that hegemonic forces in the West have no interest whatsoever in developing the rest of the world. It is as simple as that.* The underlying cause of the asymmetrical global distribution of wealth and welfare is the undervaluation of labour and natural resources (the bulk of which are in the South) and the overvaluation (gigantic overvaluation) of money capital (whose sources lie overwhelmingly in the West, nowadays including foreign reserves of China and the Gulf countries).

Third, we need to understand imperialism. Imperialism is not a fleeting phenomenon; it is a long-term structure that remains central to the present reality. Imperialism changes its form and colour, but it essentially remains the same. In his *Neo-Colonialism: The Last Stage of Imperialism*, Kwame Nkrumah, the first president of independent Ghana, said,

> The neo-colonialism of today represents imperialism in its final and perhaps its most dangerous stage. . . . The essence of neo-colonialism is that the State which is subject to it is, in theory, independent and has all the outward trappings of international sovereignty. In reality, its economic system and thus its political policy is directed from outside. (Nkrumah 1965, ix)

Fourth, decoupling from the imperial system is imperative. Of course, decoupling must be done in an intelligent manner. It must be properly strategized and sequenced. The 'value addition' must be done first at the national level: for example, using locally grown cotton in Uganda to develop textiles mills and ancillary industries (such as ginning machinery). At a higher level, value addition must be done at the regional level: for example, in the East

African region tariff barriers must first be removed intra-regionally with a common external tariff. Africa might need to levy export tariffs on raw commodities in order that these are used for value-added industrial production, nationally and regionally.

Fifth, working people must struggle for just returns to their labour. The owners of capital will not oblige by giving workers their due. Over the last three hundred years, the workers in the West have won significant battles, but they are now up against the walls of austerity by the same forces that wantonly exploit wage labour in the South. Whereas the first four points are about national resistance, this fifth point concerns resistance by the oppressed and exploited classes within nation-states. All positive developments – whether it is by women against male domination or by workers against their employers – are products of resistance.

Sixth, resistance must be non-violent. Violence – at all levels, global, national, and in the workplace – is perpetrated by the oppressing imperial nations, by neo-colonial states, and by private corporations. The oppressed nations and workers are often provoked by these acts of violence to resort to counter-violence in defence. But history shows that resistance by nations, workers, and oppressed sections of society (women, immigrants, and others) are by and large non-violent. The realization of the fruits of non-violence takes time, but when the fruits are ready to harvest they are sweeter and more enduring.

Finally, at the local or community level, ordinary people in the long run have to make a conscious effort to innovate ways and means of decoupling from the iniquitous system of market-based value. At the heart of the contemporary civilizational crisis is the reductionist logic that values everything in terms of money. Everything, including the dignity of the individual – especially vulnerable women and children – is subjected to the 'law of value'. Everything is commoditized. However, in the interstices of this globalized system, there are heroic efforts by some communities to distance themselves from the capitalist–imperialist system. These innovative approaches include production of goods and services based on exchanges without involving money. Also, where money is needed as a medium of exchange, resistance communities have created 'communal money' (a kind of labour voucher system) that is delinked from national currencies notoriously exposed, especially in our times, to fluctuations and speculations.

The ancient Chinese sage Sun Tzu said: 'When your strategy is deep and far-reaching, you can win before you even fight' (Sun Tzu 1991). His wisdom should be on the desk of every fighter against oppression and exploitation. The capitalist–imperialist ship is sinking. It is time to strategize for launching a thousand boats in the ocean.

BY WAY OF CONCLUSION

The reductionist logic that puts capital investment as the engine of growth is an ideological proposition . . . and fundamentally flawed. What is missing is an appreciation that politics, not economics, is in command. There is simply nothing like investments outside of their political context. Abstracted from the politics of power, economics is a cuckoo land.

I agree with those who argue that, if developing countries wish to participate in a globalized economy, they need to find a niche in 'global value chain'. Except that it is not that simple. Why? Because the dominant global power structure controlled by the Western imperial countries cannot allow developing countries to join the global value chain . . . except on their terms. The problem is essentially political. To the extent that the BRICS (Brazil, Russia, India, China, South Africa) have developed, it is in defiance of the power hegemons – the United States, Europe, and Japan. Appearances notwithstanding, BRICS have developed because of decoupling from the Empire-controlled global economy.

To reiterate: decoupling is not a matter of choice, but an imperative. This chapter has provided merely an outline sketch of how decoupling can be achieved by the developing countries in a non-violent, sequenced manner from local, to national, to regional levels. The policy implications of this strategy demand nothing less than a transformational re-engineering of the political economy of development.

Chapter 4

Engaging the Diasporas
An Alternative Paradigm from the Caribbean[1]

Beverley Mullings and Alissa Trotz

Drawing on the experience of the Caribbean, this chapter attends to the possible place of diaspora in conversations about structural redistribution for global democracy. We contend that, for the last thirty years, whether through coercion or willingly, nearly every nation-state in the Caribbean region has embraced a vision of development that has been unquestioning in its embrace of free markets as the main arbiter of value. Influenced by academic critiques of neo-liberalism by political economy scholars, we seek to engender conversations that explore alternative visions of social transformation, prioritize questions of social justice over market efficiency, and engage forms of democracy that embrace and include the diversity of groups that exist in the Caribbean, a formal geographic region with 39 million people and a combined landmass approximately the same size as the United Kingdom, as well as a deterritorialized diaspora of approximately 6 million people dispersed primarily across North America and former colonial powers in Europe (Nurse 2006).

DIAGNOSIS

The Caribbean is a region characterized by contemporary forms of maldistribution that bear the traces of earlier systems of plantation slavery, colonialism, and an international division of labour that historically consigned much of the region to the production of primary agricultural goods and the extraction of mineral resources. The systems of social inequality that were created during these periods also continue to haunt the region by producing new patterns of social exclusion for those at the intersection of marginalizing gender, race, sexuality, and class oppressions. While much has changed since the

1960s, when a large number of the nation-states gained their independence, the Caribbean has remained susceptible to the vagaries of a global economic system whose rules and policies continue to favour larger, more powerful nation-states and corporate interests. And these vulnerabilities have become more stark and destabilizing over the last thirty-five years, as the region finds itself increasingly entangled in the crosshairs of an ever more complex set of global rules aimed at limiting aid, deregulating trade, and disciplining indebted countries unable to attract capital to their shores. Rather than leading to expanded levels of output, inward investment, and employment, the neo-liberal policies implemented by most governments in the region have generated deep-seated economic stagnation, indebtedness, and a general loss of productive capacity.

Manifested in high levels of unemployment, poverty, crime, and, increasingly, environmental destruction, the Caribbean region in the twenty-first century faces new and intensified forms of maldistribution that increasingly pose a threat to its very existence. This is a point amply made by Norman Girvan who, in a 2012 keynote address marking the fiftieth anniversary of Jamaican and Trinidadian independence, noted that in the case of Jamaica more than half of that time had been spent under the direct management of Washington-based international financial institutions (Girvan 2012). As Girvan mused, it was ironic that Jamaican economic policy today is as much a reflection of the power leveraged by external institutions like the International Monetary Fund (IMF), as it was during the period of colonial rule when the island's policies were determined by a governor appointed from Britain.

Throughout the region's history, migration has served as an important individual and household strategy for overcoming the structural inequalities associated with high rates of unemployment, poverty, and violence. Indeed, the figures for extra-regional migration are so extensive that one could say that migration must be considered an essential feature of the region's relationship with the wider world. One has only to observe the pattern and history of Caribbean migration itineraries to get a sense of the influence that metropolitan centres, largely in the Global North, have exerted over the intensity and direction of these flows. Whether through specific recruitment drives (as was the case during the 1950s when Britain sought West Indian workers to staff its transportation and health care sectors and in the 1960s when the Canada government recruited women to work as domestic servants), or through specific immigration policies (such as family reunification or temporary farm worker or skilled worker programmes), patterns of Caribbean migration have always reflected the labour interests of metropolitan centres.

The impact of these outflows on patterns of maldistribution within the region have been significant. For some countries, emigration has been a welcome solution to problems of high unemployment, a pressure valve so to speak for potential social unrest. But, for many countries, emigration has had a deleterious effect on their stock of skilled human capital. One of the most significant characteristics of Caribbean migration has been the loss of tertiary-educated population, with the region accounting for most of the top 20 countries in the world in terms of skilled emigration rates. In 2005, Docquier and Marfouk estimated that approximately 70 per cent of the region's tertiary-educated population had emigrated (Docquier and Marfouk 2005). Topped by Guyana, where an estimated 89 per cent of tertiary-educated population had left, and followed by Jamaica, Saint Vincent and the Grenadines, and Grenada, with outflows estimated to be as high as 85 per cent, the loss of skilled human capital has been devastating.

Migration is an essential part of Caribbean culture, because it is the source of most of the network flows that are redefining the geography of region (Trotz and Mullings 2013). Through transnational flows of money, care, cultural practice, and ideas, the practices of Caribbean people living abroad have been integral to redrawing the very boundaries that define what and where the Caribbean is. For example, it is common for musicians to build careers through close engagement with Caribbean communities not only in the region, but also across a number of global cities. Similarly, the success of mega-events like Caribana and the Notting Hill Carnival is a result of the transnational and iterative flow of musicians, costume designers, and advertisers between specific islands and urban centres in the Global North. It is in large part due to these boundary-crossing migratory histories that the Caribbean can no longer be understood as simply a set of co-ordinates on a territorial map, but rather as an imagined community with ancestral pathways that connect widely disparate groups of people across space and across generations. It is the promise that these current diasporic flows offer to efforts to overcome the historic patterns of maldistribution, that has over the last decade galvanized nearly every state in the region to develop programmes and policies to incorporate migrant communities abroad as diasporic partners in development.

In what follows, we problematize current state overtures to populations overseas in the face of, and as an emergent and increasingly prominent response to, the crisis and offer some preliminary suggestions for a different kind of conversation about diasporic involvement, one that potentially opens up a space to recover 'the human' as a primary lens from which to value economic and political life. We see this alternative approach as essential to disrupting the hegemony of the market and its dominance over the ways we think about and prioritize the creation and distribution of value in everyday life. We also hope to unsettle the territorial trap that marks most contemporary strategies of diasporic engagement. We identify the region as an appropriate space for the creation of a more generative approach, and highlight a few elements and challenges that such a scaling up might entail for rethinking the involvement of diasporic populations in discussions and policies about the Caribbean's future.

Against a backdrop of economic crisis and social instability, and in the context of decreased foreign direct investment (FDI) in the Caribbean, diaspora is increasingly being named as the space of possibility, a place where emotion has increasingly become a preferred technology of the state to encourage and direct diasporic capital flows, indeed to produce overseas Caribbeans as faithful, even if *transterritorial*, patriotic subjects. In fact, such transterritoriality becomes privileged as a preferred mode of engagement, since the diasporic, fluent, networked and embedded subject in the metropolitan heartlands is not simply a potential investor. The anticipatory relationship extends beyond diasporic subjects' 'bilateral' relations with their countries of origin, to encompass how they might offer access to capital and forge effective partnerships with flows of FDI that are not 'native' to the region, as it were. In this view, diasporic subjects are also conduits that facilitate and mediate relations between international capital and Caribbean states.

Throughout the 1990s, academics and development institutions drew our attention to the transterritorial nature and importance of the categories of practice, projects, claims, and stances of increasingly multi-generational migrant communities. Recognizing the active and enduring nature of migrant connections to place, the term 'diaspora' has slowly replaced the term 'migrant community', because it draws attention to the developmental possibilities that these transnational flows offer. The shift in language from migrant to diaspora has been indicative of an increasingly instrumental approach in some quarters, one focused on orienting diasporic practices, claims, and projects towards specific material goals – primarily growth-generating ones. It is therefore not surprising that most of the attempts of Caribbean states and their development advisors to integrate diaspora into their development strategies have focused on ways to re-orient remittances towards investment ends. Remittances remain a key source of external resource flows for many Caribbean countries, far exceeding official development assistance and more stable than private debt and portfolio equity flows. Accounting for as much as 20 and 14.5 per cent of GDP in Haiti and Jamaica, respectively (IDB 2010), remittances have become increasingly attractive as a financial instrument that offers greater access to capital markets.

While many of the early policy interventions adopted by Caribbean governments focused on simplifying and reducing the transaction costs associated with sending money back home, there have been two noticeable shifts since the start of the new millennium in the way that diaspora is being imagined by Caribbean states and international development organizations. The first has been a growing interest in incorporating highly skilled and professional Caribbeans living abroad into national development plans, and the second has revolved largely around the financialization of diaspora capital. In this context, whereas the high emigration rates of the region's skilled populations would have once been regarded as a source of brain drain and a loss of capital to the region, by the end of the 1990s this way of thinking about emigrants had shifted. As the power of diasporic attachments to place became increasingly evident, and the integral role played by diaspora in the economic turnaround of countries like India and China became more apparent, Caribbean states and development institutions increasingly began to explore the possibilities of re-engaging with their middle classes abroad. The idea that diaspora could be a source of brain gain, particularly if they shared their market networks and skills, galvanized organizations like the International Organization for Migration (IOM) and the United Nations (UN) to advocate for the revitalization of migrant return policies. More recently, even these policies have undergone transformation, with governments no longer entreating skilled diasporans to return, but rather encouraging them to remain in their countries of settlement and assist from afar. Whether as ethnic lobbyists, nodes in business, or philanthropic networks, skilled migrants are increasingly regarded as potential partners of the state, offering possibilities to restore much of the human and economic capital lost to the region over the last thirty years. A number of countries have sought to re-establish a connection with their skilled populations in the hope of reclaiming some of this attrition of human and cultural capital. For example, governments in Jamaica, Guyana, Grenada, and Barbados are all in the process of developing skills databases aimed at identifying the location, size, resource level, and capacities for investment and trade among their diasporic populations. In Jamaica's most recent draft diaspora policy, the state's vision of the role that skilled diaspora might play in national development was made clear (Government of Jamaica 2015). In creating a database of skills, the Jamaican state hopes to encourage specific groups to develop knowledge networks that could be utilized to identify experts who could fill areas of labour shortage or be contracted to work on development projects funded by international development agencies and foreign investors. Diasporans are also encouraged to become active citizens in the places where they reside, so that they may engage in diasporic diplomacy – that is, forms of political engagement aimed at influencing the economic and political decisions made by the governments in the countries where they reside, that could adversely affect the Caribbean. It is envisaged that an active diaspora has the capacity to influence how states in metropolitan centres formulate policies and laws related to immigration, taxation, and investment in ways that are mindful of the harm that they may exact on the region and its development (Kapur 2010).

With regard to the second trend, since the new millennium attention has shifted to developing new policy instruments for linking remittances to financial products like micro-insurance for small enterprises and, most recently, as a means to access capital markets. Diaspora bonds are the most popular of current initiatives to financialize remittances. Diaspora bonds are debt instruments issued by a country or a private corporation to raise financing from its overseas diaspora. These bond issues tend to be targeted towards members of a national community abroad, on the presumption that their emotional ties to a country will compensate for the low creditworthiness of the bond issuer. For countries with poor credit ratings, obliged to pay high rates of interest in order to access credit in international capital markets, diaspora bonds with their lower rates of interest offer national governments a 'patriotic discount', as Dilip Ratha refers to it: that is, a discount on the value of the credit risk compensation ordinarily demanded by international creditors in the form of higher interest rates. Estimating the savings of the region's diaspora to be approximately US$ 10 billion, in a 2012 address to the Caribbean Association of Banks, Trinidad and Tobago Central Bank Governor Jwala Rambarran declared that diaspora savings represented 'a potential alternative source of long-term funding for the Caribbean' and urged banks to be innovative in their embrace of flexible bond instruments (Dickson 2013).

While most Caribbean governments see a re-engagement with diaspora as a pragmatic and innovative solution to the crises of debt, sluggish exports, and weak foreign exchange earnings that continue to stymie social transformation in the region, few have questioned the political rationalities that guide these emerging diasporic policies. Indeed, it would appear that there has been little or no critical reflection on the limits of diaspora as a space for social transformation. Could it be ethically dangerous to instrumentalize the emotional attachments to place that hold diasporic exchanges together? Thus, few scholars have questioned the extent to which efforts to instrumentalize diaspora transfers adhere to a neo-liberal frame that prioritizes forms of market engagement as the primary mechanism through which social transformation can emerge. We believe that framing the relationship primarily within the grammar of free market competition, export growth, and external direct investment limits the social transformational possibilities of diasporic engagement.

TOWARDS AN ALTERNATIVE VISION OF DIASPORIC ENGAGEMENT: THE CARIBBEAN E-DIASPORA

It is clear that discussions of social transformation in the context of the Caribbean cannot *not* engage the diaspora. As we have argued, however, the forms of diasporic engagement that are emerging are too state-driven and national in scope and excessively oriented towards the grammar of free market competition, export growth, and external direct investment. The disproportionate emphasis on appealing to diaspora members with greater potential for generating global investment capital runs the risk of replicating structures and practices that predominantly benefit elite circles at home and abroad, a trickle-down model that has not worked in the past and that will only aggravate growing inequalities within the region.

It is imperative that we *interrupt* what are still incipient processes of formal diasporic engagement in the region, if we are to imagine and work towards a different development path, one that prioritizes questions of social justice and the structural maldistributions of the region's colonial past and present. What kind of institutional architecture might best be up to the task of contributing to this much needed epistemic shift? How might we make a more diverse range of actors visible, and centre ideas and practices that contest what is fast in danger of becoming a normative neo-liberal diasporic script that frames and limits our horizons of possibility?

To answer these questions, we explore the possibilities that dialogue across the diaspora offers to the creation of a renewed and transformatively democratic sphere of interaction. Drawing on the work of radical democracy scholars (Laclau and Mouffe 1985; Rancière 2006; Dahlberg and Siapera 2007), we believe that the process of foregrounding social justice in conversations about maldistribution in the region can only begin if we change the terms of engagement, the modes of governance so to speak, in Caribbean political discourse and practice. Like radical democracy scholars, we believe that efforts to encourage greater diasporic engagement must be part of a broader vision of Caribbean social transformation, aimed at creating a political culture that welcomes the wildly different, contentious, and antagonistic views of different individuals, groups, and interests in the region and the diaspora. Such a political culture deliberately aims to reach out to previously marginalized, excluded, and dissenting voices, because of the value that a politically active citizenry offers to reshaping development trajectories.

To this end, we propose the creation of an e-diaspora: a Caribbean virtual space, embedded in local community practices whose interactions can be enhanced and extended by digital exchange. There are currently numerous websites and blogospheres where Caribbean diaspora members exchange ideas, but for the most part they exist as autonomous sites, leading to a disconnect in virtual space that is productive of and produced by offline encounters. There are also multiple government-organized websites that engage a diasporic audience, but from a distinctly national-territorial perspective (single country). Most national government sites also serve primarily as spaces for the dissemination of local event information (single issue), rather than as spaces for dialogue. Few online spaces appear to engage consistently and meaningfully with groups and organizations in the region itself, including with civil society organizations in the Caribbean, which face their own resource and other challenges with information and communication technologies (ICTs) (Hinds Harrison 2014). A Caribbean e-diaspora that focuses on the region–diaspora interface, and with a specific mandate to redirect the conversation away from neo-liberal pragmatics and the pursuit of investments and towards the longer-term participatory structures needed for global justice, can serve as one important aggregating space for sharing critical interventions. Ideas and activities generated within this virtual regional diasporic space would not need to be harmonized with the initiatives devised by each national state, but rather would serve to open up, challenge, and propose alternative ways of thinking about and engaging with particular development trajectories. What perhaps is the most important contribution that a regional e-diasporic space can offer is the opportunity for heterogenous individuals and groups, with very different ethico-political principles of freedom and equality, to bring their positions and priorities into conversation with each other.

Let us turn to an example as a way of elaborating the intervening potential of the e-diaspora. Conceiving of remittances differently from the disembodied calculations of economic value privileged by governments and international financial institutions, the e-diaspora could enable a different kind of discussion, one that foregrounds diverse stories of departure, describes the nature of the transfers home, and captures the meaning and the deep emotions that lie behind—and are the condition of possibility of—these transfers. In the first instance, such an approach underscores the crucial role that grassroots remittances (of approximately US$100–$161 per month (Thomas-Hope et al. 2009; Simmons, Plaza, and Piché 2005) have played in keeping afloat families displaced by the depredations of over two decades of structural adjustment policies. These are mostly familial transfers, but they also extend to diasporic initiatives to support communities and institutions experiencing the effects of state disinvestment (schools, churches, etc.). Importantly, it is Caribbean women (and *not* transnational capital) whose practices of transnational kinship predominantly emerge as the basis for the reproduction of families in the region. Secondly, rendering remittances as a complex set of economic, social, political, and affective practices makes it more difficult to capture these flows in strictly instrumentalist ways. *Valuing* these transfers, not just as material flows, but even more importantly in terms of the *relational ethos* that is implied in the act of remittance, is essential if recognition is to avoid efforts to simply conscript these resources in the service of dominant economic arrangements. In other words, the challenge is 'to shift our now almost instinctive understanding of dependency as something to be disparaged and avoided at all costs to a definition that speaks of a sense of interdependence, of relation that nourishes and values all lives' (Trotz 2013a). We therefore suggest that the e-diaspora can function as a space that takes the transnational survival strategies of Caribbean peoples as the starting point for re-visioning the foundation of economic, political, and socio-cultural life. What is the *human* dimension operating here, and how might it disclose a stubborn capacity to live beyond and through the current crisis facing the region?

Remittances are but one example. Other practices like *susu/partner/ box hand* – informal savings mechanisms in which members of a group contribute a set amount of money regularly over a fixed period of time, with each member drawing the full installment at each 'throw' until everyone has benefited from the bulk payout – are not only widespread in the region, but also important in diasporic communities and an avenue through which bulk purchases and contributions are sent back to the Caribbean. This is just one of a number of possible prototypes for building solidarity economies, scaling up the vital ingredients of trust and obligation that undergird these practices to develop forms of mutual welfare, regional modes of justice, and competitive (with a small c) forms of production in ways that support diaspora members across the Global North and South.

An e-diaspora can therefore have an important role to play in shifting the focus away from the state and elite diasporic actors to reveal other landscapes populated by a far more heterogeneous range of subjects. Not only does it foreground a different set of priorities and preoccupations, but it also potentially democratizes the space for social engagement, by making visible the grassroots men and (especially) women whose daily sacrifices account for household and community maintenance as well as for a significant percentage of foreign exchange earnings in the Caribbean, but who thus far have been excluded from decision-making processes. We suggest that foregrounding these actors is more conducive to making space for a different kind of diaspora discussion, one that does not insist on the primacy of 'finance, business, investment and law enforcement' over 'welfare, social justice and human rights', as has been the case in at least one of the Jamaica diaspora gatherings (Mullings 2012, 422).

As academics, we are also deeply mindful of Trinidadian economist Lloyd Best's (1967) injunction, so many years ago, that 'thought is the action for us', and situate this proposal in the Caribbean radical intellectual tradition that has left traces of its work in the *New World Quarterly* and *Fortnightly* journals it published and distributed across the region in the 1960s and 1970s, involving and challenging students and lecturers at the University of the West Indies and the University of Guyana to see public intellectual work as a constitutive dimension of their academic worlds. We see these traces in, and take our example from, such contemporary examples as the blog maintained by the late economist and New World member Norman Girvan (www.normangirvan.info); the Pan-Caribbean web forum that is a key source of regional news (www.1804caribvoices.org); and the feminist collective and online blog, Code Red for Gender Justice (http://redforgender.wordpress.com/), which is fast becoming the virtual platform for a new generation of young activists in the Caribbean.

Many critical scholars are already asking questions that trouble the immediacy and pragmatism of neo-liberal strategies for social transformation. Others have uncovered longer genealogies of Caribbean diasporic formation and organizing – like Marcus Garvey's Universal Negro Improvement Association – that sought to connect local challenges to exploitation with global concerns regarding levels of inequality and dispossession. The e-diaspora we propose also puts institutional privilege to work in the service of social justice, challenging us to creatively draw on the transnational infrastructure that we are embedded in (interacting via socially mediated network spaces such as disciplinary conferences, listservs, etc.) to make our historical and ongoing research on these key questions available and accessible to much wider publics. The academy thus has a key role to play in the elaboration of connection, helping to nurture the sorts of regional and transnational virtual exchanges that will be necessary to shift the terrain upon which conversations about diasporic engagement take place.

PROCESS

Building a sustainable space of diasporic engagement through the e-diaspora requires a vision that is Pan-Caribbean, regional rather than national, and that combines broad and critical intellectual exchange with pragmatic problem-solving strategies. Given the small size of nation-states in the Caribbean and the similarities of the problems they face, a collective approach seems most conducive to addressing the structural issues facing national economies and societies. One challenge is to dislodge the 'long-distance nationalism' (Fouron and Glick Schiller 2001) that tends to shape the imaginary of overseas communities and restricts their transnational activities to exclusive relations with the country of origin/heritage. This binary orientation is exacerbated by Caribbean state-led diaspora initiatives that for the most part involve reaching out only to 'their' citizens abroad.

One of the ironies of the contemporary moment is that, as Caribbean states attempt to transnationalize their spheres of influence, efforts to capture the attention and resources of deterritorialized populations are primarily via the invocation of nationalist imaginaries of belonging that run the very real risk of reinforcing gender, race, class, and sexuality inequalities by identifying priorities that reflect dominant concerns. Scaling up of the sort we envision here does not *ipso facto* render these forms of social exclusion irrelevant, but it offers a wider space that might better sidestep the imprisoning effects of localizing strategies at the national level. A regional approach can help to democratize the space within which diasporic exchange takes place, because many of the stubborn social divisions that influence how specific national diasporic policies are implemented would be subject to scrutiny and challenge by those who are not as intimately connected to those divisions.

It is also important to point out that, while our emphasis is on the promise of an e-diaspora space for shifting the epistemological terrain that is being used to justify the terms under which Caribbeans continue to be inserted into an already unequal system of global relations, we are not suggesting that social media are a magic bullet with the capacity to instantly transform the region (not least because not everyone has equal access to the Internet). If the e-diaspora's potential as a space of radical change is dependent on the politics that are brought to bear on the form and content of the conversations, it is also crucial to underscore that the materialization of such virtual praxis is an inextricable dimension of what we envision. That is to say, the Internet has the potential to provide the contemporary Caribbean with new forms of transnational connectivity that can bring region and diaspora together in ways that do not rely solely on the mediating, nationalizing, and disciplining presence of neo-liberal Caribbean states. But the radical democratic possibilities of an e-diaspora forum can only happen if these spaces are not striated in ways that reproduce existing and exclusionary social relations, but instead work to facilitate broader modes of political participation that extend beyond states and political parties. In this regard, democratization will be critically dependent on such virtual engagement being regularly connected to, and drawing from, activities in localities and communities on the ground. It is the synergy between the virtual and the real that has the potential to shift a playing field that for far too long has excluded the majority of the region's population. In short, this is about changing a political culture by the iterative engagement of Caribbean peoples both online and offline.

There are a few hopeful indicators in the region, such as the groundswell of opposition to the September 2013 ruling of the Constitutional Tribunal of the Dominican Republic that threatened to render hundreds of thousands of Dominicans of Haitian descent stateless. After initial hesitancy on the part of the Caribbean Community (CARICOM), the regional integration organization representing fifteen Caribbean countries, a statement was issued close to a month after the decision merely expressing regret and calling upon the Dominican Republic 'to adopt measures to protect human rights and interests of those made vulnerable by this ruling and its grievous effects'. By November, however, CARICOM would take a much stronger stand, one that included a clear condemnation of the Constitutional Tribunal ruling, along with a suspension of consideration of the request by the Dominican Republic for membership in CARICOM.

This shift in CARICOM's position cannot be seen outside of a series of actions, several of which were co-ordinated across Caribbean and diaspora communities. These included well-placed editorials, newspaper columns, and investigative reports of conditions in the Dominican Republic following the ruling, as well as dissemination of critical perspectives through various blogs. Two online petition campaigns were initiated: the first was by an organization in Trinidad and Tobago (*Jouvay Ayiti*) that was also staging demonstrations, while the second was by university students and women activists across Guyana and Grenada, calling on Caribbean citizens at home and in the diaspora to demand that CARICOM unequivocally oppose the decision (Trotz 2013b). Additionally, activists across the Caribbean, North America, and Europe were meeting online to help co-ordinate the pressure for a CARICOM Bureau meeting to discuss the ruling, which was first planned for 19 November in Trinidad and Tobago, and which eventually took place on 26 November. A public forum was held in Guyana, following which the second petition was presented to the CARICOM Secretary General. Meanwhile, a day before the Bureau meeting, a public meeting was held at the University of the West Indies that was streamed live over the Internet. Professors at the Institute of International Relations also signed and issued an open letter expressing their opposition to the judgement in the Dominican Republic. The CARICOM Bureau members agreed to receive a delegation from civil society, including members of the co-ordinating group, who handed over both of the petitions. At a press conference convened at the conclusion of this meeting, CARICOM Bureau Heads (the President of Haiti and Prime Ministers of Saint Vincent and the Grenadines and Trinidad and Tobago) issued the condemnation of the ruling.

A Caribbean e-diaspora offers possibilities for a revitalized regional sphere of deliberation and cooperation, and can importantly contribute to building more inclusive, just, and innovative modes of participation. Such broad deliberations also have the capacity to invest public discussion with a practicality it might otherwise lack. Engaged carefully, it is, we think, also a key site for inter-generational learning and a way of tapping into the skills, vision, and energies of young people who have been alienated from political processes across the Caribbean. To be sure, it will not be an easy task to create the architecture for working through the 'difficult conversations' and agreeing on the principles upon which a sustainable Caribbean future can be built. These difficulties are rooted 'somewhere' in the messy and painful histories of colonialism, indigenous displacement, slavery, indentureship, and their associated and ongoing forms of violence and dispossession that continue to haunt the region across her linguistic divides. The example of the Dominican

Republic tribunal ruling shows how diasporic–regional conversations were able to successfully put pressure on regional governments to take a stronger stand. The question of citizenship for Dominicans of Haitian heritage offered a focal point for a diffuse transnational network that was able to share and distribute information, linked in immediate and concrete ways to groups and individuals on the ground, and offering an excellent example for the radical potentiality of an e-diaspora capable of invigorating new conversations and offering visions for alternative and sustainable Caribbean futures.

NOTE

1. We dedicate these reflections to the memory and work of Norman Girvan (1941–2014) and Stuart Hall (1932–2014).

Chapter 5

Corruption of Anti-Corruption
Deconstructing Neo-liberal Good Governance

Pınar Bedirhanoğlu

Combating corruption has been a central 'reform' target of international financial institutions (IFIs) such as the World Bank and the International Monetary Fund (IMF) since the 1990s as part of their wider declared aim of ensuring good governance in the global economy. In this vein, many IFI-supported programmes have sought to increase the transparency and accountability of state institutions through more openness and visibility in public procurements, privatization processes, political campaign finances, and enhanced civil society participation in policy making.

Not everyone has accepted at face value the IFIs' emphasis on 'good governance'. Critics across the left–right spectrum have in various ways questioned its logic and implications. Indeed, some have argued that the IFIs themselves should first implement transparency and accountability in their own operations, before pushing such policies onto their member-states (Stiglitz 2003; Woods 2000; Vestergaard and Wade 2013).

Yet, strikingly, a rather limited number of critics (see Brown and Cloke 2004; Hindess 2005; Harrison 2006; Bukovansky 2006; Bedirhanoğlu 2007; Roden 2010; Bratsis 2014) have targeted the international anti-corruption agenda directly. This lack of critical response can be explained by the apparently apolitical character of the problem of corruption. After all, corruption generates deep feelings of injustice in everyone and seems to harm society as a whole. Hence, the IFIs' attention to corruption has generally been viewed positively, regardless of the nature and effectiveness of anti-corruption strategies. Moreover, the international anti-corruption agenda has often empowered opposition movements that contest authoritarian governments in different parts of the world. The result has been that long-term or indirect implications of anti-corruption policies have not been questioned.

This chapter problematizes this general approval of the international anti-corruption 'crusade' (Brown and Cloke 2004; Roden 2010), viewing it as a counter-productive and Eurocentric initiative driven by neo-liberal interests. Anti-corruption prescriptions proposed by the IFIs tend to curtail rather than enhance the reforming countries' prospects for democratic development, inasmuch as these measures reproduce existing power relations, which favour capital and the West and paralyse attempts to find other routes towards a non-corrupt society.

For instance, Bukovansky argues that by imposing 'contingent standards on societies that are not fully participating in defining those standards', a few countries and institutions have set the general framework within which civil society forces have to operate, thereby limiting civil society institutions' abilities to pursue innovative change (Bukovansky 2006, 184). Thus,

> advanced industrial countries implicitly and unjustifiably claim the moral high ground [on anti-corruption] for themselves ... [and] deny the capacity and agency of the actors in developing countries to determine for themselves the contours of political authority and the distinctions between public good and private interests, between gifts and bribes, between legitimate and illegitimate patronage. (Bukovansky 2006, 198)

This critique implies that the standard liberal definition of corruption as 'the use of public office for private gain' (Huther and Shah 2000, 1; Jain 2001, 73), which is based on a modern public–private divide, does not necessarily fit the political realities of many reforming countries, as these countries sometimes even lack such a divide. In such cases, the IFIs have preferred to impose a Western model as the norm on non-Western societies (Hindess 2005, 1396), with the argument that globalization demands harmonization of standards and norms (Camdessus 1999).

This predominant political and ideological approach to corruption helps reproduce existing global inequalities, and thus limits prospects for global democracy. Thus if, as the opening chapter of this book maintains, 'global democracy ... demands that everyone has adequate – and equitably shared – material means for effective political involvement', then a comprehensive critique of the rules and policies governing the conventional anti-corruption agenda would contribute to social struggles for more equitable distribution of resources. This approach requires, besides the criticism of present-day policies, the production of critical knowledge-for-action to combat corruption beyond the boundaries set by the existing power relations at global, national, and local levels. To this end, this chapter highlights the inherently corrupt and undemocratic nature of capitalist relations of production and proposes that the scope of anti-corruption agendas should be broadened accordingly.

The first part of the chapter examines the political implications of the international anti-corruption agenda by stressing its neo-liberal and Eurocentric underpinnings as well as its internal inconsistencies. Arguments developed here are supported by historical examples from various Southern countries, including a specific emphasis on Turkey. This critical analysis, improving the arguments made in Bedirhanoğlu (2007) and Bedirhanoğlu and Angın (2012), also shows how corruption has become a master key used by neo-liberals to deflect criticism directed against neo-liberalism in particular and capitalism in general during crisis periods.

The second part of the chapter proposes a class-based and social justice-oriented alternative agenda to combat corruption, within the context of social struggles against neo-liberal capitalism. Taking as an illustrative case the privatization of large-scale state enterprises in Turkey in 2005, part two highlights the fact that specific processes of neo-liberal transformation are potential sites to pursue such a critical reformulation. Within these processes, the conventional anti-corruption agenda disciplines inter-capitalist rivalries and labor–capital confrontation to the benefit of internationalized capital by imposing *market justice* as the cure for corruption. A critical engagement with this anti-corruption agenda would contest these practices and help attract attention instead to the more fundamental corruption, which is the exploitative nature of capitalist relations of production. This analysis helps us move beyond a statist critique of the neo-liberal anti-corruption agenda that simply rests on a North–South divide. Such a critique can also prevent this critical inquiry being abused by corrupt authoritarian governments to legitimize themselves. The concluding section of the chapter proposes some strategies through which such an alternative agenda for anti-corruption can be constructed.

CRITIQUE OF THE NEO-LIBERAL DISCOURSE AND AGENDA OF CORRUPTION

Why Neo-liberal?

Corruption attracted the attention of international institutions such as the IMF, the World Bank, and the Organisation for Economic Cooperation and Development (OECD) in the early 1990s, though it had already become a central issue in many Southern countries as early as the 1980s. Many of the countries that launched policies of neo-liberal transformation after the 1980s also experienced a simultaneous aggravation of the problem of corruption. Some obvious examples would be the Menem period in Argentina, Collor de Mello's rule in Brazil, the Perez period in Venezuela, the Özal years in Turkey, and Yeltsin's shock therapy in Russia. Even though neo-liberals have long argued that the upsurge in corruption was not an outcome of their reforms, but rather a consequence of incomplete or unsuccessful implementation of policies by the reforming states, the World Bank had to accept in 2000 that 'the simultaneous processes of developing a market economy, designing new political and social institutions and redistributing social assets have created fertile ground for corruption' (World Bank 2000a, xvi).

Here Harvey's conception of accumulation by dispossession can help us understand the mutually constitutive nature of corruption and neo-liberalism. He attracts attention to the permanence of the conditions of primitive accumulation in capitalist development, and reminds us how non-economic forms of appropriation of surplus value through violence, fraud, and corruption have been endemic to capitalist relations of production, particularly in times of radical transformation (Harvey 2003).

Contrary to Harvey's analysis, IFIs have defined neo-liberalism as a cure for corruption. They have proposed that combating corruption requires the institutionalization of neo-liberal policies in line with transparency and good governance. According to the World Bank (1997, 21–23), a multi-pronged strategy has to be pursued to combat corruption that aims at 'enhancing state capacity and public sector management, strengthening political accountability, enabling civil society, and increasing economic competition' (World Bank 2000a, 39). The best tools to attain these goals are defined as 'deregulation and the expansion of markets' (World Bank 2000b, 35), hence the standard neo-liberal restructuring prescriptions for states.

It is important to note that international interest in corruption first arose in the 1990s with a specific focus on bribery. The OECD Working Group on Bribery in 1994 aimed to 'end the tax deductibility of bribes and criminalize the bribing of foreign officials', an initiative which ultimately in 1997 produced the OECD International Convention on Combating Bribery of Foreign Public Officials in International Business Transactions. Other early international actions on corruption included the Council of Europe Programme of Action against Corruption, adopted in November 1996, the United Nations Declaration against Corruption and Bribery in International Commercial Transactions, adopted in December 1996, and the European Commission's Communication to the Council and the European Parliament on a Union Policy against Corruption, in May 1997. These moves targeted bribery as a legally definable, technical form of corruption which could be cured by the disciplining of the private sector (World Bank 2000b, 60–61). Vito Tanzi, a former director of the IMF's Fiscal Affairs Department, informs us that these initiatives were brought to the international agenda essentially by US politicians and exporters, who were complaining about the unfair competition they faced vis-à-vis other OECD countries and exporters on the question of bribes to foreigners. They were critical of some OECD exporters' legal ability to deduct the bribes they paid from their business costs, while bribing foreign officials was illegal for US exporters according to US laws (Tanzi 1998, 561–63). Hence, it can be argued that these early international concerns about corruption aimed to regulate inter-capitalist rivalry in a period when competition for newly opened markets in the post-socialist countries was increasing. As Bukovansky (2006, 188) notes, after moving to a secondary position for a while throughout the 1990s, this supply-side focus on corruption re-emerged in the early 2000s, possibly due to various corporate scandals that shook Europe and the USA, such as the Enron case in 2001 and the Worldcom scandal in 2002.

This bribery-focused anti-corruption agenda acquired a political content in the wake of the 1997 financial crisis in East Asia by replacing business with the state as the main target of reform. Indeed, the IMF responded to the criticism that its reforms had caused the crisis by arguing that the real trigger of the problem was to be found in the 'crony' state-business relations in East Asia, which impeded the creation of 'a sound financial system, and the removal of economic distortions, as well as progress in transparency and disclosure on the part of governments and financial institutions' (IMF 1998, 27). Thus, anti-corruption became an important reference to ensure the continuation of the second generation of neo-liberal reforms in the South, a move that has also meant the politicization of the anti-corruption agenda (Marquette 2004).

This novel anti-state rhetoric of the anti-corruption agenda rests on the rentier state assumptions that identify the resources distributed by states as the main basis of their political authority (Rose-Ackerman 1999; World Bank 2000a; Jain 2001, 79). The neo-liberal quality of this state perspective is evident in its direct association of the state with exploitation and corruption, insofar as this analysis sees the state as nothing more than the simple sum of egoistic state bureaucrats and politicians in search of the maximization of their private interests (North 1994). This shift of emphasis in the anti-corruption agenda has indeed better complemented the neo-liberal call for limiting state interventions in markets through the latter's deregulation and expansion (World Bank 2000b).

The IFIs have continued to systematically abuse the problem of corruption as the main scapegoat in times of financial crisis after the proved success of this strategy in East Asia. Thus, corruption has become an effective crisis-management tool appealed to during other financial crises experienced in the South thereafter (Bedirhanoğlu 2007). This strategy has not only helped deflect criticism directed against neo-liberalism, but also ensured new impetus for its accelerated implementation. It is interesting to observe that a similar logic has been at work in neo-liberal explanations of the 2007/8 global economic crisis. 'Corrupt' and 'greedy' financiers have been found guilty of triggering the crisis, rather than the processes of financial liberalization and the internal contradictions of capitalist relations of production in general.

Why Eurocentric?

One of the other identifying characteristics of the neo-liberal anti-corruption discourse and agenda has been its Eurocentrism, which treats Western capitalist institutions as ipso facto superior over others (Amin 2009). This is reflected in the association of corruption with the Southern and transition states primarily, whereas neo-liberals have seen corruption in the North as largely an exception. This perspective is made explicit by Tanzi, who associates the rising international interest in corruption with the end of the Cold War, for it 'has stopped the political hypocrisy that had made the decision makers *in some industrial countries* ignore the political corruption that existed *in particular countries*' (Tanzi 1998, 560, emphasis added). In another case, Transparency International (TI), a prominent NGO in the field of anti-corruption, has argued that 'if the matters are serious in industrialized countries, they are in crisis in much of the developing world and in countries in transition' (Hindess 2005, 1390 quoting from TI 2000, 1).

According to another neo-liberal argument that complements this position, the sources of corruption need to be investigated within the historical or cultural specificities of the countries concerned. As the World Bank states,

> The causes of corruption are always contextual, rooted in a country's policies, bureaucratic traditions, political development, and social history. Still, corruption tends to flourish when institutions are weak and government policies generate economic rents. Some characteristics of developing and transition settings make corruption particularly difficult to control. (World Bank 2000b, 12)

Such circumstances include the heritage of 'the strong state tradition' in Turkey, 'the communist past' in Russia, or the 'corporatist past' in Latin America (Dinler 2003; Bedirhanoğlu 2002; Jones 1996). Obviously, this biased perspective puts the burden of corruption on the individual countries' domestic conditions rather than on the processes of financial liberalization or privatization. It thus represents a contemporary version of the modernization perspective that serves to reproduce an idealized Western model as an end to be attained by the rest of the world (Theobald 1999, 492).

In short, the neo-liberal discourse and agenda of anti-corruption is Eurocentric insofar as it glorifies an idealized Western political model as largely non-corrupt and takes this model as a reference point while making sense of the state–society and state–business relations in non-Western contexts. The discourse is also neo-liberal, as its underlying assumptions rest on a non-problematized belief in the merits of free markets in ensuring societal development.

Hence, as aptly stated by Harrison (2006, 16), international anti-corruption strategies are shaped by the 'disciplining agendas of northern powers'.

For the Southern states, however, levelling the playing field for capital in the name of anti-corruption has practically meant opening up more profit opportunities for transnational capitalist interests relative to local and domestic ones, given the former's comparative advantages. As the next section will problematize, this process has created both challenges and novel opportunities for corruption in the so-called 'reforming' countries.

Inconsistencies of the Neo-liberal Anti-Corruption Agenda

Liberal critiques of the IFI-imposed anti-corruption agenda argue that the implementation of neo-liberal reforms in developing countries since the 1990s has aggravated rather than diminished opportunities for corruption in these countries (Harriss-White and White 1996, 2–3; Jones 1996; Manzetti and Blake 1996). Thus, neo-liberalism has to be analysed as the reason for the problem of corruption rather than its cure.

This criticism can be explained on the basis of the 'orthodox paradox', which Kahler (1990, 41) has developed to problematize the challenges neo-liberalism has created for 'reforming' governments. According to him, while following the dictates of the markets in line with neo-liberal prescriptions, reforming governments are faced with the challenge of implementing *economically rational but politically irrational* policy choices, due to the unpopularity of market-based redistributions, eroding ultimately their own legitimacy. As Manzetti and Blake (1996, 673) show, this paradox was practically resolved in Latin America with the move towards authoritarian regimes in which the executives were strengthened at the cost of the emergence of a new form of 'neo-liberal' corruption. The experience of Russian capitalist transformation even provides evidence of the possibility of promoting corruption as a conscious political strategy during the early years of a transition to capitalism, in order to ensure political support for the process through the creation of specific 'bounded interests'. In those years, Russian President Yeltsin's advisors, who had been alarmed by the possibility of the former *nomenklatura* acquiring control of state assets in Poland and Russia during the privatization processes, publicly announced that unless these people 'are appeased, bribed, or disenfranchised, privatization cannot proceed' (Blanchard *et al.* 1993, 39).

Another important inconsistency of the IFI-imposed neo-liberal anti-corruption agenda is related to the fact that the scope of corruption has rarely been extended to include those civil society institutions which work to check state corruption or those regulatory agencies formed by the public and private agents with the purpose of managing a non-corrupt and competitive deregulation in targeted sectors. There is no meaningful explanation for this policy preference, as there is no theoretical argument available to free civil society institutions from behaving in a corrupt manner. Empirically, on the other hand, several critical studies have already highlighted the corrupt practices of the 'autonomous regulatory agencies' (Bayramoğlu 2005) and the new 'regional development agencies' (Turan 2005) in various countries. It is thus clear that the IFIs' anti-corruption agenda is shaped by ideological preferences, as it targets only states rather than also civil society institutions for reform.

NEW FORMS OF CORRUPTION IN TURKEY IN THE NEO-LIBERAL ERA

The integrated history of corruption and neo-liberalism in Turkey dates back to the early 1980s. Specific corruption claims and scandals occupying a significant space in Turkish public debates in this decade were the bribes that State Minister Özdağlar took from a navigation company, bribes paid by the General Dynamics company in Turkey during the public procurement process of F-16 airplanes, the bankruptcy of Kastelli, fictitious export practices to get state incentives for export promotion, and the dead loans provided by state banks to the business groups close to government circles (Şener 2001).

Corruption claims and practices in the 1980s and 1990s in Turkey can be associated with the earlier necessity to implement neo-liberal policies through specific state cadres, who would work within the state against the state at large due to the latter's loyalty to practices of import substitution, financial control, and public interest. This problem, which is not specific to Turkey, has been resolved by neo-liberals through the strengthening of the executive branches of the state at the expense of the legislature and judiciary at the macro level and the recruitment of neo-liberal-minded new cadres at the micro level. Having been accompanied by processes of privatization, deregulation and liberalization of finance and trade, this entire process created appropriate conditions for a substantial increase of corruption in Turkey.

The aggravation and institutionalization of corruption under the Islamist rule of the Justice and Development Party (AKP) in the 2000s has been related with the neo-liberal processes of re-regulation, urban restructuring, flexibilization of labour markets, and large-scale privatizations. The AKP has utilized these processes to support Islamist business groups through the growing construction sector (Buğra and Savaşkan 2014, 21) and to provide charity to the poor in return for votes. These policies have helped the party establish conservative bonds of dependency with the society. The economic support provided to politically loyal domestic investors in establishing links and ensuring markets in the Arab world, as well as in the Islamic states of Africa, has strengthened this new and corrupt form of political command in the country. It is evident that only those companies which are loyal to Islamic culture are given such privileged treatment, while other businesses are excluded. The symbiosis between the AKP and 'green' capital, which would normally be defined as corruption, is accepted as legitimate in the eyes of the AKP's Islamic constituency due to the common normative ground they share and the practical gains they would get out of it. This symbiosis also gives Islamic businesses the responsibility to mobilize their individual economic resources and collective powers in favour of the party through direct membership and/or active involvement in politics to support government policies (Buğra and Savaşkan 2014, 10–13). This ironically highlights the corrupt roots and vulnerable nature of the long-praised 'political stability' in Turkey, which ensured that hot money stayed in the country until the global capitalist crisis hit Europe in 2009.

As this short evaluation of the increase of corruption in Turkey during the neo-liberal era indicates, state and capital are two inseparable sides of the relation of corruption, and the unpopular character of neo-liberal transformations that favour transnational capitalist interests vis-à-vis labour and the less competitive domestic enterprises seems to force governments to manage the reactions of the latter through various corrupt tactics.

CONTESTING THE CORRUPT 'NORMAL': FROM A STATIST TO A CLASS-BASED CRITICISM

Critics who diagnose the neo-liberal and Eurocentric content of the international anti-corruption agenda are faced with the danger that their arguments will be abused by corrupt authoritarian governments on nationalist grounds. One way to overcome this problem would be to introduce a labour perspective and formulate alternative class-based and social justice-oriented definitions of corruption, which expand the scope of anti-corruption by underlining the fundamentally corrupt nature of capitalist relations of production.

With these concerns in mind, this part of the chapter will demonstrate how neo-liberal discourse and the IFI-imposed agenda of corruption help reproduce legitimacy for capitalist relations of production at large. To this end, the privatization of large-scale state enterprises in Turkey in the 2000s is taken as an illustrative case, a practice which is in no way specific to Turkey, so that its conclusions can also be rethought in other socio-political contexts.

Large-scale privatizations constitute critical junctures in which the *conventional narrow* and *class-based broader* definitions of corruption practically face and latently contest each other. These are historical moments in which the corrupt nature of capitalist market exploitation becomes ever more visible on the one hand, and the ruling bloc's concerns to ensure the formal legitimacy of these privatizations through apparently open and competitive auctions increase on the other. In this contestation, the former and the latter moments fiercely work against each other for the reconstruction of social reality. Thus, if they are not radically challenged from the perspective of labour, the neo-liberal comprehension of these privatization processes turns into real practices in which 'a specific pro-capital "normality", . . . [drawing] the boundaries between the legitimate and illegitimate, just and unjust; and corrupt and uncorrupt in capital–labor–state relations' (Angın and Bedirhanoğlu 2012, 143) is effectively reproduced. Expressed in Gramscian terms, these are moments in which ideologies turn into lived, habitual practices in support of the hegemonic reproduction of historic blocs (Eagleton 1991: 112–15), in which 'material forces are the content and ideologies are the form' (Gramsci 1971, 377).

Privatization of Large State Enterprises in Turkey: Reproduction of the Corrupt 'Normal'

In Turkey's controversial neo-liberal transformation process since the early 1980s, privatizations constitute significant historical thresholds within which the question of corruption has become a top concern in public debates. The AKP's 'privatization season' in 2005 was one such moment, when four large-scale and profitable state enterprises (Türk Telekom, ERDEMİR, TÜPRAŞ, and PETKİM) were privatized by block sales. As a result, 55 per cent of Türk Telekom shares were sold for US $6.550 billion to Oger Telecoms, which is a joint venture predominantly owned by Saudi capital; 51 per cent of TÜPRAŞ shares were sold to the Koç-Shell Joint Venture for US $4.140 billion, of which a majority of the capital was derived from Turkey; 46.12 per cent of ERDEMİR shares were sold for US $2.770 billion to the Turkish Armed Forces Assistance and Pension Fund (OYAK); lastly, 51 per cent of PETKİM shares were sold for US $2.04 billion to the Socar and Turcas-Injaz Joint Venture, predominantly owned by Azeri capital. The high volume of sales revenue was frequently celebrated by liberal circles and government officials in public debates as one of the most important accomplishments of these privatizations.

Accompanying this liberal approval, however, there were serious concerns over the possibility that corruption might have been involved in these privatizations. In response to such considerations, the Privatization Administration (ÖİB) tried to assure the transparency of the tenders through their live broadcasts on television. Even though this did not prevent many corruption claims and criticisms, these privatizations were praised by various international organizations including the IMF and the OECD due to their transparency and the expected positive impact on the flow of foreign direct investment to Turkey (OECD 2006; IMF 2007, 37).

Without rejecting the importance of conventional corruption claims in the forms of bribery, fraud, or rent-seeking, this part of the chapter takes the discussion of corruption to a broader level. For the narrow and established focus on corruption indeed creates the illusion that once bribery and fraud are eliminated, these privatizations can be accepted as legitimate, right, and just. Hence, the liberal obsession with the transparency of these transactions can also be seen as a – not necessarily conscious – concern to normalize the underlying corrupt social relations, constituting perhaps one of the most important moments of ideological reproduction within these processes.

To elaborate on this argument, firstly the critical role that the aforementioned enterprises play in shaping the competition and employment conditions within their own sectors in Turkey needs to be contrasted with their market-determined sale prices. Prior to their privatizations, all of the four state enterprises had strategic roles in the Turkish economy. Türk Telekom was the fixed-line telecommunications monopoly. TÜPRAŞ was the largest industrial company of Turkey, with crude oil processing capacity of 28.1 million tons in total per annum and four oil refineries. ERDEMİR was holding 80 per cent of the iron ore reserves in Turkey. PETKİM was one of the leading petrochemical companies, producing more than fifty inputs for various sectors, including textile, automotive, agriculture, and electricity. When considered together with these features, market values obtained in the block sales seemed to be considerably disproportional to the political and economic role that these companies had played in Turkey, leaving aside the contribution that they made to the strategic development of the companies to which they were sold. To illustrate the latter argument, in the privatization of TÜPRAŞ, Koç Holding purchased a company as large as itself in terms of its annual earnings for only US $4.140 billion (Öztürk 2010, 229). Similarly, the purchase of PETKİM has led to the total reconsideration of the overall investment strategies of Socar and Turcas. Thus, rather than seeing such practices of immediate enrichment as ordinary aspects of market dynamics, Boratav *et al.* (1998, 120–21) prefer to define them as corrupt and predatory acts.

Another important market injustice normalized and hence justified during the privatization processes in general is the reduction of employment in the privatized enterprises for the sake of increasing productivity. Within two years following its block sale, employment in Türk Telekom was reduced to 37,035 from 51,737, for instance (Karataş and Ercan 2008, 370–71). This practice has been legitimized on account of the assumption that employment levels prior to the privatizations were inflated due to political interventions of the government. The history of privatizations is full of the legal and practical struggles of workers, who do not accept this situation as normal. However, these types of struggles cannot easily become visible, and the workers who are dismissed or transferred to other state enterprises through legal regulations are converted into simple statistical data according to their total numbers. What such specific moments help ensure is the legitimacy of eliminating and/or restructuring the conditions of the labour force according to the profitability concerns of capital, even though this would cause deep trauma in the lives of the workers. This basic capitalist market reality is obviously not new, though its harsh implications on the real-world conditions of labourers necessitate persistent reproduction of this practice as 'normal'. Moments such as the block sales of the large state enterprises provide ample opportunities for this.

On the basis of this discussion, it can be argued that the conventional anti-corruption rhetoric used during such large-scale privatization processes, in which corruption is defined as the differentiated treatment of potential buyers by the state, helps veil the socially corrupt nature of these privatizations themselves. To contest this, we need to move beyond the technical evaluations and arguments made in relation to the efficiency, productivity and/or the valuation calculations of these enterprises during the privatizations, and effectively delegitimize the market justice that these technical calculations impose by revealing their political content.

What this critical investigation into the practice of large-scale privatizations tells us about the anti-corruption struggle is that, whenever concerns about corruption in its conventional neo-liberal and competition-driven meaning rise in politics, it is possible to challenge and redefine them through a radical definition of corruption. This can be done by questioning the *market justice* imposed on social relations and replacing it with one that emphasizes the importance of *social justice*. The question of how each specific case can be rethought and reconfigured with such political concern would only be resolved in practice by the innovative and insistent interventions of the labouring classes in social struggles. This resistance would also be one in which the content of 'social justice', hence of a non-corrupt social existence with its appropriate political forms, would be defined in praxis.

CONCLUSION: HOW TO CONSTRUCT AN ALTERNATIVE ANTI-CORRUPTION AGENDA

This chapter has argued that the conventional anti-corruption agenda with its Eurocentric and neo-liberal conceptualization of corruption helps to legitimize and normalize the corrupt nature of capitalist relations of production.

To go beyond the corrupt market justice that this agenda imposes, there is a need to construct an alternative practice that would radicalize the meaning of corruption with reference to social justice. Various social struggles fought against privatizations, financial and trade deregulations, urban gentrification, labour market flexibility, and commodification of land, health, education, or rivers all over the world are potential sites of contestation for such a radical reformulation. Given that processes of neo-liberal accumulation by dispossession redistribute wealth in favour of capital at the expense of labour, it is imperative to show the incompatibility of market justice with social justice in each of these cases.

Besides this radical strategy, there are also things to be done to force the conventional anti-corruption institutions beyond their established positions. The IFIs' call for enhanced civil society participation in anti-corruption can be, for instance, rethought in relation to this moderate strategy, and the IFIs' selective inclusion of civil society organizations into the process would be contested in favour of a more inclusive list with representatives of labour organizations and the unemployed. Another such attempt would be to take active part in the campaigns of TI and to intervene in the agendas of local TI organizations. It is true that TI, as a conventional non-governmental organization founded by a former World Bank official, Peter Eigen (2013), embraces the mainstream conception of corruption which is criticized in this chapter. This, however, should not blur the fact that local TI offices mostly employ critical people who are capable of making sound interventions in local politics. As a result, a rather conventional international institution such as TI would be forced to get involved in radical politics at the local level. On the other side, TI has also been concerned about the protection of basic liberal democratic rights such as fair elections, freedom of speech, press, and assembly as effective tools to identify, publish, and protest corrupt government activities. These liberal-democratic institutions, which were originally products of nineteenth-century class and social struggles in Europe, can be embraced by all the oppositional forces in Southern countries today in their struggles against authoritarianism, inequality, coercion, and corruption.

Chapter 6

An Alternative Global Money
Special Drawing Rights or Bitcoin?
Taoxiong Liu with Mendang Huang

From the viewpoint of economics, money is conventionally recognized to serve three basic functions: as a unit of account; as a medium of exchange; and as a store of value. Global money performs these three roles on a world scale. As a unit of account, global money is used to denominate trade contracts and to calculate the par values for exchange rates between national currencies. As a medium of exchange, global money serves as a vehicle for transactions between countries. It is also bought and sold by central banks to intervene in foreign exchange markets or to balance international payments. Finally, as a store of value, global money can be held by private agents as assets, as well as by central banks as reserves.

From the perspective of political economy, the international monetary system also has the attribute of power. Different international monetary systems give countries and individuals different capacities to influence the economy and society. The monetary regime can furthermore allocate the benefits of international trade asymmetrically, so that participating countries and individuals gain or lose depending on their relationship to the core currencies. The international monetary system can also impose different levels of risk on the economies of different countries. Thus, global money is a highly political matter.

The nature of global money and the way that it is managed can have major consequences for the distribution of resources and power in the world economy. An undemocratic global reserve system could encourage global economic and political inequity. Conversely, democratizing the global monetary regime could be an important step towards structural redistribution for global democracy and greater global justice, as articulated in the opening chapter of this volume.

The international monetary system has evolved over time, but until now the global reserve system has always been undemocratically controlled by developed countries through a core and periphery structure. Under these rules, core countries and periphery countries have shared benefits and costs asymmetrically. This has generated global economic imbalance and inequity, which has also encouraged major instability in the international financial system.

A democratic global reserve system needs to meet two objectives. The first objective is to offer a stable and reliable unit of account, medium of exchange, and store of value. Such a global money will promote international trade and financial transactions. The second objective is to have a global monetary regime that provides due voice and control for all affected participants. In practice, this means raising the influence of developing countries, especially low-income countries, which in turn will encourage a more equitable distribution of resources and power in the world.

This chapter explores what such a more democratic global monetary regime could entail. The first section below describes the current global reserve system and analyses its fundamental equity and democracy problems. The second section explores in detail the characteristics of an alternative and more democratic global reserve system. It is proposed that the ideal solution would be to build a supranational currency and a corresponding global reserve system. The third section focuses on two candidates to underpin this supranational reserve system: (a) a reform and expansion of the Special Drawing Right (SDR); and (b) the development of digital currencies such as Bitcoin. The fourth section outlines the process by which the transition to the new arrangements could occur.

DIAGNOSIS: INEQUALITY IN THE CURRENT GLOBAL RESERVE SYSTEM

Today's global reserve system is still primarily based on the United States dollar (USD). Although in recent years the USD has been challenged in this role by the euro and the Japanese yen, it remains the world's leading international currency. The USD was initially accorded this role at the Bretton Woods Conference of 1944. Actually, at that conference, John Maynard Keynes proposed an alternative supranational currency, which he called bancor. However, US hegemonic power won the day, and the USD rather than bancor became the central currency for the postwar international monetary regime (Dormael 1978). Seventy years later, the USA is still the world's largest national economy, and its financial markets are deep, open, and well developed. As a global money, the USD has advantages of high efficiency and low cost compared with other national currencies.

Nevertheless, the current USD-based global reserve system has several fundamental problems (Krugman 1984, 262). One is that the dollar-based global reserve system has a core-periphery structure which is undemocratic and induces inequitable distributions. The USA is at the centre; currencies of Europe and Japan lie close to the centre; and other countries, including those with export-oriented development strategies, are in the periphery. The lack of democracy in the current global reserve system is obvious, since it gives core countries such as the USA enormous privilege to control the issuance and governance of international money, while countries in the periphery have almost no access to this process.

How does this arrangement produce unjust distributional inequalities? How do the USA and to lesser extents the European Union (EU) and Japan gain unfair advantages by having their monies as core currencies, while periphery countries – especially those developing countries with export-oriented development strategies – lose benefits in the world economy? For one thing, in contrast to the core countries, peripheral countries have to buy the core monies in order to use them. For example, if India needs USDs for its reserves, it has to buy them on foreign exchange markets. The same does not hold for the USA. Since the USD is the global money, the USA does not need to reserve rupees and can spend the rupees it earns whenever and however it wishes, while India has to reserve the USD for future needs. Hence, India pays costs that the USA does not face.

In addition, since the USD is much more convenient for international payments under the dollar-centered system, the US money will normally be more expensive than the rupee, even if the two currencies have the same purchasing power for goods. In economics language, the USA (and also the Eurozone and Japan) earn large amounts of seigniorage income from their role as issuers of global money. Besides, the USA can finance its fiscal deficits for economic and social objectives at lower cost through the issuance of low-interest bonds held by the periphery countries. However, for the periphery countries, it is relatively more difficult to get substantial financing from world markets. They are forced to accumulate large amounts of foreign exchange reserves for self-insurance. At the same time, they have to bear the risk of the devaluation of USD-denominated reserve assets and the costs caused by countercyclical policies of the US government. In short, the core-periphery structure of the global monetary system creates transfers of resources from developing economies to the USA, a situation which critics have termed 'reverse aid' (Ocampo 2007, 74).

Another key problem of the current global reserve system lies with its instability, which results from the dual roles of the USD as both a national currency and the dominant international currency. In this circumstance, the USA monetary authorities always face tensions between pursuing domestic objectives (regarding employment and inflation) and providing international public goods (regarding a stable currency and financial stability) (Alessandrini and Fratianni 2009, 3–6). Sometimes these two objectives cannot be reconciled, and on such occasions the USA monetary authorities may have little incentive to meet the needs and interests of other countries. Looking back over history, the USA monetary authorities have usually enforced monetary policy to meet domestic economic objectives, with much less if any consideration of the international repercussions. If the US economy falls into recession or financial crisis, the USA monetary authorities would increase the dollar supply to stimulate domestic demand and promote domestic recovery, whereas the resulting fluctuation of the value of the USD may destabilize the global reserve system, or even induce a global financial crisis. Thus, with the USD at the centre of the global reserve system, international monetary conditions are largely determined by the policies of one country, with little if any regard to its international repercussions (Erten and Ocampo 2012, 3). This intrinsic instability arises whenever a global reserve system is based on a national currency.

Is the solution to these problems to expand the range of national currencies that serve as a global reserve currency? For example, it might be argued to add the renminbi (RMB), given the rise of China in the world economy. However, this alternative is not optimal, since any global reserve system in which a national currency is the key international money would have similar problems to those described above in relation to the USD. What is needed is not another nationally based global currency to supplement or replace the USD, but a supranational global reserve currency that is not tied to any single country.

PRESCRIPTION: TWO ROADS TO A MORE EQUITABLE DISTRIBUTION

In recent years, the global financial crisis has fully exposed the defects and drawbacks of the current international monetary system based on the USD, thereby highlighting the necessity and urgency for reform. In response, many economists and political economy researchers have once again put their attention on this subject. The many proposals can be divided into two main categories. The first category proposes to establish a multiple reserve currency system, in which the euro, renminbi, pound sterling, yen, and possibly other national monies would be key reserve currencies together with the USD (Alessandrini and Fratianni 2009, 20; Bird 2011, 201). The second category advocates the establishment of a supranational reserve system and setting up a global central bank (or expanding the competences of the International Monetary Fund, IMF) to govern the operation of the global currency (Cooper 2010, 69; Zhou 2009).

Analytic Framework: Global Reserve System and Economic Democracy

Before comparing the above two categories of proposals, it is necessary to outline a set of evaluation criteria for the global reserve system. In other words, what kind of global reserve system is wanted? Three dimensions are key.

The first dimension is economic efficiency. The global reserve currency should have the advantages of low transaction cost. The reserve money should as an international settlement currency be freely convertible into other reserve assets. The reserve currency should also be widely used in international trade and financial transactions, which would increase its network externality (meaning that people want to use something more if more people use it).

The second dimension is risk. The most important risk concerns the stable value of the reserve currency. The volatility of the reserve currency needs to be minimized. For this purpose, a mechanism is needed to govern the supply of the global reserve currency which can be based on both institutional rules and technical formulas. Reducing the risk of the reserve system reduces uncertainty for international economic activities and strengthens confidence in the reserve currency's purchasing power.

The third dimension concerns democracy and equity in wealth distribution. The global reserve system is an international public good: a common asset for the whole world. The benefits and costs that it generates should be equitably distributed among the people of all countries, regardless of the country's size within the world economy. To guarantee such fairness, the issuance and management of the reserve currency should be based on a global democratic governance mechanism. All countries can cooperate to set up an international institution which administers the reserve currency through democratic decision-making procedures. On the other side, to avoid monopolistic power, there need to be definite limitations on each country's power and privilege.

In line with the above evaluation criteria, different types of global reserve system can be compared as shown in Table 6.1. Objections to the USD system have been described above, and the system of multiple reserve currencies is not ideal either. Compared with the single currency system, the multiple currency system does, as a whole, have the advantage of relatively stable currency value. However, from the perspective of efficiency, one universally accepted currency is much more convenient than a system with multiple currencies. More than one currency performing the role of global money induces much higher transaction costs, because people often have to work with different currencies in making their transactions. Frequent exchanges between different currencies also increase exchange rate risks.

Table 6.1 A Comparison of Global Reserve Systems

	US dollar-based	Multiple reserve currencies	Supranational reserve currency
Efficiency	High	Relatively low	High
Risk	Unstable currency value	Relatively stable currency value Risk in exchange rates	Stable currency value
Democracy	Monopoly of currency supply Inequitable distribution in benefits and costs caused by core-periphery structure	Oligopoly of currency supply Inequitable distribution between regions caused by core-periphery structure	Joint decision on currency supply Non-core-periphery structure The degree of equity dependent on governance mechanisms

The comparison suggests that a global reserve system based on a supranational currency is a better choice on grounds of efficiency, stability, and – of particular interest here – democracy. A supranational money system provides more opportunities to attain the equitable participation of all countries and avoids a lock-in of the existing international oligarchy. When all countries are involved in issuing and managing the global currency, the traditional core-periphery structure can be avoided. Each country obtains a fair share of rights and responsibilities in the system.

In addition, an equitably managed supranational currency is more stable. When all countries collectively decide on the issuance and allocation of global money, then no single country can manipulate the regime. Moreover, a single globally accepted reserve currency is obviously much more convenient for international payments than multiple monies, which promotes efficiency and reduces transaction costs.

Having established the superiority of a supranational global money relative to the multiple currency approach, what kind of supranational money is to be preferred? Some economists suggest to establish the new reserve system on the foundation of the existent SDR, while others are exploring a possible brand new supranational currency. Among those innovations, digital currencies like Bitcoin warrant particular attention. Let us evaluate these two options in turn.

Prescription A: Reform of the SDR

The SDR is an international unit of account and reserve asset created by the IMF in 1969. The SDR was designed to supplement other reserve assets of member countries and to offer additional liquidity. By an amendment to the

IMF's Articles of Agreement, the SDR was to become the principal global reserve asset (Article VIII.7). The IMF allocates SDRs to its member countries, who may then hold the money as reserve assets, which can be used to cover balance of payments deficits and to pay off debts owed to the IMF (Cooper 2010: 66).

The proposal to establish a global reserve system based on the SDR suggests to build on the present regime of the IMF and SDRs (Kenen 2010, 2; Kenen 2011, 752). In the light of the evaluation criteria discussed previously – on the dimensions of efficiency, risk, and democracy – the SDR option has the following features.

In terms of efficiency, the SDR has significant limitations. For example, so far it has functioned only as a unit of account, without performing the roles of medium of exchange and store of value, except when central banks accept SDRs in settlement of international debts. Another problem is that SDRs can only be obtained through issuance and allocation by the IMF, which is a slow and politically delicate process. There have been only three general allocations of SDRs in nearly fifty years: SDR 9.3 billion in 1970–72, SDR 12.1 billion in 1979–81, and SDR 161.2 billion in 2009 (IMF 2015). A further difficulty – also from an equity perspective – is that the IMF distributes SDRs proportional to each country's quota in the institution, rather than for example in terms of the country's share of international trade. This quota-based approach reinforces rather than corrects the disproportionate advantages of the core countries. Moreover, the amount of SDRs allocated is still very small compared to other international currencies, so that SDRs account for but a negligible share of overall reserves. Also, SDRs can only be used by national monetary authorities, the IMF and certain other designated financial institutions such as the World Bank and the Bank for International Settlements (BIS). Private agents have no possibility to hold and trade SDRs.

In terms of risk and stability, the SDR has the advantage of having a more stable value than that of any national currency. The value of the SDR is based on a weighted average of four currency values: the USD, the pound sterling, the euro, and the yen. Furthermore, the allocation of SDRs is a permanent supplement to member countries' reserve assets, with no need to pay off. Consequently, the SDR reduces credit risks in the global reserve system.

As to democracy, the SDR regime has poor credentials. In the existing basket of currencies, the USD has an overly large share, and the currencies of emerging economies (let alone less-developed countries) are not included. In addition, when SDRs are allocated in accordance with each country's quota in the IMF, many developing countries do not receive the shares of SDRs that they need in order to stabilize their balance of payments and fight financial crises.

Therefore, in order to develop into a fully fledged SDR-based global reserve system, the present SDR regime requires several reforms. First, the

SDR needs to perform better as a medium of exchange and a store of value. Second, the amount of SDRs needs to expand enormously to meet the growth in demand for international reserves (Bird 2011, 212). Third, the SDR needs to attract a much larger market, which can be advanced if present limitations on the use and trading of SDRs are abolished. In particular, SDRs should be accessible to private agents, so that commercial international trade is encouraged to hold and use SDRs. Fourth, it would be helpful to develop an SDR-denominated bond market. These steps would reduce the transaction costs of the SDR and strengthen its role as an international currency.

In addition, further reforms to the SDR regime are needed to make this global money more democratic and equitable. In particular, the system needs the participation of all countries, especially those with emerging markets. The institutional mechanism which governs the SDR should provide fair opportunity for all countries that need and utilize the currency. Large countries (especially emerging economies) need better incorporation into the basket of currencies that makes up the SDR. Small countries need better borrowing rights for SDRs.

Prescription B: Decentralized Digital Currency

In recent years, digital currency transactions are emerging in many countries along with the rapid development of digital technology and the popularization of the Internet (Vigna and Casey 2015). Could digital currency open other prospects for more efficient and equitable global money? In this respect, Bitcoin, as the leader of cryptographic digital currencies, is attracting particular attention. Here we take Bitcoin as an example to explore the possibility of establishing a global reserve system based on a decentralized digital currency.

Bitcoin is a peer-to-peer (P2P) online payment system. 'P2P' implies a decentralized system with no central bank (Wikipedia 2015a). The issuance and transactions of Bitcoin, called 'mining', are carried out collectively by the network of all the participants. An encrypted algorithm ensures that every single part of the network has negligible power in the process, and the power becomes still more decentralized as the network expands (Yermack 2013, 4–6).

Since the first issuance of Bitcoin in 2009, the volume of transactions in the digital currency has increased rapidly. In January 2009, the number of Bitcoin transactions per day was only 87, but it reached as high as 63,277 in April 2014 (Bitcoin Charts 2014). The weighted market price for Bitcoin climbed to US$ 825 in January 2014, the highest price in its history, and then decreased sharply and continually, to nearly US$ 300 at the end of 2014. The scope of transactions using Bitcoin is gradually broadening, with more and more individuals, organizations, and governments accepting Bitcoin as a kind of currency that can be used to purchase products and services. On 8 May 2014, the market capitalization of Bitcoin reached US$ 5.67 billion (Bitcoin Charts 2014).

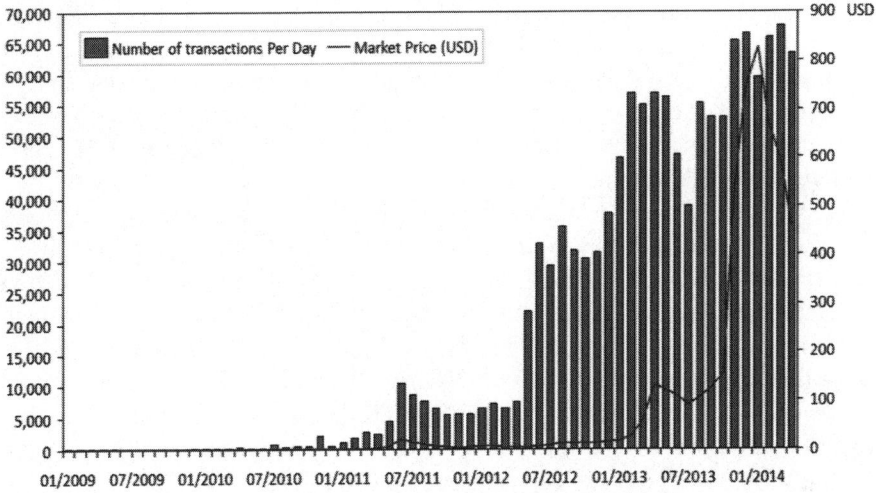

Figure 6.1 Development of Bitcoin Market. *Source*: Blockchain.info.

The current Bitcoin regime has the following features from the viewpoint of democracy, efficiency, and risk. From the perspective of democracy and equity, maybe no other form of money can better digital currencies such as Bitcoin. The decentralized quality of the Bitcoin regime puts an end to the monopoly creation of money supply. The decentralized generative mechanism and algorithm ensure that no individual or institution can ever manipulate the currency value by controlling its supply. This feature also eliminates the undemocratic distributive effect of the current core-periphery global reserve system. The algorithm of Bitcoin even gives a limit of the total possible generated amount, which is 21 million. Even though Bitcoin is thus branded as a 'deflation currency', Bitcoin's character of complete exogeneity in the process of money creation (where no individual or institution has control) is widely appreciated (Catalina *et al.* 2012, 159).

True, unequal distribution effects could be generated in the process of transactions in Bitcoin, through manipulative behaviour by a minority. However, such manipulation is inevitable in any international currency market. The severity of the problem depends primarily on the share of total market volume which is controlled by the minority. If the advantages of digital currency attract wider use, then it will be less possible for some small group to control it.

In regard to efficiency, Bitcoin realizes low transaction cost. Bitcoin is a kind of encrypted digital currency with a peer-to-peer consensus system based on the Internet. Bitcoin can be paid directly after an agreement is confirmed. The transaction cost is really low, and there is no risk of exchange rate fluctuations in cross-border transactions.

The biggest challenge for the digital currency system seems to be the problem of risk. The algorithm of Bitcoin itself technically enforces the limit of the maximum amount and the growth rate of the currency, so its value should be stable in the long run. At the moment, however, Bitcoin shows high-risk wild fluctuations in value. But are these risks inherent to Bitcoin, or can they be reduced in the long term?

One source of current risks relates to uncertainty of government policies towards digital currencies. Many governments have not accepted Bitcoin as a currency. For example, on 5 December 2013 the People's Bank of China together with four other ministries and commissions jointly issued a 'Notice on the Risk Prevention of Bitcoin' (PBC 2013). This declaration states that Bitcoin does not have the functions of currency and cannot be used and traded in the marketplace. The notice also forbade banks and third-party payment institutions to serve as Bitcoin exchanges. The RMB value of Bitcoin then plummeted.

Another source of current risk is the fierce competition among various digital currencies. After the upsurge of Bitcoin, multiple imitators appeared, including Litecoin (LTC), Ripple, and Peercoin (PPC). This competition raises the risk that Bitcoin could be substituted. Litecoin has already reached the second largest market capitalization, given its faster trade speed and lower mining difficulty (Wikipedia 2015b).

A third risk for Bitcoin comes from speculation. Like every monetary system, Bitcoin is open to speculation. Due to current relatively small trading volumes, the price of Bitcoin can be easily controlled by market speculators. However, the decentralized P2P character of Bitcoin could help to work against speculation, because no institution or person was originally endowed with more power to control it. So Bitcoin is not like a traditional centralized monetary system, in which the central bank is much more powerful than ordinary people. As the market volume of Bitcoin becomes ever larger, it will be more and more difficult for speculators to manipulate the market prices.

A fourth risk relates to technical security. Hacker attacks, network viruses, and security flaws can all harm Bitcoin owners. Even worse, these problems may break down the whole system. The largest Bitcoin exchange platform in the world, Mt. Gox, closed several times as a result of hacker attacks and security flaws, and eventually filed for bankruptcy in 2014.

Yet it is exactly the highly decentralized governance mechanism that can ensure a high degree of security in the process of generating digital currency. All of the risks around Bitcoin have occurred in respect of transaction and circulation, such as attacks on the platform and theft of user information. All of these problems are occurring in the early development of the digital currency system, without substantial international governance. Many of the difficulties can be resolved as the system matures.

Thus, with effective governance, a decentralized digital currency holds much promise as a global money. This system possesses intrinsic advantages in efficiency and equity which current global reserve arrangements cannot match. Nevertheless, this prospect can only be achieved after technical security is convincingly assured.

PROCESS: TOWARD A MORE EQUITABLE GLOBAL MONEY SYSTEM

The previous analysis advocates that future efforts focus on developing a supranational international currency system. Two main alternatives are available: an SDR-based system and a decentralized digital currency. In the long run, the decentralized digital system is more ideal for global economic democracy; however, in the short term, we still face substantial unequal development of the Internet sector among different world regions. Thus, more immediate efforts should focus on elevating the status of the SDR, which can also reduce the maladies of the current system.

The Short Term: Advancing the SDR

First, reform is needed of the SDR basket in order to acknowledge a larger number of major players in today's world economy. At present, the SDR value derives from the values of just four currencies. Yet, countries such as Brazil, China, India, and Russia now rank among the top 10 countries in the world by gross domestic product (GDP). These emerging economies also play increasing roles in global trade, finance, and investment. The SDR basket should become more diverse and inclusive to reflect this altered situation (Zhou 2009).

However, representation in the SDR basket should rest not only on economic variables, but also on political commitment. States whose currencies are added to the basket should also take greater responsibility to make the SDR regime work. For example, new players like China could promise to keep a significant part of their foreign exchange reserves in SDRs, instead of holding only the major national currencies.

The mechanism for allocating SDRs must also be reframed. Here the guiding principle should be 'those who use it have it'. At the moment, a country's access to SDRs is based on its quota in the IMF. The result is that countries who obtain the larger allotments of SDRs do not actually need them, while countries that do need more SDRs in their international transactions cannot get enough. An alternative would be to calculate allotments of SDRs partly in relation to the amount of cross-border exchange that a country denominates in SDRs. Such a rule would also encourage greater use of the SDR as a unit of account in the global economy and thereby reduce the undemocratic dominance of certain national currencies.

The Long Term: Advancing a Decentralized Digital Currency

A landmark in progress towards a digital currency will arrive when it is widely accepted and used as a medium of transaction. To reach this goal, action should be promoted on three levels: regulatory, commercial, and technical.

On the regulatory level, governance institutions in more countries need to permit the use of digital currency and protect transactions in digital currency. Currently, various states treat Bitcoin very differently. Several governments (including those of Indonesia, Russia, and Vietnam) have prohibited the circulation of Bitcoin, but the majority of states have not done so. Both the United States Treasury and the European Central Bank classify Bitcoin and similar denominations as convertible decentralized digital currency.

On the commercial level, it is very important to help people learn more about digital currency and encourage its use in transactions. The good news is that more and more commercial organizations now accept payments in Bitcoin. They include influential enterprises such as eBay, Microsoft Store, and Paypal.

On the technical level, as discussed earlier, security is a precondition for the wide acceptance of digital currency. This challenge can be overcome by two kinds of global governance mechanisms. On the one hand, effective governance needs civil society involvement, which can be achieved through comprehensive communication and cooperation between the technicians and representatives from worldwide organizations, especially the large digital exchange platforms. On the other hand, governments of all countries should strengthen their cooperation for the digital currency system. Traditionally, monetary governance concentrates on the supply, circulation, and settlement of the currency. In contrast, governance of digital currency should focus on the following issues. First, supervision of network information security should be reinforced to avoid breakdown of the transaction system. Second, legalization and government oversight of the digital currency industry should be advanced. A third requirement is to build up coordination between the digital currency transaction system and the traditional financial industry. Furthermore, government acceptance of (and effective surveillance of) digital currency as a legitimate currency would greatly expand its transaction sphere.

Finally, should Bitcoin be championed as the unique global money in the future? This remains to be seen. In any case, some form of decentralized digital currency system is better than the current international money system. But whether that would be Bitcoin, Litecoin, or some other 'coin' cannot yet be decided. The choice will emerge in the evolution of the digital currencies and through competition among different digital systems.

So there will be two phases in the path to the digital currency era. In the first phase, various digital currency systems are developed, and they bring not only great convenience, but also some chaos. In the second phase, some type of digital currency system shows outstanding qualities and gradually becomes commonly accepted. Concurrently, the necessary regulatory measures and institutional infrastructures are built up. As its volume grows tremendously and its distribution is sufficiently decentralized, the currency's value will become satisfactorily stable, and risk will decrease significantly, which in turn will strengthen the leading status of this currency. Effective regulation will be needed to ensure that the digital currency brings equitably distributed benefits to all.

CONCLUSION

This chapter has explored two proposals to reform the current global reserve system. The first proposal is to establish an SDR-based reserve system. Reforms to this supranational reserve system include augmenting the SDR's role as an international currency, as well as setting up a more democratic governance mechanism for the SDR. The second proposal is to establish a global reserve system based on a decentralized digital currency under effective governance. To implement the digital system and address its risks, reforms should concentrate on ensuring technical security through a combination of non-governmental cooperation and governmental supervision.

In the long run, a decentralized digital monetary system is more ideal for global economic democracy. While it is difficult to reach this destination in the short run, many improvements can be made in the meantime by elevating the SDR's role in the international reserve system. If the SDR and the digital currency regimes were reformed on these lines, then the global reserve system would have more equal participation. Extensive participation would in turn help to redistribute power among countries and improve welfare, especially for low-income countries. A more balanced, stable, and fair system would also benefit the West and the world as a whole.

Political economy affirms that the international monetary system is highly political. The existing international reserve system matches the present international political structure. However, it does not follow that nothing can be done. The monetary system can also be viewed as a tool of people's power, given that a currency is more powerful if more people use it. As the information society promotes processes of social flattening, opportunities for a people's transformation of global money grow.

Chapter 7

Financing Global Public Goods
The Case for a Currency Transaction Levy
Nina Hall and Inge Kaul

The world is facing global crises of epic proportions, ranging from an increased frequency of extreme weather events, due to climate change, to outbreaks of communicable diseases. Many of these crises are predicted to have, and are already having, the worst impacts on our societies, especially the world's poor. States, NGOs, and civil society are also seeking ways to reduce global inequalities and foster development in less developed nations, with the Sustainable Development Goals (SDGs) being the latest manifestation of this. Yet the international community faces a dilemma: while there is a growing list of global challenges, governments have serious financial constraints. It is thus essential to find new ways to generate global finances for global public goods and efficiently allocate these.

This chapter proposes the introduction of a modest levy on all international currency transactions to help alleviate the current resource constraints. Such a levy could raise over US $25 billion annually, as it taps into one of the largest financial markets. The size of the international currency market is striking: in April 2013, trading in foreign exchange markets averaged US $5.3 trillion per day (Bank for International Settlements 2014). Furthermore, the foreign exchange market has been steadily growing: from US $3.3 trillion per day in April 2007 to US $4 trillion per day in April 2010. The size and growth of the foreign exchange market offers great opportunity for generating finances for global public goods. The levy would operate on a user-pays basis: those who use the global economy, by making international currency transactions, would contribute to a world fund for global public goods.

Instituting such a levy is not a new suggestion. In 2009, a committee of academic experts recommended an internationally collected currency transaction levy (CTL) as the simplest, most effective way to raise finances for development. (One author of this chapter served as a member of this expert group, though not all the views expressed here are identical with those presented in the group's report.) As well as the centrally collected CTL, on which the present chapter focuses, the expert group also examined a financial sector activity tax, a VAT on financial services, a broad financial transaction tax, and a nationally collected single-currency transaction tax (Innovative Financing to Fund Development Leading Group 2009). In addition, the heads of the UK's leading development NGOs urged the Group of Eight (G8) finance ministers in 2009 to institute such a CTL to address the shortfall in global health financing (Millar et al. 2009). US and European NGOs and think tanks have also made similar demands to the US government and the European Union (EU), respectively. In the aftermath of the global financial crisis, others have also made calls and examined proposals for a broad tax on financial services. The Robin Hood Tax campaign in the United Kingdom is one prominent example, with its call for a levy of about 0.05 per cent on transactions involving stocks, bonds, foreign currency, and derivatives, which could raise £250 billion a year globally (Robin Hood Tax 2014). Scholars such as Schulmeister (2011) have also argued for the implementation of a financial transactions tax (FTT) in the EU context, building on a long-standing global campaign led by groups such as ATTAC.

However, proposals for a broad FTT differ from the narrower CTL suggested here. Their primary aim is to reduce financial speculation and volatility in the financial sector. In contrast, the CTL looks at generating funds for global public goods through a levy on just one exchange, although it may have some secondary effects on speculation and volatility (Innovative Financing to Fund Development Leading Group 2009). In short, the CTL is proposed as an effective, efficient, and technically feasible way to address the shortfall in financing for global public goods from climate change mitigation to public health.

This proposal is part of a broader normative debate, reflected in the other chapters in this book, on how we can restructure and change the global economy to ensure that it benefits everyone, and not just the richest. While others focus on the role of intellectual property regulation, microcredits, and fair trade, we look to global financial institutions to address the impacts of globalization. This chapter's unique contribution is to outline a tangible way to finance global problems outlined in this book, such as climate mitigation and adaptation. The aim is to mobilize a reliable stream of resource additionality that could foster a more inclusive, democratic global system, as the editors and other authors of this book have urged.

The rest of this chapter is structured in five sections. It begins by outlining why we need new sources of global public finance to avert global systemic crises, pointing out that donor states, even prior to the global financial crisis, were not meeting their development finance targets. The next three sections respectively explain how a CTL would work, describe how the finances generated from this levy would be governed, and argue for launching a pilot initiative. The final section identifies some of the challenges to establishing global funds for global public goods.

THE CHALLENGE: FINANCING GLOBAL PUBLIC GOODS

The history of the financing of international cooperation endeavours, including that of official development assistance (ODA), has taught us that the willingness of states to pay for international cooperation is limited. In fact, the pledge made by governments nearly forty years ago, which states recommitted to in Paris in 2005, to direct 0.7 per cent of national income is still not being met (OECD DAC 2014). Serious funding gaps have persisted even during 'good' economic times and in critical areas such as climate change, where mounting empirical evidence suggests that we are fast approaching critical tipping points. This is because states carefully guard their taxation authority and are cautious about financing projects at the international level through pooled funding. This, of course, has a positive aspect: it keeps international cooperation linked to national needs, holds international organizations accountable to citizens, and reduces the risk of over-centralization.

However, the reluctance of states to adequately fund multilateral initiatives becomes a major concern when many policy challenges, due to their global scope and interdependent nature, depend on international-level pooling of public revenue and decisive collective action. This is particularly true of global public goods, which are non-excludable and non-rival and affect all countries or anyone, anywhere. States too often pursue their own narrowly defined national interests, letting others contribute to addressing a particular global challenge, such as communicable disease control, without contributing adequately themselves. Then when the good exists, they enjoy it – free of charge, or at limited national cost. Such an approach may work in some cases for one (albeit small) country. But when all states are operating on this logic, as they currently are, it creates gridlock: no state will come forward with funds if no-one else does so. This stops states from preventing crises and leads most often to terrible consequences for the world's poor (Kaul 2013). This is clearly seen in the 2014 Ebola outbreak: states did not adequately prepare for a health crisis in West Africa, or provide finance and personnel to mitigate it at an early stage (Medhora 2014).

In addition, budgetary rules and fiscal pressures in industrial countries may prevent states from mobilizing large revenue sums through their national taxation systems, especially in issue areas that lack a powerful lobby. While huge sums of money have been mobilized for the purposes of bank bailouts, the stabilization of international financial markets, and military pursuits, there is comparatively little spent on global systemic challenges. The US government, for instance, authorized its Treasury Department to spend up to US $700 billion to purchase distressed assets, especially mortgage-backed securities, and supply cash directly to banks. This sum dwarfs the US development budget – in 2014 USAID requested US$20.1 billion from the US Congress (USAID 2014). Defence ministry budgets are also swollen when compared with their development counterparts: the German government authorized a budget of €32.44 billion for defence in 2014, compared with €6.443 billion for the Ministry for Economic Cooperation and Development (BMZ 2014).

Even though states may sometimes have compelling reasons for their limited willingness or ability to pay for international cooperation, problems like climate change, food and water scarcity, and biodiversity loss do not wait. If left unaddressed, they deepen, driving the world closer to thresholds of irreversible damage. The *Human Development Report 2014*, for instance, notes that more than 2.2 billion people (or more than 15 per cent of the world's population) are near to or live in multidimensional poverty (UNDP 2014). It is not only opportune, but also imperative to explore alternative sources of public finance in cases where a challenge is of global systemic importance.

This is especially important now, as states, notably the conventional 'donor' countries, appear to be increasingly intent on motivating the private sector to contribute more to the financing of global public policy. Again, this is to be welcomed in cases where private-sector actors are indeed the best-suited financiers to make up for the gaps in states' provision. However, we have no clear criteria on when to use public finance and when to use private finance. Furthermore, we cannot rely on the private sector to voluntarily mitigate and resolve all global crises, especially since these challenges require long-term steady commitments. We therefore need to find innovative financing solutions.

We are facing two main policy challenges: first, to identify and test ways of improving, as soon as possible, the current lack of global public financing; and second, to break out of a state-centric model of global public goods financing. We need to prevent global challenges from lingering unresolved for decades, and make it possible to generate greater public money to be allocated to crisis prevention and control. The next three sections of this chapter address the first challenge; the final section discusses the second challenge.

CLOSING THE FINANCING GAP: HOW A CURRENCY TRANSACTION LEVY COULD HELP

A CTL is a technically and legally feasible way to generate billions of dollars annually in global public finance. A CTL can be designed as a single-currency instrument levied nationally or by the member states of a currency zone. In this case, a levy would be issued at the national or regional level on all transactions from or to that currency. If the European Union (EU) established such a levy, for instance, all exchanges of another currency into euros would be taxed (by the EU) at a small rate. Alternatively, the levy can be designed as a global instrument which applies to all currency transactions at the point of their international settlement. We favour the global CTL variant, given that the CTL's main purpose is to address global problems. The proceeds would accrue and be managed internationally and, thus, obviate the need for protracted and often inconclusive bargaining with national fiscal authorities.

Such a global CTL is possible, as international currency transactions are increasingly centralized and channelled through banks such as the Continuous Linked Settlement (CLS) Bank. The CLS Bank is an industry-owned consortium with 59 member banks as its shareholders and more than 7,000 participating entities (funds, banks, and corporates) that use its services and already pay a small levy to do so. In 2009, the bank's payment instructions amounted to a daily average of US$ 3.766 trillion (CLS Bank 2009). In April 2012, this figure stood at US$ 4.47 trillion.

A 2009 study on financial levies, conducted by a panel of international economists, concluded that the CTL would be technically as well as legally feasible and generate significant resources with minimal transaction costs. The study estimated that, taking into account only the four major currencies (dollar, euro, pound sterling, and yen) and assuming a levy rate of 0.005 per cent, the annual proceeds from the CTL would amount to about US$ 33 billion (Innovative Financing to Fund Development Leading Group 2009). The levy could be reduced to 0.000 per cent, if in the future there was no longer a need for such centrally collected revenue. Adjusting the rate to this level would avoid 'moral hazard', where the presence of a global fund to address a problem, such as climate change, could engender perverse incentives (a country may decide not to invest in climate mitigation or adaptation policies if others will bail it out). However, given the scale of the problems the world faces today, it is unlikely that the levy would be reduced quickly to a zero level. Furthermore, in the interest of predictability, it would be desirable to keep the levy rate stable.

The levy would be collected by the CLS Bank in London and paid for initially by the banks when they conduct currency transactions. However, the CLS Bank's clients could pass the levy burden on to their clients, who, in turn, could pass it on to theirs, and so on. In this way, the levy would be a user fee paid by all who are involved in international economic activity, and payments would be proportional to each actor's depth of involvement. The underlying rationale for this levy is that all who participate in cross-border economic activity benefit from the provision of global public goods – whether it be global climate stability or a well-functioning trade and finance system – and should thus contribute the resources to maintain it. In addition, while the poor are often still outside the benefit streams that economic globalization creates, they tend to suffer the most due to the under-provision of global public goods.

GOVERNING THE USE OF THE PROCEEDS: ESTABLISHING A GLOBAL CTL FACILITY

While the CLS Bank could serve as the collection point, a new body, perhaps called the 'Global CTL Facility', would be needed to receive and channel the levy proceeds. This facility would be comprised of a governing board and a bank account, to which the CLS Bank would transfer the collected levy proceeds and from which the funds would be transferred to concerned operational agencies. The role of the governing board would be to ensure, in close consultation with state and non-state actors, that the funds flow to where they are most needed, taking into account established global policy priorities and the best providers.

It would be important for the CTL to gain political and public support. In particular, there would need to be broad public consultation on the criteria to allocate funds and to have a body such as the United Nations General Assembly agree on them. The Global CTL Facility should keep national parliaments informed about its spending and publicly disclose its revenues and disbursements every year. A key issue to clarify would be whether to target the funds on one major cause, such as climate change mitigation, or to allocate them to multiple concerns. As the resource volume to be generated by the CTL would be relatively modest (approximately US$ 30 billion a year), it may be best to concentrate this spending on one or two top priorities. These could include ensuring adequate funding of the Green Climate Fund and/or research development on communicable diseases, which if uncontrolled will adversely affect the health of the poor and stifle investments in poor countries.

The introduction of the CTL would not change the current multilateral decision-making patterns, nor would it affect national budgets, as it would raise the levy from so far untaxed resources. All the CTL would do is facilitate a better matching of stated global policy purposes on the one hand and financing priorities on the other.

HOW TO DO IT IN PRACTICE: A PILOT INITIATIVE

Ideally, the UN General Assembly would request the CLS Bank to collect a levy and establish a Global CTL Facility to manage the proceeds. Member states of the UN could then monitor the use of funds and ensure that they were targeted at agreed upon global problems. However, it is unlikely that industrialized states will initiate such action through the UN General Assembly. Many countries are experiencing severe fiscal constraints, and if interested in introducing a financial levy will most probably do so only for their own national good (Barker 2014; European Commission 2013). Most states are already falling behind in delivering on their announced support for the Green Climate Fund (Ryan *et al.* 2012). So how can we overcome states' reluctance to establish a new global levy which is managed by a global body?

We propose that a pilot project could be set up on a voluntary basis by states and/or banks. Someone would persuade the member banks of the CLS Bank to collect a modest levy and establish the Global CTL Facility as a pilot. Although there may be some initial reluctance from banks, the CLS and its clients could be encouraged to introduce the levy as a corporate social responsibility measure. Offering to act as the CTL collection point, the CLS Bank could also help restore the public image of financial market actors. However, the benefits for the bank, its members and its clients would be far greater, as they are among the main beneficiaries of undertakings to avert global risks and excessive instability. Accordingly, an advisory board could be selected by the participating banks, keeping in mind that for legitimacy and effectiveness reasons, it would be imperative to have a representative board.

But who will take the first step? Our proposal is that the UN Global Compact Office and the World Economic Forum (WEF), with additional nudging from the World Social Forum (WSF), could invite the world's major banks, who are CLS members, to commit themselves voluntarily to introduce the CTL. This could be their contribution to a successful implementation of the SDGs. Importantly, the CTL would be established on a pilot basis that could be easily closed down should the test phase indicate that the levy is not workable on a wider, global basis. The CTL could be initially set up for a defined number of years. The starting levy rate could be set at a lower rate in order to incentivize participation during the pilot phase. This would still generate a meaningful amount of additional resources. Once the expected positive results become visible, governments might dare to devise a longer-term institutional arrangement and increase the levy, recognizing that a more stable and sustainable world economy and polity benefits all, rich and poor alike, and also allows states to regain policymaking sovereignty. Either way, even a levy rate of 0.005 per cent would neither be market-distorting nor create any major avoidance problems.

The CTL could build on the success of other levies initiated for global public goods, such as the air ticket levy, initiated by the French government, which funds HIV/AIDS programmes. Since 2006, France has applied a levy to every departing flight, and nine other countries have also adopted it (UNITAID 2014). This levy has been established on a voluntary basis. Each country chooses the rate and ticket class which it targets, and implements the measure through the adoption of a law or decree by the national parliament. The levy is then simply added to an existing airport tax. The majority of the funds go to UNITAID, a global health agency hosted by the World Health Organization (WHO), to increase funding for greater access to treatments for HIV/AIDS, malaria, and tuberculosis in low-income countries. This is an excellent example of innovative financing to address global public goods.

CONCLUSION: OVERCOMING THE SOVEREIGNTY PARADOX TO PROMOTE GLOBAL DEMOCRACY

States today are caught in a sovereignty paradox. They are shying away from international cooperation, notably from sharing their public revenue, out of fear that they could be losing policymaking sovereignty. As a result, global challenges remain unresolved and spill over national borders, thus compelling states to be more concerned about crisis prevention and management – rather than merely pursuing narrow national priorities and goals. Instead of regaining or maintaining their policymaking sovereignty, they are losing it, bit by bit, with every new or resurgent crisis (Kaul 2013). In this process, the world's poorest are left worst off. They obtain the least from the benefits of economic globalization and suffer the most from its adverse consequences. How can we overcome the lack of finances for global crises and global public goods, given states' reluctance?

A CTL is one practical, feasible solution. By taxing international currency transactions on a user-pays basis, we could generate significant finances for global public goods. These funds would be collected centrally at the CLS Bank and dispersed by a trustee body which is mandated to channel the funds, in consultation with the concerned multilateral bodies. Following the success of the French air ticket levy, we suggest that a pilot phase could be started by entrepreneurial states or banks on a voluntary basis. In doing so, the CTL would foster global democracy by ensuring that most of the global challenges outlined in this book have a permanent, secure stream of international financing. Given the increasing problems the world is facing, now is the time to begin testing a CTL.

Chapter 8

Copyfight

Global Redistribution in the Digital Age

Blayne Haggart

Of all the issues affecting economic and social inequality discussed in this book – finance, food sovereignty, climate change, to mention only a few – copyright may seem like a marginal subject. However, as this chapter will argue, copyright, particularly as it relates to online activities, is one of the main structures shaping the distribution of wealth and access to know-ledge and culture in the twenty-first century.

Citizens around the world have grasped the importance of this issue, transforming a previously neglected area of commercial law into one of the most surprisingly politicized issues of the past decade, capable of mobilizing millions into action. On 18 January 2012, thousands of websites, including Wikipedia and Reddit, stopped operating ('went dark') in an act of voluntary self-censorship to protest against the US Stop Online Piracy Act (SOPA), a bill that aimed to achieve stronger copyright enforcement and that opponents believed could 'break the Internet' (Hruska 2011). Consequently, millions of Americans contacted their elected representatives in Washington to express displeasure over SOPA. Within a day, the bill was effectively dead, marking the largest defeat of the 'copyright industries' in thirty years (Sell 2013, 67). Thanks to the efforts of 'a transnational coalition of engineers, academics, hackers, technology companies, bloggers, consumer activists, and Internet users' (Sell 2013, 67), copyright was transformed overnight into a politically poisonous topic in the USA.

This was not an online-only issue, the purview of millennial 'slacktivists'. Less than a month after the SOPA protests, on 11 February 2012, over 100,000 Europeans took to the streets to protest an intellectual property (IP) agreement, the Anti-Counterfeiting Trade Agreement (ACTA), which was being negotiated largely in secret and was designed, among other things, to ratchet up enforcement of copyright on the Internet (Arthur and agencies

2012b). Critics contended that ACTA would have severe effects on everything from freedom of expression and privacy rights to online innovation (Carrier 2013; Amnesty International 2012). Although the European Union and many of its members have signed the treaty, ACTA has become so unpopular that it is unlikely to be ratified (Arthur and agencies 2012a).

Nor is digital copyright a preoccupation only for the Global North. Even before the SOPA protests, in July 2011, the Mexican Senate – a body that less than a decade earlier had voted overwhelmingly to extend the term of copyright to a world-leading life of the author plus hundred years – unanimously voted to reject ACTA. Mexico was one of only two developing countries (Morocco being the other) invited to the talks. Over the course of a year, a small group of activists, leveraging social media, key Senate contacts, and a keen understanding of the issue and Mexican politics, managed to orchestrate this policy turnaround. The final Senate resolution condemned the secrecy of the talks and expressed concern about how ACTA's stronger enforcement of digital copyright could negatively affect constitutionally guaranteed rights, Mexican economic development, and the 'digital divide' (Haggart 2014a; see also Haggart 2014b).

The scale and passion of these protests surprised mainstream observers, who were just catching up with what these millions of activists have realized over the past decade. The resistance responded to long-standing efforts to further tilt the global rules over copyright law and global Internet governance. These two policy domains are increasingly shaping economic and social life as it relates to the control over the creation of and access to knowledge. Property has always been a key means of controlling who gets what under capitalism, and copyright represents an attempt to commodify knowledge itself, and thus determine who will profit in the global digital economy.

Ever-stronger rules and copyright enforcement in the online world – driven by media conglomerates and developed countries, particularly the USA – put at risk not only basic rights like freedom of expression, access to culture, and privacy rights, but also the future shape of a global economy that increasingly relies in ways large and small on the decentralized platform known as the Internet. Further, the extent to which the rules reflect a specific, Western property-based regime of knowledge governance, to the exclusion of other views, raises questions about global accountability and democratic governance. While the outcome of this debate is particularly important for citizens of developing countries that have yet to realize the full benefits of broadband access, it will have long-lasting effects on the worldwide potential for economic innovation, and in determining the beneficiaries of the digital economy. Just as the debate over trade policy – another previously apolitical, technocratic subject – erupted in the 1990s, so will the debate over IP, and especially laws of digital copyright, play a significant role in global political economy debates of the early twenty-first century.

This state of affairs prompts two questions. First, what type of copyright law makes sense in the digital age? Second, given the importance of IP to the world's most powerful countries, particularly the USA, and to the interests of politically and economically powerful firms, to what extent can smaller countries influence the copyright laws under which their citizens live? In other words, are democratic laws of digital copyright possible, and what should they look like?

The authors in this volume have been asked to consider not only problems, but also to offer possible and practical solutions. In this spirit, this chapter argues that we should consider copyright policy from the perspective of the social good. Although we often think of copyright as a way to protect the work of individual creators, its actual purpose and effect are much broader, namely, promoting and regulating the creation and dissemination of knowledge and culture. Given that future innovation and prosperity depends on our ability to learn and improve, and our (legal) ability to do that depends on access to knowledge and information, it makes more sense to emphasize the need to access and disseminate knowledge, rather than continuing down the path of ever-stronger copyright protection. While loosening copyright protection will face strong opposition from entrenched and powerful interests, the SOPA and ACTA protests offer a template for successful reform that better reflects the needs and desires of the disadvantaged, and not just the privileged.

DIAGNOSIS: KICKING AWAY THE DIGITAL LADDER

Copyright as a Global Regime

Control over the rules governing knowledge – that is, control over 'the production, possession, control, communication, and above all, the legitimization of knowledge' (Tooze 2000, 187) – is, as the political economist Susan Strange (1987; 1994) identified, a key means by which structural power is exerted in the global political economy. As noted by Christopher May (1996, 192), 'Power in the knowledge structure lies as much in the capacity to deny knowledge, to exclude others, as in the power to convey knowledge.'

Forms of knowledge regulation are always historically contingent, reflecting a society's fundamental values and power structures. In today's world, copyright – and IP generally – is the primary means by which knowledge protection and dissemination are regulated, and reflects the fundamental Western values of individualism (the individual author) and private property. Copyright, for instance, is the state-backed legal means by which certain forms of knowledge (literary works, music, film, computer programmes) are commodified and rendered as property. Deeply embedded within processes of modernity and capitalism, copyright is a form of IP rights – 'the key method to assert ownership over knowledge resources' (May 2000, 13). Like all forms of property, those who control copyrights can use them to 'accumulate more resources' (May 2000, 21) and thus power to shape the future direction of the economy. Copyright, as well as other forms of IP, function as 'enclosures' (May 2000, 13), placing control of what would otherwise be freely available for all to use (what is often referred to as the global information commons, or public domain) in the hands of the owner of the copyright, who, because copyrights (like most forms of property) are alienable, is not necessarily the creator of a work. In fact, the majority of economically valuable copyrights rest in the hands of a small number of transnational corporations.

Copyright, and IP generally, usually justified as a necessary means to encourage an optimal level of creative production. The thinking is that, as creation is costly in terms of time and resources and copying is relatively cheap, the scale of creative work in a society will be suboptimal without some form of protection to prevent easy copying. IP laws also implicitly take into account that providing creators with complete protection for their works would give them a monopoly over future creation. This is why exceptions – situations in which people do not have to ask permission to copy things like short quotations in a book chapter – are built into copyright and IP laws. IP is rooted in deeply held Enlightenment views on the importance of private property and individualism (see especially Rose 1993), but the argument is based more on faith than actual evidence. A 2009 analysis of the effects of changes to US copyright law on creative work concluded that strengthening copyright does not incentivize innovation (Ku *et al.* 2009). In fact, much of what is actually created occurs without copyright acting as an incentive. Academics who produce much of the world's knowledge are often remunerated from the public purse, not copyright royalties. The folk music that served as the engine for the multi-million-dollar careers of such stars as Bob Dylan and the Rolling Stones not only was created without the benefit of copyright, but once transmogrified by these artists was turned into private property, with a stream of royalties that will flow to them and their estates for years after they are dead. In the field of knowledge and innovation, copyrights controlled by a small number of academic publishers have created a walled garden around the world's knowledge (much of which is created at public expense), which the world is usually only permitted to access upon paying a toll to the gatekeeper. In the end, the biggest winners from increased IP protection are not creators (especially future creators), but rather those who own the existing copyrights and patents needed as inputs to future creative work. Given this troubling empirical evidence, current attempts to strengthen global IP protection, such as the ongoing

Trans-Pacific Partnership (TPP) negotiations, benefit those corporations that own IP rights. Strengthening IP protection 'introduces a distortion that makes the world a bit poorer' (Krugman 2015).

All knowledge-regulation regimes involve rules to promote dissemination – knowledge that cannot be shared is practically useless – and control – for instance, to ensure its legitimacy and integrity, to commodify it as in the case of IP, or to achieve a wider societal goal (restrictions on nuclear bomb making know-how is a good example). However, in the current situation, by concentrating control over who is allowed to copy what, and under what circumstances, in the hands of a small number of firms that are focused on maximizing economic returns, stronger IP laws threaten this development imperative and imperil the information commons upon which everyone must draw in order to create new knowledge and culture. It also shuts out of the debate alternative views about how the global information commons could be governed, and in whose interest.

Intellectual property (typically defined as copyright, patents, trademarks, and trade secrets) has been at the heart of all major trade agreements since the 1980s, and particularly since the mid-1990s (Drahos and Braithwaite 2002, 11). This focus on IP in economic treaties speaks to the rising importance of knowledge as property in the contemporary global political economy, especially for the most powerful economic countries. The link between trade and IP policy was due in large part to US efforts, spurred by the transnational IP-dependent firms that are the main beneficiaries of these laws (Drahos and Braithwaite 2002; Sell 2003). For example, the 1995 Agreement on Trade-Related Aspects of Intellectual Property Rights (TRIPS), which effectively was the US price for creating the World Trade Organization (WTO), 'imposed upon the world not only the economic interests of its own IP-based industries . . . but a degree of protectionism that is economically and culturally destructive to developing countries' (Towse and Holzhauer 2002, xviii). Despite the United States' strong position, some countries, such as Brazil and India, have opposed greater IP protection on the grounds that it would restrict the flow of advanced technology needed to address social issues. Since then, organizations like the World Intellectual Property Organization (WIPO) and the Office of the United States Trade Representative (USTR) have engaged in training officials from developing countries on how to implement (a particular view of) their treaty obligations, effectively socializing the elites responsible for IP issues in Western approaches to this sector of global governance. Drahos (2007) notes a similar socializing effect with respect to the establishment of patent offices in developing countries. Consequently, at times, activists even in developing countries must contend with governments that are friendly to development-restrictive IP policies.

Despite the lack of evidence that stronger IP incentivizes new knowledge creation, stronger IP protection is promoted in treaty negotiations as necessary for a country's development. However, in practice, the benefits of stronger IP rights accrue to those who hold the most economically valuable IP, which are almost uniquely in the developed countries, and one developed country in particular. In 2012, according to World Bank data, the United States received US$ 120.7 billion from other countries for the use of IP, over half of the world total flow of charges for IP. Trailing distantly in second place was Japan, at 13 per cent (US$ 31.9 billion). Singapore, the top developing industrialized country, ranked fourteenth, with 0.6 per cent of total global flows. Mexico, meanwhile, was in thirty-fourth place, with 0.04 per cent of total international IP flows (World Bank 2015).

Copyright in a Development Context

The consequences of copyright reform are particularly serious for developing countries, where access to information is key to constructing a modern economy. The most-developed states advocate or impose liberal free trade policies, because such measures provide them with a competitive advantage while ignoring the historical reality that their own economic development depended on protectionist measures (Chang 2002). Strong copyright is being pursued by those firms and countries, such as the USA, that currently enjoy a lead in information production and technology, as well as in copyright and patenting procedures.

Since the beginning of the 2000s, developing countries in particular have become increasingly aware of how copyright and IP laws affect their place in the global economy and the maintenance of global material inequality, both among and within countries (Drahos and Braithwaite 2002; Sell 2003). Story (2003, 799), for example, argues that 'copyright definitely creates a further barrier to access . . . and the global inequality in the private property rights of copyright further reinforces and, indeed, is one source of global inequality and unequal opportunity more generally'. As a result, he concludes, 'The *Berne Convention* [the main and oldest international copyright treaty] should be repealed as it does not and, in fact, cannot serve the interests of more than three-quarters of the world's population' (Story 2003, 800).

The early 2000s also saw the emergence of the 'Access to Knowledge' (A2K) movement, which 'takes concerns with copyright law and other regulations that affect knowledge and places them within an understandable social need and policy platform: access to knowledge goods' (KEI 2005). The movement is linked in part with older campaigns to provide affordable drugs to people in developing countries (a patent-related issue). The movement's main objectives, according to a 2005 A2K draft treaty created by a coalition of non-governmental organizations, academics, and activists, and spearheaded by the movement's flagship group, the US-based Knowledge Ecology International, 'are to protect and enhance [expand] access to knowledge, and to facilitate the transfer of technology to developing countries' (CPTech 2005). Furthermore, at the WIPO, developing countries are pursuing a 'development agenda', which calls for the implementation of forty-five recommendations made by the Provisional Committee on Proposals Related to a WIPO Development Agenda and accepted by the 2007 WIPO General Assembly (WIPO 2007).

The Digital Challenge to Copyright Law

The Internet is a giant copying machine, transmitting messages and information by copying them from server to server. Digitization offers the potential for inexpensive access to the world's knowledge and culture. In developing as in developed countries, the big issue in this respect is the 'digital divide': overcoming inequalities of income and availability to ensure that as many people as possible can access this repository and learn, communicate, create, and engage with the wider society, culture, and world. Although broadband penetration rates are rising worldwide, there remain gaps between and within countries, impeding the ability of marginalized peoples to access the Internet.

For the content industries, however, the digital age represents a threat to their property rights. Previously, physical scarcity could go a long way towards protecting property rights in their works: copying physical books, particularly on a commercial scale, is a costly undertaking. The Internet undercuts this scarcity by allowing anyone with a computer and an online connection to reproduce and distribute perfect copies of anything that can be digitized (which is almost everything). In response, the content industries and their government allies have pursued laws and treaties to ensure that only authorized copies circulate, effectively pursuing a policy of ever-increasing commodification of knowledge, placing a toll on the future creation of knowledge and culture by enclosing the digital commons. As Carrier (2013, 30–31) notes,

> Legislation and agreements like SOPA, PIPA [the Protect Intellectual Property Act, companion US legislation to SOPA], ACTA, and the TPP include broad, vague language that could be used aggressively by copyright holders to stifle innovation. Innovators could not clearly show that their service does not aid, abet, enable, or facilitate infringement, as the Internet itself and countless websites and services could be found liable under such a standard.

Attempts to strengthen protection of digital copyright have faced democratic legitimacy issues. At the international level, treaties such as ACTA and the TPP are being negotiated largely in secret. The official ACTA text, for example, was only released officially in April 2010, four years after negotiations began. As of September 2014, member states have yet to release the text to the IP-heavy TPP text. Thwarted by legislative processes, copyright industries are also turning increasingly to informal, 'voluntary' agreements to pursue a form of stronger, private, copyright enforcement (Tusikov 2014).

In response, new voices have risen up to defend the knowledge commons. Crucially, where previous copyright laws targeted commercial-scale infringement by firms, these new laws have directly targeted individuals, criminalizing personal digital copyright infringement (file sharing) and then suing individuals (their customers). As a result, individuals have been radicalized and copyright politicized. The digital age has also led to the creation of new Internet businesses based on the dissemination of knowledge. Some of these firms are wholly new creations (such as the US-based Google and Amazon), while others are legacy telecommunications firms in developed and developing countries that have to address copyright on a large scale for the first time. While the content, telecommunications, and Internet industries all deal with information, they tend to emphasize different values and make their money in different ways, which places them on different sides of the 'protection/dissemination' divide. If the default position for content and IP industries is to restrict and control the spread of information through ever-stronger IP rights, the position of the Internet industries is to encourage the spread of information as widely and efficiently as possible.

Digital Copyright and Developing Countries

The importance of copyright in the digital age goes beyond its effect on knowledge production and dissemination; it is a key part of the battle over the future governance of the Internet itself. As currently structured, the Internet does not discriminate between 'authorized' and 'unauthorized' content. It is also an open network, where anyone can set up shops, services, blogs, or other formats that we have not yet imagined. This open architecture has led to some remarkable economic innovations, most of which caught legacy industries by surprise.

As Internet penetration rates increase in developing countries, the open nature of the World Wide Web offers them the possibility to reap economic, social, and cultural dividends similar to those that have accrued to developed countries. There exists a tension between content owners who want Internet services like Google to police their networks for infringement activities, and to cover any related costs, and Internet firms, such as search engines and web hosting companies, who would rather not. Taken to its extreme, stringent enforcement of copyright online could require reworking the Internet so that it gives content owners a veto over what gets transmitted as well as over new technologies. Just as free trade and stronger IP 'kicked away the [development] ladder' for developing countries, so do stronger online copyright protection and enforcement policies – discussed more below – kick away developing countries' digital development ladder.

While these issues are important for all countries, they are particularly important for developing countries. In the developed countries where the Internet began, the norm of a free and open Internet has had decades to take root. As a result, one can expect continued pushback there against proposals to end net neutrality. While, as the Mexican ACTA protests suggest, these norms are likely to be popular globally, their roots are necessarily shallower. As a result, activists from developing countries must consciously promote and defend ideas that have been taken for granted elsewhere.

PRESCRIPTION: WHY COPYING SHOULD NOT BE A CRIME

Answering the question of what type of copyright law makes sense in the digital age requires addressing the fundamental paradox at the heart of every IP debate: namely, the tension between promoting protection and encouraging dissemination (Doern and Sharaput 2000). All IP rules do two things. First, they provide a degree of protection for the work in question, providing someone – not necessarily the creator – with the right to determine who can copy and use 'their' work, and under what conditions. This is the side that is most dominant in the current debate.

However, because all new knowledge is built on existing knowledge, copyright and IP laws must also encourage the use of knowledge. Trouble arises when the commodification of knowledge impedes its dissemination. Good copyright policy involves paying attention to both its protection and dissemination sides. Copyright involves a dialogue among creators, intermediaries (who publish and distribute creative works), and 'users' (who themselves may use these works to become future creators). It is *not* an author's right with exceptions carved out for users. Copyright is a law to regulate the production and dissemination of knowledge for society as a whole, and must be evaluated from this perspective.

In the case of digital copyright policy, treaties and laws like ACTA and SOPA represent an extreme bias towards the protection side of copyright's protection-dissemination continuum. In this case, the obvious first step is to work towards laws that move copyright back towards its dissemination pole, avoiding rules and treaties that impede individuals' access to knowledge online. Sufficiently loose copyright laws are a fundamental part of overcoming the digital divide and allowing everyone to benefit from the promise of the Internet as a means of accessing and disseminating information and promoting innovation. For Internet access to mean more than merely the right for people to access pre-approved content and use it in a pre-approved manner, such information must be easily available. This requires, for instance, not allowing content owners to veto new forms of technology such as BitTorrent because they could be used to infringe copyright. It also requires that any laws protecting digital locks do not prevent people from accessing and using things like e-books in ways that are legal or (taking the wider view) needed to promote the creation and spread of knowledge.

Figuring out where to draw this line, however, is complicated by several factors. There is no consensus on this point, with opinions ranging from the view, dominant among many copyright owners, that everything should be owned, to the other extreme that copyright should be abolished completely. The role of power should also not be overlooked, including the potential for proposed copyright reforms to replicate the power imbalances inherent in existing copyright laws. For example, the very popular Creative Commons licence, invented by US lawyer Lawrence Lessig, attempts to provide more flexibility in how copyright is used, granting users rights to copy without permission in certain circumstances. However, far from replacing copyright, Creative Commons licences are based on existing copyright law and 'depend on the existence of copyright to work', offering 'certain usage rights to the public, while reserving other rights' (Creative Commons 2015).

Given these considerations, and wanting to ensure that all those affected by copyright laws have a real say in what those laws do, we can suggest three principles. First, international treaties should be sufficiently flexible to ensure that states – the level at which currently there is the highest level of democratic accountability – can implement policies that fit the needs and desires of their citizens. States should implement copyright laws that they feel respond to their particular circumstances. Furthermore, even similar societies may have different views on where to draw the line between protection and dissemination, for example, when it comes to the protection of indigenous knowledge. Focusing on the state level would allow for the greatest chance to meet the needs and desires of the largest number of people. In short, states should avoid strong treaties like the TPP and ACTA. Practically speaking, states should avail themselves of all the exceptions in treaties such as TRIPS and work towards limiting further expansion of protection-strengthening policies. Finally, because copyright policy will only be as democratic as the state in which it is made, copyright reform is intimately linked to the larger issue of democratic reform.

Second, in terms of what type of copyright policies to pursue, policymakers and activists should focus on how specific copyright proposals affect society as a whole. Again, copyright is not designed only to provide protection for authors. Its objective is much larger than that, encouraging the production and dissemination of knowledge and culture for the benefit of society as a whole. Taking this approach moves us away from what can often end up as a zero-sum debate about whether copyright owners' rights should trump users' rights. This is a particularly distracting debate, since creators by definition are users, and users often use knowledge and culture to create.

Third, policymakers and activists should rely on empirical evidence when setting copyright law. All public policy is by definition political, but copyright is unusual in the extent to which it is driven almost exclusively by untested assumptions and ideological considerations. For a policy that has been around for three centuries, there is a surprising lack of evidence that copyright protection is even needed to encourage creative production, and the evidence that stronger copyright would improve knowledge production and dissemination is similarly sparse (Boldrin and Levin 2008; Ku *et al.* 2009). This is not to say that copyright should be abolished, but that the elimination of copyright should at least be on the table, and that all other alternatives should be considered in light of their actual effects on the creation, control, and dissemination of knowledge. For instance, free and open source software (FOSS) movements have demonstrated that complex computer programmes can be developed without a copyright incentive, while a project like Wikipedia has largely supplanted an entire genre, namely, encyclopaedias. This further demonstrates that copyright is neither the only nor possibly the best way to encourage creativity and innovation.

PROCESS: ALLIES, ONLINE AND OTHERWISE

Seen from one angle, the politics of positive digital copyright reform are daunting. The USA – which remains, despite its troubles, the global economic superpower – has made strong enforcement of laws on digital copyright a key demand in trade negotiations such as the TPP. The beneficiaries of these agreements are well-funded and well-connected transnational firms who have at their disposal not only financial resources and political capital, but also a narrative that draws on concepts like private property, which are fundamental to modern identities. However, the successful protests discussed at the beginning of this chapter strongly suggest that healthier policies on digital copyright are not only possible, but perhaps even likely.

The success of the ACTA and SOPA protests largely resulted from three factors: a positive framing of the issue, an emphasis on democratic legitimacy, and the innovative use of social media. In terms of organization, social media was a key component to all of the protests, making it easier for previously isolated individuals and groups to coordinate and spread information both within and across borders (Haggart 2013). Digital copyright issues are a particularly fertile ground for social media-based activism, because people who understand Internet issues like digital copyright are also likely to be at the cutting edge of social media technologies.

Current stronger copyright projects, such as the TPP, ACTA, and the failed SOPA, have been characterized by excessive secrecy, with only selected parties, usually representing the content industries, allowed even to know what is being discussed. While this secrecy may seem to be a strength for IP holders, in practice activists have successfully framed it as lacking democratic legitimacy. In the Mexican case, ACTA's secrecy led the government to keep even the Senate in the dark, illegally, and caused even members of the governing party to desert the executive.

The SOPA and ACTA protests effectively countered the traditional copyright narrative – the need for ever-stronger protection of property rights – by reframing the copyright debate as a digital/Internet issue. For example, the Mexican Senate's rejection of ACTA was based partly on a concern that the agreement could limit Internet access and worsen the digital divide in Mexico, as well as restricting net neutrality and endangering the legitimate development of e-commerce, digital creativity, and the legitimate diffusion of culture (Haggart 2014a). This is not to say that substantive change is impossible, but that it is easier when norms or institutions have not yet been accepted as 'natural'.

The Mexican Senate resolution demonstrates the appeal of the norms of Internet access and net neutrality, as well as that of the 'digital divide' and online economic development, and suggests that these norms could have significant support outside the Global North, even as the Mexican executive's support for ACTA highlights how copyright debates in developing countries can pit activists against their own government. Combined with recent developments in Brazil, the ACTA experience suggests the potential emergence of a strong counter-hegemonic approach that can challenge the current US-driven strong protection view of copyright. On 23 April 2014, Brazilian president Dilma Roussef signed the *Marco Civil da Internet*, also known as the 'Internet constitution', which establishes 'rights and principles for Internet regulation in Brazil: freedom of expression, interoperability, the use of open standards and technology, protection of personal data, accessibility, multi-stakeholder governance, [and] open government data' (Moncau and Mizukami 2014). While the *Marco Civil* does not address copyright enforcement, which will be dealt with in a subsequent bill (Moody 2014), it establishes a strong precedent in favour of promoting dissemination interests, which can serve as an example for other countries.

Not Just a North–South Issue

Although the predominant role of the USA makes it tempting to see digital copyright through a North–South lens, the reality is both more complicated and more hopeful. There are key constituencies in all countries that favour a reform of digital copyright. As the successful SOPA protests suggest, the US copyright position is not set in stone. Furthermore, while US democracy may be overly influenced by money and insider influence, the changing constellation of copyright interests – particularly mass politicization and the meteoric rise to prominence of firms like Google – cannot but help change the US government's interpretation of its global copyright interests. The current US maximalist position was created by lobbying and capture of key agencies like the USTR; it will be undone in the same way.

Transnational activist networks are already active on these issues. For example, since 2011 the Global Congress on Intellectual Property in the Public Interest links activists, experts, and academics from around the world through annual meetings, the most recent being in Rio de Janeiro, Brazil, and Cape Town, South Africa. Furthermore, Internet companies such as Google, whose business models are relatively friendlier to issues of access and dissemination, stand to be potential tactical allies in the pursuit of positive reform of digital copyright.

That said, power imbalances continue to characterize both the overall debate on digital copyright, as well as the global movement for copyright reform. With respect to the former, large countries like the USA continue to possess the ability to set the debate parameters through their influence in organizations like WIPO. Furthermore, while the Mexican ACTA protests demonstrated that it is possible for smaller countries to resist the will of larger ones, dominant players like the United States can use their economic power, particularly in trade negotiations, to convince other states to implement strong copyright laws.

Regarding the latter, although Internet companies like Google can be powerful, well-resourced allies in the battle for more balanced regimes of digital copyright, their size potentially gives them a disproportionate voice in defining what is meant by positive reform of digital copyright. The same is true of Internet service providers (ISPs). As profit-seeking businesses, often with their own IP portfolios and diverse interests, ISPs approach copyright by putting their own interests ahead of the public interest. Similarly, ISPs' profit motive means that their support for increased Internet access will be limited by a their interest in controlling the market in this area.

Similarly, to date, the open-Internet debate has been driven by a relatively narrow segment of global society. The people who are most active on this issue – the ones making their voices heard on Twitter, for example – are, almost by definition, relatively technologically savvy individuals with a bias towards the idea of a free and open Internet. Whether this state of affairs should be a cause for concern is an open question. More balanced digital copyright laws are likely to benefit economically and socially marginalized groups by creating a relatively open platform to use for their self-defined purposes. As Internet penetration rates increase, marginalized citizens are increasingly making use of the Internet in a variety of contexts. For example, Grossman, Humphreys, and Sacramone-Lutz (2014, 704) find that reducing the cost of information and communication technology increases the number of people heard, without necessarily changing the types of demands that are aired. Activists and policymakers should also consider the extent to which IP laws benefit those who may not be directly involved in the debate, as well as situations where the free and open sharing of information or culture may hurt already disadvantaged groups, such as aboriginal groups seeking to protect traditional knowledge. That knowledge and culture should circulate freely is a guiding, but not absolute, principle.

Finally, the copyright-critical global discourse tends to be driven by actors and ideas originating in the Global North, meaning that the experiences of Southern contexts are not necessarily taken sufficiently into account. As already noted, Creative Commons, the dominant quasi-alternative to copyright, reflects a distinctly American view of copyright and the law. That said, larger Southern states like Brazil are beginning to implement policies, in partial response to domestic activists, which respond to their own needs and desires. Those looking to improve the global copyright situation should work to ensure that they do not reproduce the same inequalities that characterize the current regime.

CONCLUSION

One of our objectives in coming together to write this book has been to suggest real, practical, just alternatives to the status quo. Those who have reached this point of the chapter may be disappointed to read that, instead of recommendations for alternative models of knowledge governance, all I can suggest are some starting principles, based on the preceding discussion, that should be considered when thinking about the best way to regulate knowledge in a globally redistributive way.

First, a stateless, free-knowledge-sharing utopia is unlikely. All societies regulate knowledge. All knowledge-regulation regimes create winners and losers, and privilege some forms of knowledge and culture over others. And all knowledge regulation reflects the values of its society. Just as the elimination of copyright is highly unlikely in the near term, its replacement – whether by formal state-based regulation, or by community-driven informal rules – will almost certainly reflect existing power distributions.

That said, these regimes can be more or less unjust. Consequently, we can evaluate proposed changes to copyright rules by the extent to which they balance the desire to protect knowledge with the need to encourage its dissemination. However, while an overemphasis on one side over the other is fundamentally damaging to society, neither one should be privileged *a priori* over the other. Access to knowledge is critical for societal improvement, but restrictions on the free dissemination of knowledge and information may be legitimate in some circumstances (though these restrictions must be justified with an appeal to evidence).

On a related point, the complexity of these issues cannot be reduced to 'Internet freedom' versus 'copyright holders'. 'Internet freedom' is itself a politically contested and historically situated term. For the United States, it implies a free and open – borderless – *global* Internet, dominated (at the moment) by US-based firms and multistakeholder oversight groups. This approach provides the necessary means by which copyright owners – themselves predominantly US-based – can sell their assets, being protected by strong international and domestic copyright laws (Haggart and Jablonski 2015). This is probably what former US Secretary of State Hillary Clinton had in mind when she committed the United States to 'stand[ing] for a single Internet where all of humanity has equal access to knowledge and information' (Clinton 2010).

Furthermore, as Powers and Jablonski (2015) remark, global Internet governance itself is strongly biased in favour of the current digital superpowers, despite its ostensibly multistakeholder nature. While this aspect of global knowledge governance lies outside the scope of this chapter, it suggests that, while inequitable copyright is a crucial impediment to the realization of a just global economic redistribution, much else also remains to be done.

Most importantly, striking a just balance between these conflicting objectives requires full democratic participation from all segments of society, including the voice of future creators. As a result, our knowledge-governance regimes will only be as good as our political processes. From this perspective, the secret, unbalanced negotiation of the TPP suggests that international copyright policymaking is far from just.

However, based on these criteria, it is difficult not to be encouraged by the successful political actions highlighted at the beginning of this chapter. They suggest the rising importance of individual citizens as a force for change – a crucial element of any democratic action – in correcting the decades-long dangerous ratcheting up of IP protection, as well as the importance of domestic-level politics. With criticisms rising in the USA and elsewhere, global copyright policy, which has favoured stronger global copyright protection and the interests of its content industries over those of the public at large for the past several decades, has never been more ripe for change.

Chapter 9

From Land Grabs to Food Sovereignty

Heloise Weber

This chapter examines an important aspect of the project on Structural Redistribution for Global Democracy (SRGD), the question of deprivations of fundamental life-sustaining needs of all peoples, and of the ecological challenges of a highly contradictory development project. It broadly adopts the three dimensions outlined in Chapter 1 – diagnosis, prescription, and process – as part of its specific contribution to the question of global economic justice. Integral to the analysis is that unequal relations are refracted in economic inequalities, and this in turn cannot be wholly comprehended without an engagement with the politics of global development. I demonstrate how the food sovereignty movement operates across global scales in ways that pose a democratic challenge to conventional political institutions and relations, including with regard to questions of sovereignty, substantive democratic practices, and justice (social and ecological).

In recent decades, the issue of food security has been gradually and persistently gaining attention, as has the rise of concerns about how to balance development objectives and ecological problems. These issues overlap with projections of global population growth, expectations of increasing (and uneven) urbanization, and more diffuse unease over questions of 'ecological limits' and their impact on food security. In this context, dominant actors and institutions from the World Bank to investors and international consultancy firms (such as KPMG, see UN 2008, 11), and stakeholders in food production are becoming more intensely involved in debates about, as well strategies around, food production and the promotion of private investment more generally (for good critical discussions, see Akram-Lodhi 2012; Patel 2007; McMichael 2012b, 2013a, 2013b). In their different ways, these actors and institutions are engaging with (and, as we shall see, in some cases contributing towards) what has been seen as a central paradox in the global political economy of development: 'hunger in the midst of plenty' (Sahlins 1974, 36). For these actors, neo-Malthusian approaches offer the best explanations for hunger; hence, they focus not on questions of redistribution, but on the availability of the physical magnitude of food in relation to population (for a good critique, see Sen 1983). Thus, the most common policy response to the 'food problem' at the level of international development institutions is to focus on methods that industrialize food production. For example, the United Nations Millennium Project has explicitly advocated the conversion of 'subsistence farming to market-oriented farming' (UN Millennium Project 2005, 7). Others, however, working from more critical approaches, foreground questions of rights and entitlements to both produce and consume food through more democratically, cooperatively oriented, and ecologically balanced mechanisms (e.g. Weber 2015). The two distinctively different approaches to food and hunger are now caught up within a more recent dynamic, namely, what critics refer to as the global land grabs.

Since the so-called 'global food crisis' of 2007–08 (though Akram-Lodhi 2012, 129 cautions against this label), and the subsequent global financial crisis, there has been renewed interest in 'global food security' that is closely aligned with the 'land grabs', or 'new enclosures'. Contemporary land grabs parallel historical cases of the expropriation of lands through colonialism, dispossessing peasants and peoples from the bases of subsistence and livelihoods (Li 2011). In the contemporary context, the actors behind large-scale land acquisitions include corporate investors, joint venture companies, and/ or states (through sovereign wealth funds). The deals occur predominantly (though not exclusively) in the 'Global South'. In many cases, the deals have involved the displacement of local populations, often targeting rural subsistence communities or indigenous peoples in the process (Wolford *et al.* 2009; Vermeulen and Cotula 2010; Lyons and Westoby 2014). Such practices thus contribute directly to the exacerbation of Sahlin's paradox, constituting a political economy that reproduces inequality and deprivation.

In what follows, I take the lead from Julian Saurin's challenge with regard to such developments, when he argues that: 'to the extent that contradictions between hunger and plenty can be explained, then the paradox disappears' (Saurin 1997, 107).

I initially reconstruct the social and political implications of the 'new' land grabs in development from a critical political economy perspective. I situate this discussion within a broader paradox which is expressed by the continued adherence by dominant actors in global development to the imperatives of neo-liberal modernization approaches to development. I draw on some examples to illustrate what is at stake, and how these continuities affect the perpetuation of Sahlin's paradox. Contemporary land grabs are related to the reorientation of agricultural staple production to biofuels and carbon offsetting, the procurement of food and feed by expanding 'ghost-acres' (McMichael 2012a, 20), and the rise of speculative investment in agricultural land (McMichael 2012b, 2013a; Sassen 2013). I identify justifications offered by governments and investors involved in such large-scale and long-term land deals and show how Sahlin's paradox is organized and extended, facilitating the ongoing maldistribution of basic entitlements, while also increasing adverse ecological impacts.

In the second part of the chapter, I examine the case of the food sovereignty movement as an alter-development strategy. The food sovereignty movement has been active and gaining momentum globally since the early 1990s. Its aims, objectives, and strategies reach beyond narrow sectoral concerns, expressing social, political, and ecological values that are about much more than achieving equity in food consumption. Rather, food sovereignty movements espouse a distinctive, holistic approach to living with and off the land, combined with a participatory democratic conception of political organization and self-empowerment. In so doing, participants in the movement seek to overcome non-material inequalities (e.g. with regard to gender and collective identities), and retrieve practices that respect the intrinsic value of ecological integrity and diversity (Desmarais 2008). Food sovereignty movements in this sense arguably offer a positive and inclusive response to what has been described as 'the one truly universal human right', one that crosses cultural boundaries and is the one necessity of all human beings 'from birth to death': food and shelter (Grovogui 2011, 63). Given the challenges entailed in what Mike Davis has aptly described as the rise of a *Planet of Slums* (2006), it is imperative to consider the alternatives posited by the food sovereignty movement, which entail possibilities and practices that are at once progressive *and* more democratic than the development model offered through mainstream organizations and their dominant sponsors (whether private or public). The food sovereignty movement, understood in this context, is a highly significant and instructive example of a political, economic, and ecological alter-development project.

In the final part of the chapter, I consider possible practical political strategies to enhance the critical struggles of La Vía Campesina as the major exponent of the food sovereignty movement. In keeping with an understanding of this movement as offering a critical *systemic* challenge to development thinking over issues of food production, distribution, consumption, and ecological situatedness, I locate the *democratic* significance of the food sovereignty movement in its facilitation of counter-hegemonic practices. That the movement is involved in tackling internal issues, such as gender equity, by facilitating a global solidarist exchange and transformation is indicative of its potential. I conclude by drawing out some of the main challenges that the movement faces, and how these might be met.

STRUCTURAL (MAL)DISTRIBUTION IN GLOBAL DEVELOPMENT

It is incumbent on any analysis of the problems and implications of contemporary practices of land grabbing to consider their wider historical context, and in particular colonialism and its legacies, including associated practices of expropriation and forced social and economic transformations. Although there are significant differences between historical 'land grabs' and the current rush to conclude long-term leases on agricultural land in countries predominantly still working through the legacies of colonial domination, there are also striking similarities, particularly when the question is considered of who suffers the most from the adverse implications. Research concerned with this issue has hence frequently drawn parallels between these practices of 'new enclosures' and a transnationally reconstructed account of the 'original' enclosures in the context of the rise of agrarian capitalism, first in England, and subsequently in the rest of colonizing Europe (see, indicatively, Makki 2014). The magnitude of the land grab phenomenon is aptly captured by a World Bank report suggesting that in the year from March 2008 to April 2009, twenty times more land was sold and bought than the annual average over the preceding forty years (Wolford *et al.* 2013, 190; also Sassen 2013, 29–39; McMichael 2013b). Forced displacement of subsistence agriculturalists, pastoralists, and indigenous peoples has accompanied recent land deals either in actual practice, or as a threat still looming large (on the latter, see for instance the situation faced by Kenyan Maasai herders, whose pastures were sold to investors without their knowledge; see Galaty, 2011). Adding to such instances of human suffering in the context of the political economy of contemporary land grabs is the issue of their ecological implications, which raises a whole new dimension of problems as a result of the spread of highly capitalized monocultural agriculture.

In order to understand what drives the recent surge in land deals, we can distinguish three broad trends, related to wider issues in the global capitalist economy: (a) the emergence of a new market in biofuels (predominantly bioethanol, but also wood pellets and other bio-combustibles) in the context of the climate change debate, rising prices for carbon-based energy, and the anticipated shift to post-carbon economies; (b) the acquisition by institutional investors and global corporations of additional agricultural land for the purpose of ensuring food security to growing populations with few prospects of increasing agricultural production domestically (ghost-acres, with prominent buyers based in South Korea, Japan, and the United Arab Emirates (UAE)); and (c) the re-orientation of speculative finance towards asset-based leverage in the wake of the global financial crisis (GFC), which saw major banks and hedge funds, particularly from Europe and the USA, get involved in speculative acquisitions of land and primary materials, predominantly in countries of the Global South, where such assets were secured relatively cheaply, and thus constitute enormous potentials for investment returns (cf. McMichael 2013b; Sassen 2013).

Climate Change and the Rise of Biofuels as a Driver for Land Grabs

In the run-up to what became referred to as the 2008 food crisis, a trend emerged which has seen private as well as public investors move into large-scale agricultural land deals in developing countries, with the specific purpose of securing investment opportunities for biofuels. For developed countries – and the European Union (EU) as a region is important here – biofuels offer a pathway to greener solutions to their own development challenges, associated in particular with the need to find new ways to reduce their carbon emissions and transit to cleaner energies. By investing in biofuels in developing countries, and more specifically in low-income countries (LICs), and in Africa and in Southeast Asia in particular, the EU and its member states can move closer to meeting their greenhouse gas (GHG) emission targets, while simultaneously addressing their international development assistance commitments (Franco *et al.* 2010). Developing countries for their part, and LICs in particular, are actively engaged in pursuing new land deals linked to investments in biofuels and/or agricultural products (see, for example, joint ventures in Madagascar between German and local companies to produce oil from Jatropha) (GRAIN *et al.* 2010). For LICs, these investments offer an opportunity to facilitate rural development and modernization, and, by raising the prospect of the emergence of what has been called the 'Green OPEC', also enhance their relative bargaining power *vis-à-vis* developed states. The policy instruments of the United Nations Framework Convention on Climate Change (UNFCCC) facilitate such deals, for instance, under the Clean Development Mechanism (CDM). For the proponents and advocates of such deals, which often include the governments of the targeted (host) countries, climate change politics has resulted in a win-win situation for North–South relations. Developed countries can meet their development goals in line with commitments to GHG emissions targets, and developing countries can benefit in terms of the contributions which biofuels investments make to raising revenue for their own development objectives, such as meeting the Millennium Developments Goals (MDGs) and/or the post-2015 Sustainable Development Goals (SDGs) (Weber 2014, 2015). However, while aggregate (economic) benefits to national development indicators may (most plausibly) register, there is increasing evidence linking investments in biofuel land deals with adverse social and political implications for local inhabitants, including small-scale farmers, and food insecurity (McMichael

2010). It is this (second) aspect that is the main focus of critical interests in the 'new enclosures': that is, the contributions of biofuels markets and associated land grabs more generally to unequal relations of development (local and transnational).

From such a perspective, the win-win scenario regarding biofuels in development is challenged, prompting some commentators to refer to 'agro-fuels', a reference intended to (polemically) highlight the adverse social, economic, ecological, and political implications of this development strategy. A number of studies have examined this trend, including major investigations conducted by the United Nations Food and Agriculture Organization (FAO), Friends of the Earth (FOE), the International Institute for Environment and Development (IIED), and the United Nations Conference on Trade and Development (UNCTAD), as well as by individual academic researchers. These studies have drawn attention to causal linkages between the trend to produce agro-fuels and rising food prices, with a direct effect of greater food insecurity for many and especially the vulnerable in many host countries. The studies have also documented evidence of forced displacement of peasants from their lands, often leaving 'farmers with no income and no source of food' (Friends of the Earth 2010). Additionally, there is evidence of growing instances of manifest violence at the community level in the context of resistance to displacement and/or land acquisition. As some researchers have noted, the social impact is particularly problematic in contexts where customary land rights prevail, including where these are part of commons-type management systems, often involving pastoral grazers as well as indigenous populations. From such perspectives, there are wide-ranging sustainability questions (social, ecological, economic, and political) at stake in the biofuel-led, land-grab-based development strategy.

Food Security, Ghost-Acres, and Land Grabbing for Food and Feed

A second cluster of motivations behind investors pursuing land deals, and governments of 'land-rich' developing countries agreeing to these, stems from wider concerns over the near future of food security. Several trends come together here. As a new 'middle class' is set to emerge in and among the BRICS countries (China and India in particular), further changes in dietary habits are anticipated, which will reorient global food consumption patterns towards more meat-based diets and an accelerated increase in per capita calorific consumption. This is assumed to lead to price increases, with wealthier consumers becoming able to redirect more staple foods towards use as animal feed for meat production (McMichael 2013a). Key players in the global food regime have responded by seeking to expand agricultural production, specifically of 'multifunctional crops'. Among the latter are, for instance, corn and soybeans, which can be inserted into food and feed production in versatile ways. They are also particularly useful in the procurement of processed foods. In order to be economical for large commodity trading companies, these foods have to be produced in expansive monocultures amenable to industrialized farming practices. With suitable land in many wealthy countries becoming either increasingly expensive, or simply not being available due to geographic circumstances, companies and governments have looked to 'land-rich' countries in the Global South (and specifically Africa) in order to start production there.

Land grabs of this kind have sometimes been referred to as the creation of 'ghost-acres', referring to acreage secured over and beyond the domestically available ecological resources of any given country. From the perspective of food security, ghost-acres contribute to maintaining low (or lower) food prices, also for populations living through increasing gaps in wealth and disposable income. In order for meals of processed foods to remain available to working-class, low-income customers in otherwise 'rich' capitalist economies, cheaper means for producing calorific input are secured by acquiring cheap land. Reminiscent of the role of sugar in sustaining calorific input for poor workers in Britain, and its connection to the triangular trade (especially enslavement) and plantation systems (see Mintz 1985), the global food regime's use of versatile staple crops for input into processed foods (and the fast-food industry) is hence also implicated in the perpetuation of crises of malnourishment, where low-income people are trapped in a cycle of consuming unhealthy foodstuffs, whether in rich or poor countries (see Patel 2007).

Land Grabs for Speculation

A third cluster of land grab deals in the Global South was driven by the GFC of 2008–9 and the subsequent crisis in investor confidence. As the trends mentioned under the previous two headings became more obvious and publicly well established, land (whether for agricultural use or for other ventures such as resource extraction) came onto the radars of banks and investment fund managers, who were looking to move out of what had turned out to be unsustainable investment schemes implicated in creating the GFC's overinflated bubble of multiple-leveraged debt obligations, and into what could be seen as asset-based markets with high growth potential. While some banks went as far as acquiring (or building) warehouses to 'bunker' raw materials for future sale, others as well as hedge funds directed their attention to land acquisition. Sovereign wealth funds are also among institutional investors in land grabs, in a context where many deals amount to establishing 'holding rights' for the purpose of future sale, rather than the 'development' of the land in question, or any investment in using it agriculturally (for a good overview, see Sassen 2013). Typically, such deals may involve the people who currently *live* on the land in question, and who often may have no idea that a deal has been concluded. Where land is used as a speculative asset in such ways, the implied development benefits of 'new enclosure'-type land deals for the receiving country are even more diminished. Nevertheless, such speculative investment deals do require the adaptation of domestic laws on trade and title, in order to reassure investors with regard to their expected returns. The deals may also, at any point, involve the further lease to business investors seeking to start production of agricultural commodities, thus leading again to land clearances, displacement, and an exacerbation of maldistribution. The magnitude of this component in the land grabs is difficult to ascertain, with many of the deals agreed currently at different stages of implementation. Some suggest that the percentage figure on 'pure' speculative investment (without commencing to produce anything) may exceed 90 per cent (see, for instance, project 'Landmatrix', accessible at www.landmatrix.com).

Unpacking the Land Grabs: Justifications and Implications

From a conventional international development and/or international relations perspective, the 'biofuels constellation' belongs to the world of 'win-win' scenarios, which are frequently emphasized for trade-led or trade-oriented development strategies. These land deals are primarily premised upon long-term leases to foreign governments or private investors for between 50 and 99 years, with some cases of actual land sales. There are clearly transformative dynamics at play in these emerging transnational coalitions and relations of governance. For example, some African countries appear to be gaining in bargaining power through what has been dubbed as the 'Green OPEC', while new international alliances are emerging in the pursuit of biofuel investment, such as between Brazil, Germany, and Mozambique, and their respective investors. All in all, it would seem that a 'new deal' is being firmly established in ways that appear to be transforming South–North relations. This dynamic, however, is met in turn by activities aimed at mobilizing and coordinating resistance through environmental justice movements, which equally manage to work across South–North relations. Such transnational alliances and linkages have been, for instance, evolving and effective between European social movements (and German groups especially) and Southeast Asian movements, especially with regard to oil palm plantations in Indonesia (Pye 2010).

Meanwhile, though, these land deals also meet the strategic interests of developed states – *and key corporations there* – enabling the formation of interesting and somewhat new alliances in the governance of development. For example, as noted above, on the one hand, investment in biofuels allows the EU to work towards meeting its GHG emission trading goals. On the other hand, it also allows for EU comparative advantage to excel by way of facilitating the interests of its key corporations engaged in direct and indirect investment in biofuels. At the same time, through such investment deals, often linked to foreign policy and international development assistance goals, developed countries can be seen to meet their responsibilities to assist LICs. Indeed, such an objective is clearly stated in the context of EU biofuels policy (Franco et al. 2010). But the issue and context is not as straightforward as it might seem if viewed from traditional international relations (realist and liberal institutionalist) perspectives. Not only are transnational coalitions emerging to resist this agenda, but these alliances and the debates they engender are now also part of wider concerns around climate justice.

If the critics of the 'new enclosures' are correct, the 'developmental states' involved in revenue raising and other development-oriented outcomes (such as infrastructure development) through such land deals are caught up in a paradox. 'Land grabs' figure as a deliberately harnessed development strategy that potentially enhances national economic growth. It is on the basis of such arguments that officials in the targeted countries defend the legal reforms and contractual arrangements underpinning long-term land leases, often in return for very little 'direct' rent. However, the national economic growth associated with entering into such arrangements appears to come at the cost of increased livelihood insecurities for many. The case of Ethiopia is exemplary here, where one such land deal brokered by a wealthy Saudi-based Ethiopian to produce both biofuels and food on more than 100,000 acres of land for export to Qatar (on a 99-year exclusive lease arrangement) occurs in the context of a country with one of the highest levels of food insecurity. Other similar examples are being increasingly documented, effectively highlighting the increasing footprint of 'ghost-acres' (McMichael 2012a, 20; for further examples from Africa and Latin America, documenting also repressive use of force in the context of population displacements, see GRAIN 2014). Recognizing the depth and adverse implications of the new land deals, the former Special Rapporteur on Food Security to the United Nations, Jean Ziegler, referred to these land investment-oriented development strategies as 'one of the greatest crimes against humanity' (McMichael 2010, 610). Ziegler's critical concerns have been reinforced further by his successor, human rights lawyer Olivier De Schutter, who drew the following conclusion from a comprehensive study of recent trends in land distribution and food production: 'development models that do not lead to evictions, disruptive shifts in land rights and increased land concentration should be prioritised'. De Schutter made this recommendation in one of his submissions on food (in)security and land deals to the United Nations General Assembly (UN 2010).

Critics of the new land grabs consistently highlight that these deals contribute to a further distortion of the already highly problematic constellation of the global food regime. While smallholder farmers produce, according to the FAO, over 70 per cent of the world's food, they do so under conditions of increasing pressure from large agribusiness players, and on less than 25 per cent of the available agricultural land (GRAIN 2014). Nevertheless, and in no small measure due to the lobbying power and financial influence of the major players in the industry (from seed companies through biotech giants, insurance companies, and commodity traders to global food producers and supermarkets), the agro-industrial complex continues to be the model supported by major development players at the expense of smallholder farmers everywhere. Indicative of this are, for instance, the role of the World Bank in switching its attention from considering the potential of small-hold agriculture (still documented in 2007) towards the financialization of agriculture, and an economies-of-scale argument conducive to further entrenching industrial practices and, ultimately, monocultures (see Akram-Lodhi 2012, 129). Together, the agro-industrial complex, multilateral development institutions, global initiatives such as the one for the 'second green revolution' (this time targeting Africa), and local governments are hence involved in reconfiguring agricultural production for the purpose of attracting investment, with the consequence that smallholders, despite their enormous contribution to global food security, are squeezed out and forced to join the ranks of the urban poor.

However, today a formidable force is challenging this model, aiming at a renewed empowerment of smallholder farming and a new appreciation of equitable, progressive, and ecologically sensitive development.

FOOD SOVEREIGNTY AS ALTER-DEVELOPMENT

A large global movement for 'food sovereignty' is a vital part of the challenge to the land grabs (even as the land grabs are a challenge to food sovereignty movements). This movement promotes alternatives to industrial production, distribution, and consumption of food. Prominent in this mobilization is La Vía Campesina ('The Peasants' Way'), which encompasses more than one hundred and fifty organizations from seventy countries, between them involving 200 million farmers. The food sovereignty movement has also attracted support from many NGOs, think tanks, and universities. It even has the backing of some official circles at the FAO.

Food sovereignty movements advocate continued local custody of land. Peasants thereby not only retain more control of their destiny, but also practice small-scale and low-input agriculture that is more ecologically sensitive, more biologically diverse, and also more productive in terms of food yields per acre. Industrial agriculture produces high carbon emissions, contributes to topsoil erosion, strains water supplies, and reduces biodiversity. In addition, the intensive use of pesticides and herbicides has been shown to lead to decline in insect and bird populations and to the emergence of 'super weeds', sometimes rendering whole agricultural tracts unusable. Smallholder practices very often score immeasurably better on all these counts. Smallholder farming is also not inherently less productive than high-input industrial agriculture. Scientists at Cornell University have established in long-term studies that organic farms outperform industrial farms in terms of output after four years and outperform them instantly on ecological criteria (see Pimentel *et al.* 2005).

The food sovereignty movement challenges orthodox accounts of the causes of hunger. Its critical analysis particularly emphasizes structural inequalities in global political economy and highlights the paradox where mainstream approaches to 'development' actually leave many poor people hungry. Land grabs disrupt the food security that exists when land, labour, community, and food are united in a coherent integrated web.

To reverse food insecurity, undermine the tide of land grabs, and advance its alternative vision, the food sovereignty movement seeks to create new tenure systems or to reinvigorate existing or defunct arrangements that can secure local claims to the land. La Vía Campesina is also exploring how the formal institutionalization of other traditional models of cooperative village-based agriculture could raise legal barriers against land grabbing (GRAIN 2014, 60–64).

The food sovereignty movement in addition promotes seed banks as well as alternative approaches to creating and sustaining food markets, relating with consumers, and integrating farmers with societies at large. La Vía Campesina supports novel local ways to connect consumers and producers of food. For instance, box schemes that link producers directly with consumers have helped to re-educate consumers about annual food production cycles, nutrition, and varieties of produce.

All of these practices are oriented towards the collective self-empowerment of smallholder farmers, who are activist producers and collaborators in maintaining a value-based challenge to the highly problematic ecological, social, and economic implications of the late-capitalist food regime and its modes of production. By facilitating experimentation with, and the spread of, alternative institutional arrangements based on solidarity, collaboration, and the sharing of information in a spirit of mutual aid, they are also involved in already implementing lessons elsewhere harnessed by heterodox economists in the context of challenging the presumed superiority of neoclassical approaches (see, indicatively, Ostrom 1990 for a defence of cooperative and collective institutions using scarce resources). It is in such practices that the food sovereignty movement constitutes itself as a political force advancing real change for its participants while transforming perceived institutional possibilities and constraints.

Food sovereignty activists collaborate with researchers to assess and demonstrate the ecological value of smallholder agricultural production. For instance, academics have helped to gather, pool, and protect peasant expertise, techniques, and systems of exchange. The movement promotes information sharing among its following regarding farming practices, land management, and traditional techniques of plant breeding and tending. La Vía Campesina coordinates opportunities for smallholder farmers to engage in site visits and other exchanges with members across the world.

In sum, food sovereignty promises a better food production socially, ecologically, morally, politically and – once considered in all its implications – also economically. All of this is achieved through substantive democratic relations and processes. The food sovereignty movement is more than an issue-based alternative project in development. Rather, it is *a comprehensive alter-development movement*.

THE DEMOCRATIC CHALLENGE OF THE FOOD SOVEREIGNTY MOVEMENT

As McMichael has stated, the 'food sovereignty vision, for the long term, unsettles the state-centric mold' (McMichael 2013a, 59). Viewed from the perspective of contending positions on democracy, the movement is comprehensively oriented towards a popular sovereignty model sustained by shared values and outlooks. 'Sovereignty', in this context, is neither directed at nor channelled through the state (as in representative models), but rather constituted as the political practice of mutual empowerment. As McMichael shows, the movement inadvertently involves a 're-territorialization of states through the revitalization of local food ecologies and recognition of the rights of people of the land' (2013a, 59). He goes on to affirm further (quoting Wittman 2009), that the 'food sovereignty movement, recognizing state complicity in the neo-liberal market project, seeks to reconstitute the state (and its spatial relations) via a politics of 'agrarian citizenship'. McMichael notes in this context the significance of the argument by Marc Edelman (2009) that '"peasantness" is a political rather than an analytical category' (McMichael 2013a, 59). Conceiving of the food sovereignty movement in these terms constitutes a radical break from conceiving of sovereignty and development in terms of the state. Thus, the food sovereignty movement is a practically existing alter-development model and one that proactively seeks to challenge and transform the structural inequalities and limitations of the current democratic model associated with state-led development. This might appear at first glance to be an improbable case of overcoming asymmetric power relations, as between David and Goliath! The challenges met by movement participants reflect this, with many experiencing repression in different forms, including disappearances, killings, forced evictions, or deeply unfair legal procedures and arrangements (see, indicatively, GRAIN *et al.* 2014). The adversaries of this movement have formidable financial and political resources at their disposal.

Yet, it is not utopian to dream of success. The food sovereignty challenge to the 'development project' is already in the making, and comprises what is easily the largest social movement in the world today. Drawing on McMichael (2013a, 83), we can illustrate the political significance of the food sovereignty movement in terms of its wider implications for contemporary world politics, including its transformative potential for more just social and political relations:

> The food sovereignty movement transforms the way we think about possibilities for a sustainable socio-ecological future. It is not a movement simply about food; rather it has broader civilizational claims, precipitated by the deepening contradictions of the food regime. It politicizes the agrarian condition in relation to the overall social structure of capital accumulation. If one views these dynamics solely through the capital/labour lens, substantive food and ecological relations are rendered inconsequential or invisible. Arguably, it takes the voice of a mobilized peasant and landless labour movement to articulate a more complex agrarian question regarding the contemporary crisis of capitalism, and to posit an alternative ontological path.

In keeping with these sentiments, a report by the United Nations Special Rapporteur, Olivier De Schutter, noted that there is a 'strong overlap between recommendations made in' various documents he cites relating to 'human rights challenges of large scale land acquisitions or leases of land' (UN 2014, 12, para 27) and 'the Declaration of the Rights of Peasants – Women and Men, adopted in 2008 by the international network of peasant organizations, Via Campesina, which the Human Rights Council Advisory Committee attached to its final study on the advancement of the rights of peasants and other people working in rural areas' (UN 2014, 12, para 28). It is further noted that this 'declaration now forms the basis of the discussions launched on 15 July 2013 within the open-ended intergovernmental working group mandated by the Human Rights Council in its resolution 21/19 to negotiate a United Nations declaration on the rights of peasants and other people working in rural areas' (UN 2014, 12, para 28).

THE WAY FORWARD TO ALTER-DEVELOPMENT

While the challenge identified above is big, it is not insurmountable. There are already proposals and initiatives to advance the food sovereignty movement. For example, as McMichael (2013a) notes, these steps could include proposals put forward by Jose Bové of the Peasant Confederation in France and could include 'alternative multilateral institutions such as a Convention of Food Sovereignty and Trade in Food and Agriculture, an International Court of Justice, a World Commission on Sustainable Agriculture and Food Sovereignty and so forth' (McMichael 2013a, 59–60; quoting Bové and Defour 2001). These more macro-political proposals would need to be linked with support mechanisms for community-level practices as envisioned by the food sovereignty movement.

Part of realizing the way forward requires working on different social and political scales and combining different modes of critical reflective practice. I offer some initial thoughts in this regard:

1. Pursue options to connect the food sovereignty movement with other similarly oriented alter-development approaches (such as the Rastafarian Co-operative Movement for Food Sufficiency) in order to develop stronger transnational and horizontal alliances (on this movement, see Shilliam 2012, esp. 341–42).
2. Develop and pursue deeper linkages between the food sovereignty movement, researchers/academics, and supportive public political figures (such as the UN Special Rapporteur, Olivier De Schutter, who has already been an outspoken critic of the land grabs and a strong proponent of the food sovereignty movement and the 'right to food' (UN 2010).
3. Develop deeper connections between critical lawyers, activists, and the food sovereignty movement. These linkages are especially relevant to ensure that through legal fiat the food sovereignty movement is not undermined, sidelined or otherwise constrained. These collective efforts will also assist in holding global governance institutions to account, such as the World Trade Organization (WTO), which at its Ministerial Conference at Bali in December 2013 'failed to place food security above trade concerns' (UN 2014, 19, para 48).
4. Tackle divisions and disagreements within the food sovereignty movement, and develop greater transparency and capacity with regard to processing internal conflicts among member groups and organizations. While La Vía Campesina has been tremendously successful in galvanizing and energizing political agency over land, food production, and agro-ecology, there have also been challenges, with some member organizations sidelined or leaving the movement. (For an overview of such issues, see Desmarais 2008.)

5. Develop deeper connections between (critical) progressive media outlets and the food sovereignty movement.
6. Continue to nurture counter 'public opinions', especially with regard to those who influence knowledge about development within development institutions. More specifically, this would entail a revival of debates about the question of food as intrinsically political and as an integral dimension of the legacy of the enclosures, thereby challenging the framing of food in apolitical, ahistorical, and 'technical' terms.

It is clear that the food sovereignty movement articulates nothing less than a paradigm shift. It is an example of a global political movement which aspires to counter the structural inequalities that undermine substantive global democratic practices and relations. It shines a light on the contradictions of the global 'development project' while advancing an alter-development politics.

Chapter 10

Global Redistribution through Climate Justice

Dorothy Grace Guerrero

The need to stabilize greenhouse gas (GHG) concentrations in order to prevent catastrophic global warming is acknowledged by 196 member states that have since 1992 pursued climate agreements in the annual Conference of the Parties (COP) under the United Nations Framework Convention on Climate Change (UNFCCC). The UNFCCC is the principal intergovernmental effort to tackle climate change. However, the undeniable fact is that, since the issue of climate change was mainstreamed in various policy circles after the Earth Summit at Rio de Janeiro in 1992, and despite over twenty years of meetings at the UNFCCC, total global anthropogenic (human-made) GHG emissions have continued to increase. Annual GHG emissions grew to an average of 1.0 gigaton of carbon dioxide equivalent per year during the years 2000–2010 as compared with 0.4 gigaton per year in the period 1970–2000 (IPCC 2014a, 8).

As our planet continues to warm, with 2014 as the warmest year on record since 1880 (NASA 2015) the climate talks have become one of the most high-profile annual multilateral meetings of governments, business, and civil society organizations. However, the increasingly worrying climate situation and the lack of progress in the climate talks have made a number of environmental NGOs, movements, and campaign groups see each conference since COP15 in Copenhagen, Denmark in 2009 as a failed chance to prevent the growing crisis. The climate situation now occupies top, front, and centre among policy initiatives and development concerns due to frequent and increasingly devastating natural disasters affecting millions. Nevertheless, and in spite of having the most updated and sophisticated information and analyses available, governments do not take adequate actions.

Yes, the COP meetings continue. The 21st edition gathered in Paris as this book went to press. In addition, United Nations Secretary General Ban Ki-moon called a Summit of Leaders on Climate Change in September 2014.

This prompted around 400,000 people from 1,574 organizations to rally in the streets of New York, as well as 2,646 other events in 162 countries, all urging world leaders to address the problems of climate change (People's Climate 2015; see also Climate Space 2014).

Many environmental activists are increasingly losing faith in the climate negotiations and are critical of current solutions. The failure to reach such solutions is largely due to corporate capture of UN climate processes and other relevant policy arenas. Instead of the required binding commitments, the UNFCCC is moving closer to a corporate agenda of voluntary pledges and market-based initiatives that tend to do more harm than good with respect to the global climate system (Climate Space 2014). Hence campaigners argue that nothing less than a systemic change in the political economy can address the climate crisis. Binding targets are not being realized in respect of emissions reductions, appropriate technology, and financial transfers from developed countries to developing countries to support the costs of mitigation and adaptation for climate change. If no drastic reduction in emission levels occurs, GHG equivalent of CO_2 will total 57 gigatons by the end of the century, which is 13 gigatons more than the 44 gigatons of CO_2 that would give a reasonable chance of remaining below the 2°C maximum of global warming (UNEP 2013). The overwhelming evidence that ongoing climate change is driven by human activities is also being widely ignored, as are suggestions to keep below the 2°C global average warming, as recommended in the Fifth Assessment Report of the Intergovernmental Panel on Climate Change (IPCC 2013, 2014b), the World Bank (2012), the United Nations Environment Programme (UNEP 2011), and many other climate studies.

Climate change is producing unequal impacts across regions and social classes. Already poor countries and poorer sectors within countries are experiencing the earliest and more severe damages to their lives and livelihoods. Although parties agreed at COP16 in Cancun to a maximum 2°C rise in global temperature, this level is not actually safe and could produce catastrophic impacts, as disclosed in a 2015 report by a team of climate scientists led by former NASA climatologist James Hansen. This report suggests that feedback mechanisms produced by the warming of oceans could raise sea levels ten times faster than previously predicted, that is, 10 feet by 2065 (Holthaus 2015). Climate change is a very complex and complicated phenomenon that produces different effects in different places. A 2°C rise will further damage already water-challenged countries and produce more demands on sanitation and health services in poor countries (World Bank 2009). As a United Nations Development Programme (UNDP) report says, global warming most threatens the poor and the unborn, the 'two constituencies with little or no voice' in governance (UNDP 2007, 13).

Many market-based responses to climate change have so far been proposed, including the Clean Development Mechanism (CDM), Reducing Emissions from Deforestation and Forest Degradation (REDD), Climate-Smart Agriculture (CSA), and various carbon market schemes. However, these initiatives will likely not reduce emissions, but rather allow business as usual and create profits for companies in the name of climate improvement (Focus on the Global South 2012). Moreover, such measures will further increase inequality, as they disproportionately target forests, territories, and lands of indigenous peoples and small-scale farmers. The widely embraced new concept of a 'green economy' is likewise little more than business as usual. The idea is merely a reconfiguration of capitalism, which seeks to reduce nature and nature's services to tradable commodities (Solon 2014b).

In its underlying causes, climate change is the result of an unjust economic system that prioritizes overproduction and overconsumption. Although global warming is anthropogenic, people do not generate it equally and democratically. Footprints vary dramatically. For example, the 19.5 million inhabitants of New York State consume more energy than the 900 million inhabitants of Sub-Saharan Africa, and a single average resident of the United States emits more GHGs than 500 residents in Ethiopia, Chad, Afghanistan, Mali, or Burundi (Malm 2015). Imagine the equation if we talk of how much a US millionaire emits compared to poor people in Laos or Cambodia.

As observed in the last two decades of climate negotiations, three steps must be made to start solving the climate crisis and realize climate justice. One is a drastic emissions reduction, which should be at least 40 per cent below 1990 levels by 2020, as stated in the 2007 and 2013 IPCC Reports. The reductions must be legally binding and without the possibility of offsets, and they need to be undertaken especially in developed countries. The rest of the world will then follow based on capacities and development needs. A second key step is to leave 80 per cent of currently known fossil fuel reserves under the ground (IPCC 2014a). Third is to start a shift towards a low-carbon society by changing the way we approach development, production, and consumption, as well as related governance. These steps need a transformative politics that will promote alternatives, some of which are already being articulated by NGOs, social and ecological movements, and their supporters. The rest of this chapter elaborates these dynamics of change.

DIAGNOSIS: CLIMATE CHANGE IS REAL AND RAPIDLY ADVANCING

Global warming was already predicted in the 1960s and 1970s as a consequence of increasing GHG concentrations in the earth's atmosphere. Now, fifty years later, climate change is real and in fact advancing at a faster rate than previously predicted (Archer and Rahmstorf 2010; also Costa 2013). Frequent and stronger tropical cyclones (typhoons in the Pacific or hurricanes in the Atlantic), severe and longer droughts, hotter temperatures, and heavier snowfalls are the new normal. Small-scale farmers, fishers, women, indigenous populations, and those living in vulnerable places increasingly brace themselves against such weather events many times in the year.

According to the 2013 Fifth Assessment Report (AR5) of the IPCC, each of the last three decades was warmer than all of the preceding decades going back to 1850 (IPCC 2014b, 3). The first decade of the twenty-first century was the warmest thus far. The IPCC is a UN body, made up of scientific experts, tasked with producing five-yearly updates of knowledge on the scientific, technical, and socio-economic aspects of climate change. The IPCC has three scientific working groups, each producing a detailed report, which are then synthesized into one document. Over 600 authors from 32 countries contributed to AR5, and over 9,200 scientific publications were cited. The summary report was agreed by all 196 UNFCCC member states (IPCC 2013a, 1).

The average temperature of the earth's atmosphere has risen by 0.8°C since the late 1800s. The IPCC Report also concludes that the current emission pathway points to more than a doubling of CO_2 concentrations, which would generate 4–6°C of warming this century (IPCC 2014b, 10). The International Energy Agency has also advised that failure to reduce fossil fuel consumption would result in at least 6°C of global warming (IEA 2013, 2). The AR5 indicates that CO_2 emissions from fossil fuel combustion and industrial processes contributed 78 per cent of the total GHG increase from 1970 to 2010 and that about half of the cumulative anthropogenic CO_2 emissions between 1750 and 2010 have occurred in the last forty years (IPCC 2013a, 7). Atmospheric temperatures are rising, particularly over landmasses. The oceans are acidifying. The Arctic Ocean ice retreat has doubled, and the Antarctic and Greenland ice sheets are shrinking (IPCC 2013b, 252).

The melting ices in the polar regions and the rapid disappearance of ice sheets in Greenland are producing 'tipping points' (Lenton 2011). The process itself accelerates climate change. As ice melts, methane gases that were frozen into the Arctic are released into the atmosphere. Methane gas is twenty-five times worse for global warming than carbon dioxide (ScienceDaily 2014). As more ice melts, more methane gases are released and produce more rapid melting. This spiralling dynamic could reach a point beyond control.

The sea surface has been warming up at an average rate of more than a tenth of a degree Celsius per decade since the 1970s (IPCC 2013b, 253). The IPCC modelling data already shows that this warming has direct connection with the increasing number of cyclones. New studies also indicate that sea levels are actually rising 60 per cent faster than previous predictions, with average annual increases of 3.2 millimetres instead of 2 millimetres (Hanna 2012). Many capitals and key cities are near seas or rivers. If the lands that support lives and human activities submerge under water, there could be hundreds of millions of climate refugees.

If all of these impacts are already happening at current levels of global warming, what more will a rise of between 2 and 6° C bring – or as high as 8° C if the Copenhagen and Cancun COP promises are not met? It would be catastrophic for people like communities in the Central Philippines that were affected by super storm Haiyan in November 2013 (Costa 2013). This strongest and most destructive recorded storm to have ever hit land killed more than 6,200 people, displaced 650,000, and destroyed 1.1 million homes (ABC 2014). Total economic losses, including damage and reconstruction costs, were estimated at US$ 5.8 billion (PR Newswire 2013). Many public facilities like schools, hospitals, roads, airports, and piers were destroyed (Buchanan *et al.* 2013). On some islands, nothing was left standing. The coconut industry, a major source of livelihood in the affected islands, was destroyed and will take a minimum of five years to restore.

A report by the Climate Vulnerability Forum (2012), a platform of countries most at risk from global warming, concludes that five million deaths occur each year from air pollution, hunger, and disease as a result of climate change and carbon-intensive economies. That toll would likely rise to six million a year by 2030 if current patterns of fossil fuel use continue. More than 90 per cent of those deaths will occur in developing countries (CVF 2012, 18). Climate change is already costing the global economy a potential 1.6 per cent of annual output, or about US$ 1.2 trillion a year, and this could double to 3.2 per cent by 2030 if global temperatures are allowed to rise (CVF 2012, 17). Even big developing countries will be affected in terms of potential GDP loss. China could see a 2.1 per cent reduction by 2030, while India could experience a more than 5 per cent loss of potential output (CVF 2012, 20).

Poor and vulnerable people are already dying, and communities are losing resilience amidst ever increasing impacts of global warming. Still, even many poor and developing countries have yet (or outright refuse) to question, challenge, and problematize the key role of capitalism in climate change. It has long been acknowledged that climate change affects people differently and that the poor who contribute very little to its causes are the first to suffer its impacts. The principle of 'common but differentiated responsibilities' was already mentioned at the first Earth Summit in Stockholm in 1972, well before the UNFCCC adopted it as a basic principle in 1992. The main task now is to devise equitable burden-sharing mechanisms.

The outcomes of the UNFCCC negotiations do not match the urgency of the situation. It took until 1997 to achieve the Kyoto Protocol as an implementation measure (UNFCCC 1997). In the First Commitment Period of the

Protocol, which covers the years 2008–2012, the parties pledged to reduce emissions by an average of 5.2 per cent below 1980s level. However, since the 2005 COP in Montreal, Annex 1 countries (i.e. 37 industrialized countries) have found ways to avoid deep emission cuts.

To stay below a 2°C average warming of the global temperature by 2050, the IPCC has prescribed that Annex 1 countries should reduce their GHG emissions by as much as 40 per cent of their 1990 level by 2020 in the Second Commitment Period (IPCC 2007). However, this advice has been largely ignored, and instead offset mechanisms like the CDM were introduced. The CDM is a carbon-trading tool that allows polluters, mostly from rich countries, to purchase credit through projects, mostly in developing countries, rather than actually reduce emissions. The already weak Kyoto Protocol was further watered down in 2010, when non-binding pledges at the Cancun COP amounted to only a 15 per cent emissions reduction by 2020. By the 2011 COP in Durban, major emitters such as Japan, Russia, Canada, and New Zealand had abandoned the Kyoto Protocol, on top of the United States, which never ratified the agreement in the first place. What is left is a mere *laissez-faire* regime of 'voluntary pledges' for emissions reduction.

Recent years have seen still further intensification of dirty energy production like fracking. Annex 1 countries remain reluctant to pledge deeper cuts in their emission levels (without offsets and loopholes). Also lacking is appropriate financial and technology transfer to developing countries to help the latter adapt to the already felt impacts of climate change. Instead, the focus is on profit-oriented, market-based, and destructive public-private partnership initiatives such as carbon trading, CDM measures, REDD+ initiatives, CSA, etc.

Case studies on the CDM in Asia show that most of these projects do not actually reduce emissions, are ill conceived, and do not follow diligence and participatory processes already followed by international financial institutions (Focus on the Global South 2010, 2012). According to research by International Rivers, CDM projects have failed to meet their goals. Structural flaws and cheating by project developers have wasted billions of dollars, as credits are sold to projects that do not really need CDM assistance and cause serious environmental and social harm (International Rivers 2008).

The main argument against REDD+, another offset mechanism, is that it does not reduce emissions, but merely moves them from one place to another (Friends of the Earth 2008). Promoters of REDD+ have a very poor understanding of what a forest is. Their ideas of opportunity costs are also flawed, as they merely view forests as carbon sinks, instead of appreciating their full value to the ecosystem and humanity. In March 2014, more than one hundred organizations from all over the world requested that the Food and Agriculture Organization (FAO) change its misleading definition of forests (WRM 2014). The FAO employs a reductionist definition based solely on the presence of trees, disregarding the fact that forests are also spaces for different kinds of flora and fauna, as well as home to local communities. Under the FAO and CDM definition of a forest, large-scale monoculture plantations of fast-growing eucalyptus trees, managed with toxic agrochemicals, are 'forests'. Indigenous peoples are already losing their ancestral domain as forests are transformed into plantations. The losses to biodiversity and the ecosystem of diminishing natural forests have complex environmental, sociopolitical, and economic consequences.

Critics denounce 'green economy' approaches such as the CDM, REDD+, and CSA as false solutions that lead to further destructive commodification of life and nature (Climate Space 2013). Indifference to justice issues (environmental and social) and low consideration of social, economic, developmental, and ethical dimensions of climate change provide opportunities for corporations to push their agenda of endless profits. Corporations are profiting from insufficient actions by governments. The fossil fuel industry is unapologetic. The business-as-usual attitude is very clearly summarized when ExxonMobil President and CEO, Rex Tillerson, declared in an interview: 'My philosophy is to make money. If I can drill and make money, then that's what I want to do' (Rose 2013).

The failure of the COPs violates the fundamental principles of the UNFCCC, as stated in Article 3, and in particular Paragraph 1 (UNFCCC 1992):

> The Parties should protect the climate system for the benefit of present and future generations of humankind, on the basis of equity and in accordance with their common but differentiated responsibilities and respective capabilities. Accordingly, the developed country Parties should take the lead in combating climate change and the adverse effects thereof.

Offered solutions must be appropriate to the enormity of the crisis, just, and sustainable. Climate change is not just an environmental issue; it threatens people's livelihoods and the possibilities for development of the poor. To stop climate change, it is necessary to alter current economic, social, and environmental policies. It is becoming abundantly clear that partnerships between the UN, governments, and transnational big business are unable to handle catastrophic global warming. Tackling the crisis requires that solutions must also address the root causes, which can only come about with a change of the system. Climate science and the ethical dimensions of the crisis are not being met by climate politics, because our system is captured by big business, which is coming up with new development concepts like the 'green economy' that promote the commodification of all aspects of life.

Frontline communities and justice movement activists have long complained that, with neo-liberal globalization, the state has transformed its role into being a facilitator of corporate interests through policies and priorities for the capitalist elite. This corporate capture of governance did not happen overnight. Several decades of conscious and elaborate preparations have built an economic architecture that supports the current system: (a) a global trade and investment regime; (b) economic policies of 'opening' encouraged by international financial institutions; (c) a hegemonic development paradigm; and (d) the solutions now offered to address global warming.

The increasing capture by large transnational capital of various policy spaces and decision-making processes related to climate change poses big challenges for democracy in developing and developed countries alike. Issues such as climate and energy are not even on the electoral agenda. It would be very difficult, if not impossible, for progressive parties to win on a climate and energy platform. Almost all governments, if they discuss energy politics at all, separate it from general development discourse.

Governments are increasingly complicit with corporations through the signing of aggressive and comprehensive trade and investment agreements that further environment destruction. People who act collectively to promote ecological integrity often face the force of the military or police. In this crucial struggle to resist the system, the relationship between government and people becomes problematic. If the priority is that of upholding the rights of the people, then there must be an appreciation for the people's right to resist the existing system and the agents who uphold it.

PRESCRIPTION: THERE ARE SOLUTIONS AND THEY ARE DIVERSE!

A key question in the effort to halt and reverse global warming then is: what does an anti-capitalist, system-change struggle for climate justice involve? The key component is a paradigm shift towards more democratic, inclusive, collective ownership and control of resources and more equitable access to their benefits. What kind of politics is strong enough to realize that process of change, ensure its course, and defend it against attacks from forces for the status quo? It is not enough just to be convinced and want this change. The actors, institutions, and processes that support the status quo are powerful, and they will not easily give up their privileges.

The patterns of vulnerability from climate change vary in relation to class, race, gender, and geographical location in the world economy. For example, coastal Filipino fishers lost their boats, homes, and family members in Haiyan. When reconstruction started, these poor people discovered that their former home areas had been reclassified and sold to big real estate developers. Their former coastal communities are to be replaced by hotels and high-rise apartments, which they can never afford to buy. Some families continue to live in cramped evacuation centres, and some were relocated miles from the sea. Many widowed women prostituted themselves to feed their children. Even in a rich country like the United States, it was poor and black families who suffered more and got the least priority during hurricane Katrina in 2005.

The proposed alternatives from social and ecological movements and NGOS are diverse as well as numerous. As Patrick Bond has said, 'There is paralysis from above, but there are dynamism and movements below' (Bond 2012,185–214). The NGOs and movements that push for climate justice are not waiting for governments to act; they know that the official climate negotiations will not produce sufficient actions. The most appropriate response to the current climate crisis is to change the system, and a growing block within the climate justice movement is now mobilizing around this agenda. In *This Changes Everything*, Naomi Klein has described the climate crisis as a confrontation between capitalism and the planet. The problem is our unsustainable neo-liberal capitalist development model. It needs to be transformed into a system that aims not for infinite growth, but for harmony between human beings and nature (Klein 2014, 6, 152, 450). Promoting climate justice with systemic change has many components, five of which are described below.

Acknowledging the Climate Debt by Rich Countries to Poor Countries

One of the foundational principles of the network Climate Justice Now! (CJN) is that rich countries owe a climate debt to poor countries. Climate debt has historically accrued to rich countries owing to their disproportionate contribution to the causes of climate change. This debt has two aspects. On the one hand, an emissions debt accrues to rich countries for overusing the atmosphere with their high carbon footprint, substantially diminishing the earth's capacity to absorb GHGs, and in the process denying developing countries the atmospheric space that they need in the course of their development. On the other hand, an adaptation debt accrues to rich countries for the adverse effects of their excessive emissions, which are contributing to the escalating losses, damages, and reductions of development opportunities for poor countries. The sum of emissions debts and adaptation debts constitutes the 'climate debt' of developed countries (Stilwell 2012).

The concept of climate debt has been submitted to the UNFCCC in 2008 by over fifty countries, including Bolivia, Bhutan, Malaysia, Micronesia, Sri Lanka, Paraguay, Venezuela, and the Group of Least Developed Countries, which represents forty-nine of the world's poorest and most vulnerable countries. By submitting very low (and voluntary) emission targets, the already rich countries are effectively transferring a huge burden of GHG reductions to poor countries and to future generations, while continuing to consume far more than their fair share of fossil fuels and atmospheric space.

Just Transition to a Low-Carbon Society

Fossil fuel production and consumption is interlinked with global capital circuits that are dependent on fossil fuel. The world should start a just transition to a low-carbon society based on renewable energy. In this vein, Bill McKibben's arguments on resisting fossil fuel addiction to save the planet have powered the youth movement 350.org, which he co-founded (McKibben 2012). The eco-socialist discourse of building a low-carbon society is promoting imaginative counter-narratives of environmental justice, energy democracy, and food sovereignty. Although renewable energy development is gaining leverage, it faces huge obstacles from powerful capitalist interests in the fossil fuel sector. Urgent issues exist around access to and management of the process of building renewable energy, as well as democratizing the necessary technology and finance and addressing other connected issues like jobs and land rights.

That said, not all renewable energy is climate-friendly. For instance, methane emissions from big hydroelectric dams in the tropics outweigh the benefits that this form of renewable energy provides. According to the Brazilian National Institute for Space Research, the world's largest dams emit 104 million tons of methane annually and are responsible for 4 per cent of the human contribution to climate change (Brown 2014).

A growing number of climate campaigns are now advancing calls for deindustrialization in the North and sustainable industrialization in the South in order to achieve a just global transition to a low-carbon society. Both processes are imperative for addressing social problems, especially inequality and the need to tackle issues of ownership, access to resources, democratic control of energy, and ending extractivism (i.e. development-based extractive industries such as logging and mining). Participants in the Climate Space at the World Social Forum in Tunis in 2013 and 2015 viewed consumption as a political question that cannot be sufficiently addressed by advocacy for alternative normative lifestyles alone. Fundamental change in the ways of production and consumption is needed in order to realize the low-carbon society (Climate Space 2013).

Food Sovereignty

Other key contributions to climate justice can come from agriculture. A major component of food production is not foreign investments, as most governments believe, but rather a healthy ecosystem and the capacity of small-scale farmers to continue feeding the world. The close relationship between climate change, food production, and land use made farmers groups like La Vía Campesina incorporate climate justice into the heart of their campaign for food sovereignty.

Food sovereignty refers to the right of people to define their own food and agriculture systems. It involves healthy and culturally appropriate food produced through ecologically sound methods. As more elaborately discussed by Heloise Weber in this volume, food sovereignty is a political project and campaign, an alternative, a social movement, and an analytical framework.

Food sovereignty is to be contrasted with the previously mentioned CSA initiatives. The CSA approach promotes the corporate production of genetically modified (GM) crops and the conversion of land for biofuels production. Yet small-scale farmers offer a much less costly and more effective alternative by feeding more people using local seeds (Ahmed 2014).

Deglobalization

More than a decade ago, Focus on the Global South, an international NGO based in Bangkok, proposed that social and ecological movements should join in a collective struggle for deglobalization. This concept rests on a twofold process of both deconstructing and reconstructing the prevailing development paradigm (Bello 2002; Focus on the Global South 2003). Deconstruction refers to the dismantling, paralysis, or drastic reduction of the power of the current structures and institutions that support neo-liberal governance. This is imperative in order to undermine the old system focused on growth and to provide space for alternative paradigms.

Neo-liberal global governance is a complex of world-scale economic regulation that is executed through institutions such as the International Monetary Fund (IMF), the Organisation for Economic Co-operation and Development (OECD), the World Bank, and the World Trade Organization (WTO). Together these global bodies are a major force promoting climate-destructive policies of liberalization, privatization, and general marketization of society. For example, the World Bank and other multilateral development banks finance many projects such as coal and hydropower plants that induce climate change. International financial institutions are also major promoters of the flawed CDM. Thus, any programme of climate justice needs to include a dismantling of neo-liberal global governance.

Deglobalization argues that we must transform the framework of political economy by protecting and prioritizing domestic economies and local needs. Instead of overproducing for export, reorient the economy and support small, local, peasant, and indigenous community farming. Dismantle big agribusiness that deforests, destroys soils, eliminates indigenous crop species, heats the planet, and pollutes waters and air. Promote local production and consumption by reducing long-distance trade that uses millions of tons of carbon dioxide. Steeply decrease extractivism and leave 80 per cent of the fossil fuel reserves under the soil. Stop the exploitation of tar sands, shale gas, and coal. These steps are painful but necessary for an effective and fairly shared response to the climate crisis.

Buen Vivir

Vivir bien (as it is called in Bolivia) or *buen vivir* (the equivalent phrase in Ecuador) is a Spanish term that emerged in the late twentieth century to refer to the practices and visions of indigenous peoples of the Andean region. The Aymara people call it *sumaqamaña*, the Quechua speak of *sumakkawsay*, the Peruvian Amazon embrace *kametsa asaiki*, and for the Guaraní it is *ñandereko*. The term can be translated into English as 'living well', 'good life', 'knowing how to live', 'inclusive life', and 'sweet life', among others. The practice of *vivir bien* or *buen vivir* may differ in various areas of Latin America, but across the particularities are some common elements that have been identified and developed into a concept now codified in the constitutions of Ecuador and the Plurinational State of Bolivia (Focus on the Global South 2014).

Living well contrasts with capitalist ways of life. In this alternative paradigm, humans are an integral part of nature, and society and nature are not taken to be separate entities. The goal of humans is not to control nature, but to take care of nature as one takes care of the mother who has given one life. The rights of nature and the ecosystem must be respected as much as those of humans.

In this spirit, *buen vivir* highlights the expression 'Mother Earth' (cf. Cochabamba Declaration 2010). For 'living well' the goal is harmony, not growth (Solon 2014a). Without growth, the current capitalist system cannot exist. The 'living well' vision pursues exactly the opposite: humanity can only live if it achieves balance within the overall web of life. Harmony is not an idyllic status or an end to history. In harmony, different sides and emerging contradictions need to be rebalanced, protecting the environment for the benefit of all and not growth for the profit of corporations.

Reconstructing society in the vein of *buen vivir* is challenging but imperative. *Buen vivir* is not a single fixed formula, but an array of diverse and evolving responses that one finds in nature itself. Already movements for transformation have had good discussions and agreements on principles and practices of 'living well', though much more needs to be done.

PROCESS: HOW TO GET THERE

Given the needs, the realities on the ground, and the current status of climate negotiations, big tasks of climate justice lie ahead for everyone. None of the Annex 1 developed country governments in the UNFCCC process are presenting concrete plans to meet the required 40–45 per cent of emission reductions. None of the 196 parties have mentioned the need to keep 80 per cent of known fossil fuel reserves in the ground. The prescriptions described above have few government and business champions. Hence it lies mainly with social and ecological movements to push for and pursue systemic alternatives of climate debt, a low-carbon society, food sovereignty, deglobalization, and *buen vivir*.

According to the Global Justice Ecology Project (2010), a just and equitable reduction of emissions must be driven by communities:

> It is imperative that the [Global] North urgently shifts to a low carbon economy. At the same time, in order to avoid the damaging carbon-intensive model of industrialization, countries of the Global South are entitled to resources and technology to make a transition to a low-carbon economy that does not continue to subject them to crushing poverty. Indigenous Peoples, peasant communities, fisher folks, and especially women in these communities have been able to live harmoniously and sustainably with the Earth for millennia. They are now not only the most affected by climate change, but also the most affected by its false solutions, such as agro fuels, mega-dams, genetic modification, tree plantations and carbon offset schemes.

Collective demands for change and people's empowerment must be creatively shaped through political organizing, development education, and cross-movement solidarity. Campaigns must take account of existing political conditions, but at the same time also remain firm on the goal of putting life and the environment first. The challenge is great. The structure and institutions of neo-liberal capitalism have perfected the art of sustaining the status quo: not only through their control of policy processes, but also and more importantly by presenting themselves as knowledge-bearers and experts on solving the economic crisis, poverty, climate change, and upholding social and economic rights. Insistent resistance to neo-liberalism is the only option.

Some incremental steps towards a climate justice paradigm are possible immediately. One is to promote safe, clean, and sustainable energy production through more subsidies for the development of renewable energy. A second is to develop public transport systems that discourage the unsustainable dependence on automobiles. This does not mean that social movements should disregard the climate negotiations, but rather that they should accept that the UNFCCC process will not deliver system change that is not in the interest of the rich and powerful. Engagement of the UNFCCC remains important in order to ensure that bad outcomes do not become worse.

CONCLUSION

Realizing climate justice requires nothing less than a fundamental transformation of economy, democracy, law, mass media, popular culture, and everyday habits. A growth-driven and market-dependent social system is incompatible with the reality of a finite ecosystem. States and society need – in the light of a reevaluation of nature – to rethink how resources are allocated and used.

Current policies protect the interests of the transnational capitalist class, which also includes elements from economically emerging countries like China, India, Brazil, and South Africa, as well as a small number of super-rich families in poor countries. Climate change requires that people veer away from Western lifestyles and patterns of wealth accumulation and consumption that are associated with resource-intensive growth. The climate crisis is not just an environmental issue, but an overall global ecological and societal issue. Millions of lives are already at stake, mainly among poor people, and without change the very future and form of life on earth will come into question. Solutions to climate change extend beyond markets and technology to almost every aspect of our societies and ecosystems. A total overhaul of the global political and economic system is required, and that process must start as soon as possible.

The link between climate change and social justice through global redistribution is key. A radical anti-capitalist analysis of the problem leads to out-of-the-box solutions which favour equity and sustainability. The current climate crisis has revived eco-socialist arguments that capitalism not only generates war, poverty, and insecurity, but also potentially threatens human survival in vulnerable areas. The right to development and the need for alternative development also raise class issues, where the divides lie not only between rich and developing countries, but also between rich and poor within countries.

There is no alternative, from a climate justice perspective, but to resist exploitative capitalism. To this end, each person has a responsibility to educate oneself; to be a conscious political subject; to organize, mobilize, and forge unities (including beyond one's usual partners); and thereby to avoid further harm to the planet and all living beings. Political and development education plays a big role in building a collective voice and sense of agency. It is vital for the deglobalization process to challenge received accounts of reality, to ask the question of who wins and who loses in certain social arrangements, and to identify which actors and institutions dominate and gain from current injustice. It is a complex and challenging task that cannot be comfortably undertaken. Yet, we have our planet and our humanity to lose if this is not achieved.

Chapter 11

Governance Innovation
Enabling Collective Action for Structural Redistribution

Lorenzo Fioramonti and Alfred G. Nhema

This book contributes to the quest for a more just global governance system premised on progressive people-centred redistribution. The various chapters have critically examined issues of contemporary relevance, such as climate change, land, food, corruption, digital information, finance, money, investment, and migration. Each chapter has developed fresh perspectives that can help policymakers and other stakeholders think out of the box.

Through this volume, a diverse group of authors from across the globe have proffered a well-informed treatise on what can be done to counter ongoing maldistribution patterns. The prescription has focused on promoting structural redistribution through a nuanced definition and examination of new rules for global justice. The analysis has proceeded according to three steps: the identification of various forms of global maldistribution; the description of potential solutions; and, whenever possible, the outline of 'actionable' recommendations for implementation.

The analysis has highlighted issues of power, access, and distribution of resources, in line with a political economy approach. All contributions to this book, in one way or another, conclude that only structural change can generate the rules, incentives, and behaviours needed to produce a more equitable global economy in the public good. It is clear that there are no easy fixes. What is needed is a combination of people-centred transformative energies and institutional reforms. In this process, collective action and civil society contestation, together with progressive research and advocacy, are key drivers of change.

This closing chapter builds on the various specific proposals developed in the volume to suggest a new conceptual framework of governance innovation that can promote structural redistribution. By showing the intimate links between rules and action in the quest for a more just global economy, the concept of governance is re-conceptualized as a contested terrain of interaction among a wide variety of societal stakeholders. Not only must governance processes adapt to changing needs, but they must also build new ways to incorporate the participation of groups previously excluded from decision-making processes, from local to global levels. Without such shifts in the ways that rules are made, there is indeed little hope that collective action will lead to deep and lasting redistribution of resources and power in the global economy.

THE POTENTIAL AND LIMITS OF COLLECTIVE ACTION

Redistribution has become especially topical since the 2008 financial crash. Not only have 'new economy' think tanks, foundations, and alliances proliferated, but social movements such as Occupy have also spread across the globe. Best-selling books have examined the links between inequality and economic failures, lack of innovation, and plummeting well-being (Wilkinson and Pickett 2009; Therborn 2013; Piketty 2014). Shrinking economic growth in much of the world has underlined the need to redistribute wealth as the only feasible way forward, since growth has been traditionally presented as an alternative to redistribution (Fioramonti 2013). Even the World Economic Forum, certainly not a promoter of revolutionary ideas about wealth redistribution, has identified extreme inequality as the prime threat to global stability (WEF 2014). Moreover, recent elections in countries like Greece, Spain, Italy, Denmark, and Turkey, which have seen a growth of social justice movements and networks of 'netizens' (i.e. citizens who use the Internet as their main tool for organization and deliberation), have attested to the view that structural changes are needed to make the global economy serve the needs of a just society in the twenty-first century.

Yet, all these phenomena highlight that structural redistribution is unlikely to happen in the absence of a system of governance which enables collective action not only to occur, but also to sustain itself and limit the capacity of entrenched interests and powerful actors to capture political and economic institutions. Indeed, while many groups contest the current system of rules and distribution at national and global levels, those who benefit from the status quo seek to maintain existing arrangements or to concede only cosmetic changes. The massive concentration of wealth at the very top (not just the 1 per cent, but even the 0.1 per cent) indicates that unprecedented financial resources are available to maintain the current model. Moreover, the very language and tools of 'hypercapitalism' have influenced (and in some cases entirely colonized) traditional sectors of progressive collective action (Fioramonti 2014). Nowadays, most major non-governmental organizations

(NGOs) receive the bulk of their funding from so-called philanthrocapitalists, whose market-driven approach to social change has become dominant in most charitable work and social progress initiatives (Edwards 2008; Fioramonti 2014).

Although collective action is key to addressing injustices and distributional inefficiencies in the global system, not all counterforces share the same objectives and principles (Fioramonti 2007; Scholte 2002). As the contributions to this book show, some forms of intellectual and collective action may pursue reformist approaches, while others may be keener to advance transformative solutions. Importantly, not all actors have the resources to voice their grievances and the capacity to mobilize with the intensities that are required for change to occur. This makes governance-for-change particularly complex. Again, there are no easy fixes.

Regardless of the specific issue focus, the interconnection between interests, resources, and power is evident in all of the proposals put forward in this book. For instance, the idea of a global social democracy presented by Valentina Fedotova builds on a tradition of progressive finance and labour practices championed through co-operatives, microcredit, and fair trade. Proposals for an alternative global money system, as advocated by Taoxiong Liu and Mendang Huang, or a currency transaction levy, as advanced by Nina Hall and Inge Kaul, would greatly reduce inequalities through diffused monetary governance and the generation of resources for the provision and protection of global public goods. Common-good approaches to intellectual property and alternative systems of remittances, discussed respectively by Blayne Haggart as well as Beverly Mullings and Alissa Trotz, significantly reframe development paths of the global economy. These proposals afford a central role to traditionally excluded actors such as peer-to-peer knowledge producers and the diaspora. Additionally, Yash Tandon promotes local community-based investment as a powerful alternative to current commodification patterns and mainstream approaches to foreign direct investment. The very language of neo-liberalism should also be challenged, as it often leads to foregone conclusions with respect to key concepts like 'development', 'efficiency', and even 'transparency' and 'corruption' (as argued by Pınar Bedirhanoğlu). Such discourses distract society from the very structural injustices that a neo-liberal market-based economy produces. In this vein, Dorothy Guerrero identifies potential catalysts for radical change in justice-centred approaches to climate change. Similarly, Heloise Weber's focus on land governance and agricultural production points to food sovereignty as an innovative alternative to the prevailing development models.

As underlined throughout this book, governance is crucial to achieve structural redistribution in the global economy. Yet, for governance to become a useful concept in this regard, its very meaning has to be redefined. As discussed at various earlier points in this volume, the neo-liberal concept of 'good governance' has been employed to support a system of rules that entrenches inequalities, more often than not through the redefinition of constructs such as 'markets', 'efficiency', 'productivity', and 'growth', which have been developed in mainstream approaches to the global economy. In this vein, 'governance' has been traditionally presented as nothing but a set of tools to promote fast-growing market economies. However, governance is a much more nuanced concept: it is fundamentally a dynamic process of adaptation, contestation, and re-elaboration of how social, economic, and political actors shape the rules of engagement at local, national, regional, and global levels. Governance is continuously evolving in line with the pressures and contributions exerted by a wide variety of stakeholders, which makes governance *innovation* crucial to structural change. Some of the proposals put forward in this volume are novel ideas which address new problems, while other proposals have a longer history (in one form or another) and have regained currency due to the persistence of the maldistributions that they aim to redress. Indeed, the rules that govern our decision-making procedures shape the capacity of the system to adapt. If we are to successfully alter the current distribution of power and resources at the global level, it is not enough to mobilize collective actions for short periods of time. There is a need for ongoing governance innovation, which has the capacity to develop adaptable mechanisms of decision-making that foster empowerment and inclusivity through inputs from a wide variety of stakeholders.

GOVERNANCE INNOVATION AND STRUCTURAL REDISTRIBUTION IN THE GLOBAL ECONOMY

The term 'governance' has arisen over recent decades to indicate the complexity of decision-making processes in contemporary society. While some analysts still use the term to indicate the 'government's ability to make and enforce rules, and to deliver services' (Fukuyama 2013), there is a growing consensus that the idea of 'governance' departs from old-style government and presupposes a fragmentation and diffusion of authority. No government nowadays can govern 'alone': it is bound to share 'bits and pieces' of authority with other entities, including NGOs, regional and global intergovernmental institutions, private corporations, and other citizen organizations. Governance may take many forms, along a continuum from a vertical multilevel architecture of decision-making to a horizontal structure of diffused networks. As pointed out by Manuel Castells, governance reflects the emergence of a 'network society' in which public and private authorities are increasingly intertwined (Castells and Cardoso 2006).

In the international political and economic debate, the term governance has related to decision-making in the absence of an overarching (and therefore exclusive) political authority (Rosenau 1999). Since the early 1990s, researchers have observed fundamental change in the global arena, especially due to the rising power of multinational corporations and transnational civil society movements. For some, international politics has witnessed an era of 'turbulence' since the fall of the Berlin Wall (Rosenau 1990), and our societies have been entering a 'global age' (Albrow 1996). In this process, the traditional emphasis on national sovereignty that characterized world politics since the Treaty of Westphalia in 1648 has gradually given way to a 'postnational constellation' (Habermas 1998; Zürn 2002). States have become managers rather than monopolists of authority (Genschel and Zangl 2008), with private corporations accruing unprecedented power and resources, while new opportunities have also been afforded to civil society.

Participation in global politics by individuals and organized groups (largely supported by technological innovation) has increased to a point where they now play a significant role in decision-making, a process which has intensified the breakdown of traditional state-centred authority relations (Held et al. 1999; Zürn 1998; Castells and Cardoso 2006). It is now widely recognized that effective and efficient governance of a global world requires capabilities that are spread across a broad range of actors (Dingwerth and Pattberg 2009). Some of these arrangements may be formal and involve a wide variety of actors such as state ministries, international institutions, corporations, non-governmental groups, and even individuals. Other arrangements may be informal and even temporary, as is the case with some civil society coalitions (Karns and Mingst 2004). In the field of collective action theory, Elinor Ostrom has shown various ways in which governance plays out at the local level (Ostrom 1990). In particular, she has pointed out how top-down systems of control, such as those exerted by the state or by market actors, are not necessarily the most effective to create order and compliance. Local communities and civil society groups can indeed develop shared institutions that are often more adaptive, more accountable, and more creative than those developed by states and markets. In particular, Ostrom has highlighted that governance is more hybrid than we often think, where the distinction between public and private authority is blurred by overlapping roles, fuzzy memberships, and direct participation. Indeed, associations, public offices, and a myriad of private agents continuously interact to shape collective choices and behaviours at all levels of governance. It is precisely this system of 'horizontal' governance, with its inherent integration of interests and roles, which explains the resilience of some forms of bottom-up cooperation, especially in the management of shared resources (e.g. the commons).

In such a multilevel and multi-actor system of decision-making, one can distinguish between different orders of governance (Kooiman 2003). First-order governance is the level at which the actors involved identify problems and enact responses. The first order indicates the more substantial element of governance, that is, its capacity to produce particular outcomes. Second-order governance refers to the set of rules governing the decision process. It underlies the fact that decisions do not take place in a vacuum, but rather within clear institutional boundaries, although these institutions may not necessarily be tangible or perpetual, which therefore underlines the capacity of governance to change. The reflection on second-order governance thus adds another layer of complexity, as it points to the influence of institutional parameters on the capacity of actors to affect decisions. Finally, one can distinguish a meta-governance level, as 'the governing of governing' (Kooiman 2003: 170), that is, the set of structural (both normative and resource-based) boundaries within which governance processes are conducted, including global standards as well as shared beliefs and values within public opinion.

Governance therefore encapsulates a fragmentation of central authority, thus giving way to more inclusive and more multifaceted forms of decision-making. The multiplication of sources of authority and the capacity of these sources to interact in decision-making processes (whether at the macro level of the political sphere or at the micro level of individual organizations) is by no means an indication that governance is a collaborative process. In fact, the interaction can be highly conflictual, and domination by one sector over another is always possible (cf. Scholte 1997; 2005). Moreover, different forms of governance can enjoy varying degrees of inclusivity, with some arrangements forcing the various actors into highly rigid structures, thus limiting the capacity for meaningful participation. This is why innovation in governance is crucial.

Organizational theorists such as Kanter were among the first to highlight the distinction between popular perceptions of innovation and its actual meaning in social theory. As she notes,

> The term 'innovation' makes most people think first about technology: new products and new methods for making them . . . . Fewer people would mention new tax laws or the creation of enterprise zones, even though these are innovations too. Fewer still, if any, would be likely to mention such innovations as quality circles and problem-solving task forces. (Kanter 1983, 20)

From a broader angle, innovation can be also defined as 'the development and adoption of new and improved ways of addressing social and economic needs and wants' (Kuhlmann, Shapira, and Smits 2010, 1). But what is improvement? Innovation for whom and for what purpose?

Clearly the best way to capture the intersection between governance and innovation is to focus on inclusivity premised on empowerment, which are defining characters of the fragmentation of authority underlying the concept of governance. Innovation in this context is therefore about developing processes that increase inclusivity, thus deepening the horizontal distribution of power against the always-present push for vertical control. A focus on higher degrees of inclusivity allows governance innovations to increase the legitimacy of decision-making: that is, to increase the acceptability of decision-making processes in the eyes of a wide range of stakeholders. Inclusivity is also crucial to help redefine the rules of engagement that allow sustained collective action in the pursuit of structural redistribution, which in turn create conditions for further innovations in governance (as shown in Figure 11.1).

The various studies in this book seek to proffer new rules for the global economy which, along with enhancing structural redistribution of resources, also deepen participation by a wide variety of stakeholders. Tandon's chapter is refreshingly blunt in its critical reflections on the various structural redistribution challenges facing developing countries. He highlights the so-called 'North–South' pattern of unequal global distribution. Cognizant of the persistent outflows of capital, mostly from the South to the North, Tandon urges not only to rethink the configuration of foreign direct investment, but also to innovate in investment practices, policies, and laws, for both source and recipient countries. In this context, governance innovations should aim to break North–South dependence patterns. Regional systems of cooperation, strengthening ties among like-minded countries in clearly defined regional areas, could help foster a dynamic industrial and investment coordination, thus reducing the need for 'poor' countries to borrow from international institutions and require massive inflows of distant foreign investment.

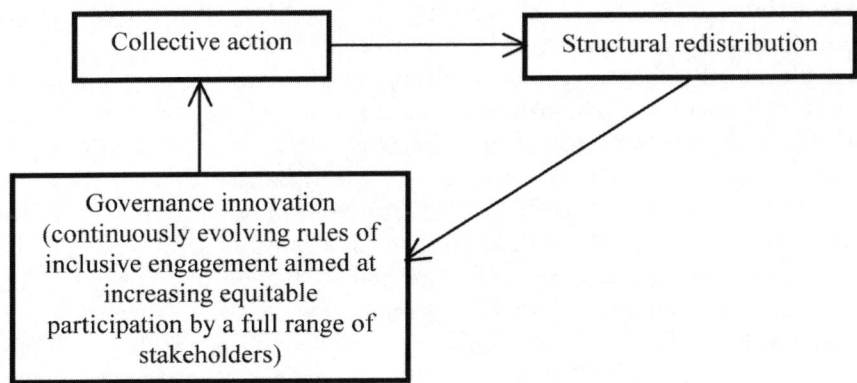

Figure 11.1 Dynamics of Change

Experiments such as the Chiang Mai Initiative and the Asian Infrastructure Investment Bank in East Asia and the New Development Bank (popularly known as the BRICS Bank) are examples of regional and global investment initiatives aimed at supporting the sustained mobilization of resources for hitherto developing and emerging countries. Similarly, traditional debt-cancellation campaigns as well as civil society's initiatives on climate debt could become governance innovations able to redirect significant resources away from wealthy circles in the North towards the generation of sustainable and equitable development opportunities in the South.

Fedotova's contribution also highlights global inequality between 'rich' and 'poor' countries across the globe. In her case, innovation focuses on scaling up social democracy from a national level to a global strategy for redistribution from North to South. Here too, regional integration examples like the European Union (with all its limitations and contradictions) can show potential ways to achieve social policy improvements that transcend national borders and create incentives for cross-subsidization between more and less wealthy areas of the world. Among other initiatives, basic income grant campaigns have mushroomed around the world, from Europe to Africa and North America, proposing practical ways to redirect funds from natural resources revenues and excessive wealth concentration towards the economic uplifting of all individuals (see, for instance, the Basic Income Earth Network). In this regard, alternative indicators of economic performance, which complement or replace the gross domestic product (GDP) to put well-being and sustainable development at the centre of policy formulation, can provide additional incentives to support social policy mechanisms, while constraining policies that fuel inequality (Fioramonti 2013).

The adoption of the Sustainable Development Goals in September 2015 may also contribute to reinforcing the causes of civil society and social movements committed to the fight against inequality and environmental degradation. As Weber shows in this book, the dramatic rise in land acquisitions by foreign (often private) actors has become a major concern in the quest for a sustainable global redistributive agenda. Similarly, the global food system is not only inflicting a heavy toll on human rights and nutrition for millions of people, but also becoming a major cause of environmental destruction. Guerrero's chapter addresses the (re)distributive challenges posed by climate change. She notes that if the unequal impacts of climate change are not addressed, they will further undermine development aspirations across various geographical and social structures. Guerrero highlights that climate change most disrupts livelihoods in poor countries and among poorer sections of the community within those countries. The chapter underlines that climate change is the result of a global economic system that prioritizes overproduction and overconsumption and that any redistribution programmes must take this reality into account.

So, what alternatives are possible? Certain national governments have accorded nature 'fundamental rights', thus giving land and all the produce emerging from it a 'public good' profile. Both Bolivia and Ecuador have incorporated sustainable development into their constitutions. New Zealand has afforded rights to certain ecosystems (notorious has been the case of the Whanganui River). First Peoples in both Canada and the United States have used legal avenues to reaffirm their control over land that had been appropriated by fossil fuel and gas companies (Klein 2015). Moreover, as Weber shows, food sovereignty movements are growing in the four corners of the world, not only demanding a radical restructuration of the mainstream food system, but also supporting social enterprises that deliver local, organic, healthy food to millions of people every day.

The marginalization of alternative thinking and practices is also the focus of chapters by Bedirhanoğlu, Haggart, and Mullings and Trotz. Bedirhanoğlu deconstructs the neo-liberal good governance doctrine against corruption. She asserts that the prevailing anti-corruption crusade is curtailing rather than enhancing the targeted countries' prospects for democratic development. Instead, corruption must be combatted from a holistic perspective that highlights the class dimensions of corruption and social struggles against neo-liberal capitalism. Haggart's contribution contends that the prevailing copyright enforcement regime in the online world, driven by media conglomerates and industrial countries, is paradoxically curtailing basic rights like privacy, freedom of expression, and unfettered access to culture. According to him, an innovative alternative would emphasize the need for all to access and disseminate knowledge, rather than the wish by narrow entrenched interests to have strong copyright protection. Mullings and Trotz highlight the potential of diaspora engagement. Their critique of neo-liberalism explores innovations that prioritize social justice over market efficiency. This transformative strategy is inclusive of a diversity of groups in the Caribbean, as well as the diaspora community in North America and Europe. The proposition is to create an e-diaspora, a Caribbean virtual space and digital exchange platform that enables enhanced global interactions among Caribbean peoples.

These cases are complemented by other chapters that examine innovative perspectives on alternative global redistributive systems for money and finance. Taoxiong Liu and Mendang Huang posit that a redistributive global monetary regime is vital for global democracy and global justice. The contention is that the current global reserve system has major maldistributive effects that can only be addressed through a democratic global governance supported by a supranational global currency reserve system. Hall and Kaul advocate for the introduction of a levy on international currency transactions. The levy, operating on a progressive 'user pays' basis, could raise over US$ 25 billion annually. Their contribution outlines why new sources of global public finance are needed and then critically examines how the currency transaction levy would work.

Redesign of the global money system is critical to all areas of human sustainable development and could potentially reinforce the calls made above for more accountability, participation, and inclusion. The dominant money system is, indeed, a perfect example of a top-down, highly concentrated structure of governance. As a system of social organization, current fiat money has attributed immense powers not only to central bankers and their stakeholders (which often are not just states, but private individuals). It has also given commercial banks the power to create money through the issue of loans to the general public. It is therefore worth asking what would happen to this hierarchical governance if the introduction of cryptocurrencies and alternative/complementary currency networks was to continue apace in various regions of the world. Digital currencies are becoming particularly en vogue these days, with Bitcoin being the best known but by no means only case of global digital money. Moreover, local currency networks are proliferating in Europe, Africa, and the Americas, providing much needed impetus to local economic development, especially in crisis-stricken areas (Fioramonti 2013). These alternatives are not only creating a parallel 'market', but also providing more transparency and more possibilities for democratic control of the money supply.

Together the chapters in this book show that truly transformative governance innovations cannot be driven by the maximization of utility of a limited privileged group of individuals who currently control the lion's share of the world's wealth. Rather, a broader set of stakeholders – including the citizenry at large – needs to drive the new rules for global justice. The innovations presented in the various chapters contribute to developing governance in ways that systematically sustain collective action for long-term structural redistribution in the global economy.

CONCLUSION

The chapters in this book have focused on developing redistributive measures that would empower marginalized groups in today's global world. Reconfiguring global investment is now much more within reach than a few decades ago. As argued by Tandon, ordinary people 'have to make a conscious effort to innovate ways and means of decoupling from the market-based iniquitous value system'. This move blurs the distinction between consumers and producers, paving the way for individuals to become 'prosumers' in many different fields.

Nowhere is this blending as evident as in the reinvention of money, especially through the proliferation of alternative currency systems. Since the

2008 global financial collapse, non-fiat currencies have emerged in most countries around the world, taking a phenomenon that has deep roots in many societies to a new global scale (Fioramonti 2013). Whether through local community currencies or through cryptographic systems such as Bitcoin, the new currencies allow users to transcend both the regulatory frameworks devised by public institutions as well as the financial system controlled by private corporations. The resulting system of more evenly distributed power has the potential to redesign national and global economic governance. Similarly, innovative forms of direct investment such as offered by the BRICS New Development Bank hold the potential to revolutionize the traditional role played by private corporations.

As governance innovations make more interaction across sectors and networks possible, the innovation therein is likely to produce hybrid models, to promote cross-fertilization, and increasingly to decentralize and de-sectoralize decision-making. More diffused forms of governance, supported by innovations that make collective action not only possible but also sustainable in the long run, hold the potential to profoundly tilt the power distribution away from the few. The traditional advantage of vertical systems of social organizations – which has always fuelled concentration of power and resources at the top – is increasingly challenged by forms of organization that develop horizontally and challenge the centre–periphery structure. As accountability demands increase and new technologies emerge, the process of structural redistribution is likely to evolve to a new level, in which individual citizens transcend the intermediary role traditionally played by the state, the market, and civil society to become proactive actors in governance processes at interconnected local, national, regional, and global levels.

Bibliography

Aday, Sean, Henry Farrell, Marc Lynch, John Sides, John Kelly and Ethan Zuckerman. 2010. *Blogs and Bullets: New Media in Contentious Politics.* Washington, DC: United States Institute of Peace.

Ahmed, Nafeez. 2014. "UN: Only Small Farmers and Agroecology Can Feed the World." Accessed September 1, 2015. http://permaculturenews.org/2014/09/26/un-small-farmers-agroecology-can-feed-world/.

Akram-Lodhi, Haroon. 2012. "Contextualizing Land Grabbing: Contemporary Land Deals, the Global Subsistence Crisis and the World Food System." *Canadian Journal of Development Studies* 33 (2): 119–42.

Albrow, Martin. 1996. *The Global Age: State and Society beyond Modernity.* Cambridge: Cambridge University Press.

Alessandrini, Pietro and Michele Fratianni. 2009. *International Monies, Special Drawing Rights and Supernational Money.* Social Science Research Network Working Paper. https://www.researchgate.net/publication/46547332_Dominant_Currencies_Special_Drawing_Rights_and_Supernational_Bank_Money.

Almond, Gabriel A., and Sidney Verba. 1963. *The Civic Culture: Political Attitudes and Democracy in Five Nations.* Princeton: Princeton University Press.

Amin, Samir. 2009. *Eurocentrism.* 2nd ed. New York: Monthly Review Press.

Amnesty International. 2012. "EU Urged to Reject International Anti-Counterfeiting Pact." News release, February 10. Accessed September 1, 2014. https://www.amnesty.org/en/news/eu-urged-reject-international-anti-counterfeiting-pact-2012-02-10.

Andersen, Torben M. 2008. "The Scandinavian Model – Prospects and Challenges." *International Tax and Public Finance* 15 (1): 45–66.

Angın, Merih and Pınar Bedirhanoğlu. 2012. "Privatization Processes as Ideological Moments: The Privatization of Large-Scale State Enterprises in Turkey in the 2000s." *New Perspectives on Turkey* 47: 139–67.

Archer, David and Stefan Rahmstorf. 2010. *The Climate Crisis: An Introductory Guide to Climate Change.* Cambridge: Cambridge University Press.

Arthur, Charles and agencies. 2012a. "Acta Unlikely to be Ratified in Europe, Says Kroes." *The Guardian*, May 8. Accessed September 1, 2014. http://www.theguardian.com/technology/2012/may/08/acta-europe-kroes.

Arthur, Charles and agencies. 2012b. "Acta Criticised after Thousands Protest in Europe." *The Guardian*, February 13. Accessed September 1, 2014. http://www.theguardian.com/technology/2012/feb/13/acta-protests-europe.

ABC. 2014. "UN Warns that 100 Days after Typhoon Haiyan Hit the Philippines, Millions of Survivors Still Need Shelter." Australian Broadcasting Corporation. Accessed September 1, 2015. http://www.abc.net.au/news/2014-02-16/an-phils-typhoon-haiyan-100-days-on/5262960.

Awange, Joseph L., Eshan Forootan, Jürgen Kusche, John B. K. Kiema, P. A. Omondi, B. Heck, Kevin Fleming, S. O. Ohanya, and Rodrigo M. Gonçalves. 2013. "Understanding the Decline of Water Storage across the Ramser-Lake Naivasha Using Satellite-Based Methods?" *Advances in Water Resources* 60: 7–23.

Baker, Gideon and David Chandler, eds. 2005. *Global Civil Society: Contested Futures*. New York: Routledge.

Bank for International Settlements. 2014. "Triennial Central Bank Survey of Foreign Exchange Turnover in April 2013." Accessed September 20, 2014. http://www.bis.org/press/p130905.htm.

Barker, Alex. 2014. "Eurozone Divided over Financial Transaction Tax Deal." *Financial Times*, May 6. Accessed January 16, 2016. http://www.ft.com/intl/cms/s/0/d8a5d630-d529-11e3-9187-00144feabdc0.html#axzz3xPNQxAxe.

Bayramoğlu, Sonay. 2005. *Yönetişim Zihniyeti: Türkiye'de Üst Kurullar ve Siyasal İktidarın Dönüşümü* [The Mentality of Governance: Higher Councils and the Transformation of Political Power in Turkey]. İstanbul: İletişim.

Bedirhanoğlu, Pınar. 2002. "Rusya'da Kapitalist Dönüşüm Süreci, Yolsuzluk ve Neoliberalizm" [Capitalist Transformation Process, Corruption and Neoliberalism]. *Toplum ve Bilim* 92: 217–33.

Bedirhanoğlu, Pınar. 2007. "The Neoliberal Discourse on Corruption as a Means of Consent-Building: Reflections from Post-Crisis Turkey." *Third World Quarterly* 28 (7): 1239–54.

Bello, Walden. 2002. *Deglobalisation: Ideas for a New World Economy*. London: Zed Books.

Best, Lloyd. 1967. "Independent Thought and West Indian Freedom." *New World Quarterly* 3: 13–36.

BGD. 2015a. "Building Global Democracy Library." Accessed September 2, 2015. http://www.buildingglobaldemocracy.org/building-global-democracy-library.

BGD. 2015b. "Building Global Democracy Programme." Accessed September 2, 2015. http://www.buildingglobaldemocracy.org.

Bhagwati, Jagdish N. 2007. *In Defense of Globalization*. 2nd ed. New York: Council on Foreign Relations.

Bird, Graham. 2011. "Prospects for the Evolution of Global Reserves." *World Economics* 2 (3): 191–212.

Bitcoin Charts. 2014. Accessed September 2, 2015. http://bitcoincharts.com/charts/bitstampUSD#rg360zczsg2012-06-21zeg2014-12-31ztgSzm1g10zm2g25.

Blanchard, Olivier, Maxim Boycko, Marek Dabrowski, Rudiger Dornbusch, Richard Layard and Andrei Shleifer. 1993. *Post-Communist Reform: Pain and Progress.* Cambridge, MA: MIT Press.

Blockchain.info. 2014. "Number of Transactions Per Day". Accessed September 2, 2015. https://blockchain.info/charts/n-transactions?timespan=all&show DataPoint s=false&daysAverageString=1&show_header=true&scale=0&address=.

BMZ Ministry Budget. 2014. Accessed September 8, 2014. http://www.bmz.de/en/ministry/budget/.

Boldrin, Michele and David K. Levine. 2008. *Against Intellectual Monopoly.* Cambridge: Cambridge University Press.

Bond, Patrick. 2012. *Politics of Climate Justice: Paralysis Above, Movement Below.* Durban: University of KwaZulu-Natal Press.

Boratav, Korkut, et al. 1998. "Kamu İşletmeleri ve Özelleştirme Deneyimi: Sorunlar ve Politika Seçenekleri" [Public Enterprises and the Privatization Process: Problems and Policy Choices]. *Toplum ve Bilim* 77: 100–133.

Bourguignon, François and Christian Morrison. 2002. "Inequality among World Citizens, 1820–1992." *American Economic Review* 92 (4): 727–44.

Bratsis, Peter. 2014. "Political Corruption in the Age of Transnational Capitalism." *Historical Materialism* 22 (1): 105–28.

Bresser-Pereira, Luiz C. 2001. "The New Left Viewed from the South." In *The Global Third Way Debate,* edited by Anthony Giddens, 358–71. Cambridge: Polity.

Brooks, Thom, ed. 2008. *The Global Justice Reader.* Oxford: Wiley.

Brown, Ed and Jonathan Cloke. 2004. "Neoliberal Reform, Governance and Corruption in the South: Assessing the International Anti-Corruption Crusade." *Antipode* 36 (2): 272–94.

Brown, Paul. 2014. "Drowned Tropical Forests Add to Climate Change." *The Daily Climate,* September 11. Accessed September 1, 2015. http://www.dailyclimate.org/tdc-newsroom/2014/09/tropical-hydro-methane.

Buchanan, Larry, Hannah Fairfield, Alicia Parlapiano, Sergio Peçanha, Tim Wallace, Derek Watkins and Karen Yourish. 2013. "Mapping the Destruction of Typhoon Haiyan." *New York Times,* November 11. Accessed September 1, 2015. http://www.nytimes.com/interactive/2013/11/11/world/asia/typhoon-haiyan-map.html?_r=0.

Buğra, Ayşe and Osman Savaşkan. 2014. *New Capitalism in Turkey.* Cheltenham: Edward Elgar.

Bukovansky, Mlada. 2006. "The Hollowness of Anti-corruption Discourse." *Review of International Political Economy* 13 (2): 181–209.

Camdessus, Michel. 1999. "Second Generation Reforms: Reflections and New Challenges." Opening Speech for the IMF Conference of the Second Generation Reforms. 8 November. Accessed September 20, 2014. http://www.imf.org/external/np/speeches/1999/110899.HTM.

Caney, Simon. 2005. *Justice beyond Borders: A Global Political Theory.* Oxford: Oxford University Press.

Caplan, Bryan. 2012. "Why Should We Restrict Immigration?" *Cato Journal* 32 (1): 5–24.

Carrier, Michael A. 2013. "SOPA, PIPA, ACTA, TPP: An Alphabet Soup of Innovation-Stifling Copyright Legislation and Agreements." *Northwestern Journal of Technology and Intellectual Property* 11. Accessed September 1, 2014. http://scholarlycommons.law.northwestern.edu/njtip/vol11/iss2/1.

Castells, Manuel and Gustavo Cardoso. 2006. *The Network Society: From Knowledge to Policy*. Washington, DC: Centre for Transatlantic Relations.

Catalina, Cozmei and Caloian Florentin. 2012. "The Bitcoin Economy: An Anti-Crisis Remedy?" *Journal of Economic-Financial Theory and Practice* Supplement (4): 156–163.

Chang, Ha-Joon. 2002. "Kicking away the Ladder." *post-autistic economics review* 15. Accessed August 27, 2015. http://www.paecon.net/PAEtexts/Chang1.htm.

Chase-Dunn, Christofer. 2003 "Globalization from Below: Toward a Collectively Rational and Democratic Global Commonwealth." *Social Evolution & History* 2 (1): 195–237.

Climate Space. 2013. "World Social Forum Climate Space Declaration: To Reclaim Our Future, We Must Change the Present." Accessed September 1, 2015. http://www.polarisinstitute.org/world_social_forum_climate_space_declaration_to_reclaim_our_future_we_must_change_the_present.

Climate Space. 2014. "Mobilize and Organize to Stop and Prevent Planet Fever!" Accessed September 1, 2015. http://focusweb.org/content/sign-statement-denounce-corporate-takeover-climate-summit.

Clinton, Hillary. 2010. "Internet Freedom." Speech presented at the Newseum, Washington, DC. January 21.

Cochabamba Declaration. 2010. "People's Agreement of Cochabamba." April 22. Accessed September 1, 2015. http://pwccc.wordpress.com/2010/04/24/peoples-agreement/.

Collier, Paul. 2007. *The Bottom Billion: Why the Poorest Countries Are Failing and What Can Be Done about It*. Oxford: Oxford University Press.

Cooper, Richard. 2010. "A Future for the SDR?" *Central Banking Journal* 20 (4): 65–72.

Costa, Alexandre A. 2013. "Haiyan/Yolanda: Inside Each New-Born Violent Storm Is the DNA of the Fossil Fuel Industry and Capitalism." *International Viewpoint*, November 21. Accessed September 1, 2015. http://www.internationalviewpoint.org/spip.php?article3183.

CPTech. 2005. "Draft Treaty on Access to Knowledge." May 9. Accessed September 1, 2014. http://www.cptech.org/a2k/a2k_treaty_may9.pdf.

Cramme, Olaf and Patrick Diamond, eds. 2012. *After The Third Way: The Future of Social Democracy in Europe*. London: I.B. Taurus.

Creative Commons. 2015. "Frequently Asked Questions." Accessed January 16, 2016. https://wiki.creativecommons.org/Frequently_Asked_Questions.

Credit Suisse. 2014. *Global Wealth Report 2014*. Zurich: Credit Suisse Research Institute.

CVF. 2012. *Climate Vulnerability Monitor: A Guide to the Cold Calculus of a Hot Planet*. Climate Vulnerability Forum. Madrid: DARA. Accessed September 1, 2015. http://daraint.org/climate-vulnerability-monitor/climate-vulnerability-monitor-2012/report/.

Dahlberg, Lincoln and Eugenia Siapera. 2007. "Introduction: Tracing Radical Democracy and the Internet." In *Radical Democracy and the Internet: Interrogating Theory and Practice*, edited by Lincoln Dahlberg and Eugenia Siapera, 1–15. New York: Palgrave Macmillan.

Davies, James B., ed. 2008. *Personal Wealth from a Global Perspective*. Oxford: Oxford University Press.

Davis, Mike. 2006. *Planet of Slums*. London: Verso.

Desmarais, Annette A. 2008. "The Power of Peasants: Reflections on the Meanings of La Via Campesina." *Journal of Rural Studies* 24: 138–49.

Desmarais, Annette A. 2007. *La Vía Campesina: Globalization and the Power of Peasants*. London: Pluto.

Dickson, Dixie-Ann. 2013. "Governor Rambarran: Small Economies Should Tap into Diaspora Bonds." *The Trinidad Guardian Newspaper*, January 30. Accessed May 28, 2015. http://www.guardian.co.tt/business/2013-01-30/governor-rambarran-small-economies-should-tap-diaspora-bonds.

Dingwerth, Klaus and Philipp Pattberg. 2009. "Actors, Arenas and Issues in Global Governance". In *Palgrave Advances in Global Governance*, edited by Jim Whitman, 41–65. Basingstoke: Palgrave Macmillan.

Dinler, Demet Ş. 2003. "Türkiye'de Güçlü Devlet Geleneği Tezinin Eleştirisi" [Critique of the Thesis of Powerful State Tradition in Turkey]. *Praksis* 9: 17–54.

Docquier, Frédéric and Abdeslam Marfouk. 2005. *International Migration by Educational Attainment (1990–2000), Release 1.1*. Washington DC: World Bank.

Doern, G. Bruce and Markus Sharaput. 2000. *Canadian Intellectual Property: The Politics of Innovating Institutions and Interests*. Toronto: University of Toronto Press.

Dormael, Armand van. 1978. *Bretton Woods: Birth of a Monetary System*. New York: Holmes and Meier.

Drahos, Peter. 2007. "'Trust Me': Patent Offices in Developing Countries." Working paper. Canberra: Centre for Governance of Knowledge and Development. Accessed March 18, 2015. http://www.anu.edu.au/fellows/pdrahos/pdfs/2007Drahostrustmessrn.pdf.

Drahos, Peter and John Braithwaite. 2002. *Information Feudalism: Who Owns the Knowledge Economy?* London: Earthscan.

Dür, Andreas and Gemma Mateo. 2013. "Gaining Access or Going Public? Interest Group Strategies in Five European Countries." *European Journal of Political Research* 52 (5): 660–86.

Eagleton, Terry. 1991. *Ideology: An Introduction*. London and New York: Verso.

Edwards, Michael. 2008. *Just Another Emperor? The Myths and Realities of Philanthrocapitalism*. New York: Demos.

Eigen, Peter. 2013. "International Corruption: Organized Civil Society for Better Global Governance." *Social Research* 8 (4): 1287–1308.

EJOLT. 2013. "Madagascar: To Eat or To Be Eaten". Accessed September 10, 2014. http://www.ejolt.org/2013/09/madagascar-to-eat-or-to-be-eaten/.

Elliott, Larry, Richard Murphy, Tony Juniper, Jeremy Legget, Colin Hines, Charles Secrett, Caroline Lucas, Andrew Simms and Ann Pettifor. 2008. *A Green New Deal*. London: New Economics Foundation.

Eltis, David. 1987. *Economic Growth and the Ending of the Transatlantic Slave Trade*. New York: Oxford University Press.
Erten, Bilge and José A. Ocampo. 2012. *Building a Stable and Equitable Global Monetary System*. New York: United Nations Department of Economic and Social Affairs, Working Paper 118.
European Commission. 2013. *Proposal for a Council Directive Implementing Enhanced Cooperation in the Area of Financial Transaction Tax*. 14 February 2013. Document COM, 71 final—2013/0045 (CNS). Accessed September 15, 2015. http://ec.europa.eu/taxation_customs/resources/documents/taxation/com_2013_71_en.pdf.
Fedotova, Valentina. 1997. *Modernizacija 'drugoj' Evropy* [Modernization of the 'Other' Europe]. Moscow: IPHRAN.
Fedotova, Valentina. 2002. "Evropejskij Tretij Put' i ego Simvolicheskoe Znachenie dlja Rossii i Drugih Stran." [European Third Way and Its Symbolic Importance for Russia and Other Countries] *Sociologicheskoe obozrenie* [Russian Sociological Review] 2 (1): 3–17.
Fedotova, Valentina, Vladimir Kolpakov and Nadezhda Fedotova. 2008. *Global'nyj Kapitalizm: Tri Velikie Transformacii. Social'no-Filosofskij Analiz Vzaimootnoshenij Jekonomiki i Obshhestva* [Global Capitalism: Three Great Transformations. Socio-Philosophical Analysis of Relations between Economy and Society]. Moscow: Kul'turnaja revoljucija.
Fioramonti, Lorenzo. 2007. "The Internal Contradictions of Global Civil Society: What Impact on Democracy?" *Development Dialogue*, 49: 131–141.
Fioramonti, Lorenzo. 2013. *Gross Domestic Problem: The Politics behind the World's Most Powerful Number*. London: Zed.
Fioramonti, Lorenzo. 2014. *How Numbers Rule the World: The Use and Abuse of Statistics in Global Politics*. London: Zed.
Focus on the Global South. 2003. "Programme Plan 2003–2005." Bangkok: Focus on the Global South.
Focus on the Global South. 2010. *The Clean Development Mechanism Projects in the Philippines: Costly, Dirty, Money-Making Schemes*. Quezon City: Focus on the Global South. Accessed September 1, 2015. http://focusweb.org/sites/www.focusweb.org/files/CDM%20Web%20version%20lowres.pdf.
Focus on the Global South. 2012. *Whose "Clean" Development? Communities Speak Out*. Bangkok: Focus on the Global South. Accessed September 1, 2015. http://focusweb.org/sites/www.focusweb.org/files/whose-clean-development.pdf.
Focus on the Global South. 2014. *Learning from Our Roots: A Conversation on Vivir Bien*. Bangkok: Focus on the Global South. Accessed September 1, 2015. http://focusweb.org/content/publication-learning-our-roots.
Fogarty, Edward A. 2011. "Nothing Succeeds Like Access? NGO Strategies Towards Multilateral Institutions." *Journal of Civil Society* 7 (2): 207–27.
Fouron, Georges E., and Nina G. Schiller. 2001. *Georges Woke up Laughing: Long-Distance Nationalism and the Search for Home*. Durham: Duke University Press.
Franco, Jennifer, Les Levidow, David Fig, Lucia Goldfarb, Mireille Hönicke and Maria Luisa Mendonça. 2010. "Assumptions in the European Union Biofuels Policy: Frictions with Experiences in Germany, Brazil and Mozambique." *Journal of Peasant Studies* 37 (4): 661–98.

Friedman, Thomas L. 2005. *The World is Flat: A Brief History of the Twenty-First Century*. New York: Farrar, Straus and Giroux.

Friends of the Earth. 2008. *REDD Myths: A Critical Review of Proposed Mechanisms to Reduce Emissions from Deforestation and Degradation in Developing Countries*. Amsterdam: Friends of the Earth International. Accessed September 1, 2015. http://www.foei.org/wp-content/uploads/2014/08/15-foei-forest-full-eng-lr.pdf.

Friends of the Earth. 2010. *Africa: Up for Grabs – The Scale and Impact of Land Grabbing for Agrofuels*. Accessed June 15, 2010. https://www.foeeurope.org/sites/default/files/publications/FoEE_Africa_up_for_grabs_0910.pdf.

Fuchs, Christian. 2014. *Social Media: A Critical Introduction*. London: Sage.

Fukuyama, Francis. 2013. "What is Governance?" *Governance: An International Journal of Policy, Administration, and Institutions*, 26 (3): 347–368.

Galaty, John G. 2011. "The Modern Motility of Pastoral Land Rights: Tenure Transitions and Land-Grabbing in East Africa." Land Deal Politics Initiative, Conference Paper. Accessed December 7, 2014. http://www.iss.nl/fileadmin/ASSETS/iss/Documents/Conference_papers/LDPI/42_John_G._Galaty.pdf.

Gamble, Andrew. 1979. "The Free Economy and the Strong State: The Rise of the Social Market Economy." In *The Socialist Register*, edited by Ralph Miliband and John Saville, 1–25. London: Merlin Press.

Genschel, Philipp and Bernhard Zangl. 2008. "Transformations of the State: From Monopolist to Manager of Political Authority." *TranState Working Paper 76*.

Giddens, Anthony, ed. 2001. *The Global Third Way Debate*. Cambridge: Polity.

Giddens, Anthony. 2009. *The Politics of Climate Change*. Cambridge: Polity.

Gini. 2014. "List of Countries by Income Inequality." Accessed September 28, 2015. https://en.wikipedia.org/wiki/List_of_countries_by_income_equality.

Girvan, Norman. 2010. "Are Caribbean Countries Facing Existential Threats?" Accessed September 7, 2015. http://www.normangirvan.info/wp-content/uploads/2010/11/existential-threats.pdf.

Girvan, Norman. 2011. "Existential Threats: Regionalising Governance, Democratizing Politics." CLR James Memorial Lecture, Oilfield Workers Trade Union, May 12.

Girvan, Norman. 2012. "50 Years of In-Dependence in Jamaica: Reflections." Paper presented at SALISES 50–50 Conference, "Critical Reflections in a Time of Uncertainty", Kingston, Jamaica, August 22.

Global Justice Ecology Project. 2010. 'What Is Climate Justice?' Accessed September 1, 2015. http://globaljusticeecology.org/climate-justice/.

Gorbachev, Mihail. 2002. "Social-Demokratija v Global'nom Mire" [Social Democracy in a Global World]. Accessed September 9, 2015. http://www.gorby.ru/presscenter/publication/show_423/.

Government of Jamaica. 2015. *National Diaspora Policy: Background, Policy Process, Principles, Goals, Outcomes and Actions*. Kingston: Ministry of Foreign Affairs and Foreign Trade.

GRAIN, Joan Martinez-Alier, Leah Temper, Serah Munguti, Paul Matiku, Hugo Ferreira, Oswaldo Cruz, Wagner Soares, Marcelo F. Porto, Vahinala Raharinirina, Willi Haas, Simron Jit Singh and Andreas Mayer. 2014. *The Many Faces of Land Grabbing. Cases from Africa and Latin America*. EJOLT Report No 10. Accessed December 7, 2014. http://www.ejolt.org/2014/03/the-many-faces-of-land-grabbing-cases-from-africa-and-latin-america/.

Gramsci, Antonio. 1971. *Selections from the Prison Notebooks*. Edited and translated by Quintin Hoare and Geoffrey Nowell Smith. New York: International Publishers.

Grovogui, Siba N. 2011. "To the Orphaned, Dispossessed, and Illegitimate Children: Human Rights Beyond Republican and Liberal Traditions." *Indiana Journal of Global Legal Studies* 18 (1): 41–63.

Grzanka, Patrick R., ed. 2014. *Intersectionality: A Foundations and Frontiers Reader*. Boulder: Westview.

Guardian. 2014. "Caribbean Nations Prepare Demand for Slavery Reparations." *The Guardian*, 9 March. Accessed September 2, 2015. http://www.theguardian.com/world/2014/mar/09/caribbean-nations-demand-slavery-reparations.

Habermas, Jürgen. 1998. *Die Postnationale Konstellation: Politische Essays* [The Post-National Constellation: Political Essays]. Frankfurt am Main: Suhrkamp.

Haggart, Blayne. 2013. "Fair Copyright for Canada: Lessons for Online Social Movements from the First Canadian Facebook Uprising." *Canadian Journal of Political Science* 46: 841–61.

Haggart, Blayne. 2014a. "Birth of a Movement: The Anti-Counterfeiting Trade Agreement and the Politicization of Mexican Copyright." *Policy & Internet* 6: 69–88.

Haggart, Blayne. 2014b. *Copyfight: The Global Politics of Digital Copyright Reform*. Toronto: University of Toronto Press.

Haggart, Blayne and Michael K. Jablonski. 2015. "Not So Strange Bedfellows: The Internet Freedom Initiative, US Copyright Maximalism and the Exercise of US Structural Power in the Digital Age." Paper presented at the International Studies Association annual conference, New Orleans, Louisiana, February 21.

Hanna, Edward. 2012. "Greenland Plays a Large Role in the Gloomy Picture Painted of Probable Future Sea-Level Rise." *Environmental Research Letters* 7 (4). Accessed September 1, 2015. http://iopscience.iop.org/article/10.1088/1748-9326/7/4/041002.

Hardt, Michael and Antonio Negri. 2004. *Multitude*. New York: Penguin.

Harrison, Elizabeth. 2006. "Unpacking the Anti-corruption Agenda: Dilemmas for Anthropologists." *Oxford Development Studies* 34 (1): 15–29.

Harrison, Lawrence and Samuel *Huntington,* eds. 2000. *Culture Matters: How Values Shape Human Progress*. New York: Basic Books.

Harriss-White, Barbara and Gordon White. 1996. "Editorial Introduction: Corruption, Liberalization and Democracy?" *IDS Bulletin: Liberalization and the New Corruption* 27 (2): 1–5.

Harvey, David. 2003. *The New Imperialism*. Oxford: Oxford University Press.

Harvey, David. 2005. *A Brief History of Neoliberalism*. New York: Oxford University Press.

He, Chuanqi. 2012. *Modernization Science: The Principles and Methods of National Advancement*. Heidelberg: Springer.

Held, David. 2003. "Global Social Democracy." In *The Progressive Manifesto: New Ideas for the Centre-Left,* edited by Anthony Giddens, 137–72. Cambridge: Polity.

Held, David. 2005. "At the Global Crossroads: The End of the Washington Consensus and the Rise of Global Social Democracy?" *Globalizations* 2 (1): 95–113.

Held, David, Anthony McGrew, David Goldblatt and Jonathan Perraton. 1999. *Global Transformations: Politics, Economics, Culture*. Cambridge: Polity Press.

Hill, Robert A. 2011. *The Marcus Garvey and Universal Negro Improvement Association Papers Volume XI: The Caribbean Diaspora, 1910–1920*. Durham: Duke University Press.

Hindess, Barry. 2005. "Investigating International Anti-Corruption." *Third World Quarterly* 26 (8): 1389–98.

Hinds Harrison, Kristina. 2014. "Virtual Shop Fronts: The Internet, Social Media, and Caribbean Civil Society Organizations." *Globalizations* 11 (6): 1–16.

Hines, Colin. 2000. *Localization: A Global Manifesto*. London: Routledge.

History Man. 2001. "The Triangular Trade." Accessed September 2, 2015. http://www.historyman.co.uk/tritrade/.

Holodkovskij, Kirill, ed. 2001. *Social-Demokratija Zapada pered vyzovami sovremennosti* [Western Social Democracy Facing Challenges of Our Time]. Moscow: IMEMO RAN.

Holthaus, Eric. 2015. "The Point of No Return: Climate Change Nightmares Are Already Here." *Rolling Stone*, August 5. Accessed September 1, 2015. http://www.rollingstone.com/politics/news/the-point-of-no-return-climate-change-nightmares-are-already-here-20150805.

Holthoon, Fritz V. and Marcel van der Linden, eds. 1988. *Internationalism in the Labour Movement 1830–1940*. Leiden: Brill.

Holton, Robert J. 2014. *Global Inequalities*. Basingstoke: Palgrave Macmillan.

Hope, Mat. 2013. "How the IEA Says We Can Avoid Six Degrees of Warming - In Three Graphs". Accessed September 1, 2015. http://www.carbonbrief.org/blog/2013/11/three-graphs-showing-how-the-iea-says-we-can-avoid-six-degrees-warming/.

Hruska, Joel. 2011. "How SOPA Could Actually Break the Internet." *Extreme Tech*, December 19. Accessed August 27, 2015. http://www.extremetech.com/computing/109533-how-sopa-could-actually-break-the-internet/2.

Huo, Jingjing. 2009. *Third Way Reforms: Social Democratic Welfare States after the Golden Age*. Cambridge: Cambridge University Press.

Huther, Jeff and Anwar Shah. 2000. "Anti-corruption Policies and Programs: A Framework for Evaluation." Accessed September 15, 2014. http://econ.worldbank.org/files/1311_wps2501.pdf.

IDB. 2010. *Ten Years of Innovation in Remittances: Lessons Learned and Models for the Future - Independent Review of the Multilateral Investment Fund Remittance Portfolio*. Washington DC: Inter-American Development Bank.

IMF. 1998. *Annual Report 1998*. Washington, DC: International Monetary Fund.

IMF. 2007. "Turkey: 2007 Article IV Consultation—Staff Report; Public Information Notice on the Executive Board Discussion; and Statement by the Executive Director for Turkey." 07/362. Accessed September 10, 2014. http://www.imf.org/external/pubs/ft/scr/2007/cr07362.pdf.

IMF. 2015. "Factsheet: Special Drawing Rights (SDRs)". Accessed September 2, 2015. http://www.imf.org/external/np/exr/facts/sdr.htm.

Innovative Financing to Fund Development Leading Group. 2009. *Globalizing Solidarities: The Case for Financial Levies*. Report of the Committee of Experts to the Taskforce on International Financial Transactions and Development, Paris. Accessed September 15, 2015. http://www.leadinggroup.org/IMG/pdf_Financement_innovants_web_def.pdf.

International Rivers. 2008. *Rip-Offsets: The Failure of the Kyoto Protocol's Clean Development Mechanism*. Berkeley: International Rivers.
IPCC. 2007. *IPCC Fourth Assessment Report: Climate Change 2007*. Geneva: Intergovernmental Panel on Climate Change. Accessed September 1, 2015. http://www.ipcc.ch/publications_and_data/ar4/wg3/en/ch3.html.
IPCC. 2013a. *Climate Change 2013: The Physical Science Basis. Working Group 1 Fact Sheet*. Geneva: Intergovernmental Panel on Climate Change. Accessed September 1, 2015. http://www.climatechange2013.org/images/uploads/WG1AR5_FactSheet.pdf.
IPCC. 2013b. "Summary for Policy Makers." In *Climate Change 2013: The Physical Science Basis*. Geneva: Intergovernmental Panel on Climate Change. Accessed September 15, 2015. http://www.ipcc.ch/pdf/assessment-report/ar5/wg1/WG1AR5_SPM_FINAL.pdf.
IPCC. 2014a. "Summary for Policymakers." In *Climate Change 2014: Mitigation of Climate Change. Contribution of Working Group III to the Fifth Assessment Report of the Intergovernmental Panel on Climate Change*. Geneva: Intergovernmental Panel on Climate Change. Accessed September 1, 2015. http://mitigation2014.org/.
IPCC. 2014b. *Working Group III Integrated Assessment Modelling Consortium (IAMC) AR5 Scenario Database*. Laxenburg: International Institute for Applied Systems Analysis. Accessed September 1, 2015. https://secure.iiasa.ac.at/web-apps/ene/AR5DB/.
Jackson, Tim. 2009. *Prosperity without Growth*. London: Earthscan.
Jain, Arvind K. 2001. "Corruption: A Review." *Journal of Economic Surveys* 15 (1): 71–116.
Johnston, Jake and Juan A. Montecino. 2011. *Jamaica: Macroeconomic Policy, Debt and the IMF*. Washington DC: Center for Economic and Policy Research.
Jones, Charles. 1996. "The Argentine Debate." In Barbara Harriss-White and Gordon White, eds., *Liberalization and the New Corruption*. Brighton: Institute of Development Studies, 71–7.
Kahler, Miles. 1990. "Orthodoxy and Its Alternatives: Explaining Approaches to Stabilization and Adjustment." In *Economic Crisis and Policy Choice, The Politics of Adjustment in the Third World*, edited by Joan M. Nelson, 33–62. Princeton: Princeton University Press.
Kanter, Rosabeth M. 1983. *The Change Masters: Corporate Entrepreneurs at Work*. London: Unwin.
Kapur, Devesh. 2010. *Diaspora, Development, and Democracy: The Domestic Impact of International Migration from India*. Princeton: Princeton University Press.
Karataş, Cevat and Metin Ercan. 2008. "The Privatization Experience in Turkey and Argentina: A Comparative Study, 1986–2007." *METU Studies in Development* 35 (2): 345–84.
Karns, Margaret P. and Karen A. Mingst, 2004. *International Organizations: The Politics and Processes of Global Governance*. Boulder: Lynne Rienner.
Kaul, Inge. 2013. "Meeting Global Challenges: Assessing Governance Readiness." In *Hertie School of Governance, Governance Report 2013*, 33–57. Oxford: Oxford University Press.

Ketkar, Suhas L. and Dilip Ratha. 2007. *Development Finance via Diaspora Bonds: Track Record and Potential*. Washington DC: World Bank, Policy Research Working Paper 4311.

Ketkar, Suhas L. and Dilip Ratha. 2011. "Diaspora Bonds: Tapping the Diaspora during Difficult Times". In *Diaspora for Development in Africa*, edited by Sonia Plaza and Dilip Ratha, 127–143. Washington DC: World Bank.

Kenen, Peter. 2010. "An SDR Based Reserve System." *Journal of Globalization and Development* 1 (2): 1–12.

Kenen, Peter. 2011. "Beyond the Dollar." *Journal of Policy Modeling* 33: 750–8.

KFC, 2015. Website of the Kenya Flowers Council. Accessed September 2, 2015. http://kenyaflowercouncil.org/?page_id=94.

Klein, Naomi. 2014. *This Changes Everything: Capitalism vs The Climate*. New York: Simon & Schuster.

Knowledge Ecology International. 2009. "Access to Medical Technologies." Accessed September 1, 2014. http://www.keionline.org/a2m.

Kooiman, Jan. 2003. *Governing as Governance*. London: Sage.

Krugman, Paul. 2015. "TPP at the NABE." *New York Times*. March 11. Accessed March 18, 2015. http://krugman.blogs.nytimes.com/2015/03/11/tpp-at-the-nabe/.

Krugman, Paul R. 1984. "The International Role of the Dollar: Theory and Prospect." In *Exchange Rate Theory and Practice*, edited by John F.O. Bilson and Richard C. Marston, 261–78. Chicago: University of Chicago Press.

Ku, Raymond, Jiayang Sun, and Yiying Fan. 2009. "Does Copyright Law Promote Creativity? An Empirical Analysis of Copyright's Bounty." *Vanderbilt Law Review* 63: 1669–746.

Kuhlmann, Stefan, Philip Shapira and Ruud Smits. 2010. "Introduction. A Systemic Perspective: The Innovation Policy Dance." In *The Theory and Practice of Innovation Policy: An International Research Handbook*, edited by Ruud Smits, Stefan Kuhlmann and Philip Shapira, 1–22. Cheltenham: Edward Elgar.

Laclau, Ernesto and Chantal Mouffe. 1985. *Hegemony & Socialist Strategy: Towards A Radical Democratic Politics*. London: Verso.

Lamming, George. 2000. *Coming, Coming, Coming Home: Conversations II*. St. Martin: House of Nehusi Publishers.

Lavelle, Ashley. 2008. *The Death of Social Democracy: Political Consequences in the 21st Century*. Aldershot: Ashgate.

Lenton, Timothy M. 2011. "Early Warning of Climate Tipping Points." *Nature Climate Change* 1: 201–09. doi:10.1038/nclimate1143.

Li, Tania M. 2011. "Centering Labor in the Land Grab Debate". *Journal of Peasant Studies* 38 (2): 281–98.

Lundberg, Erik. 1985. "The Rise and Fall of the Swedish Model." *Journal of Economic Literature* 23 (1): 1–36.

Lyons, Kristen and Westoby, Peter. 2014. "Carbon Colonialism and the New Land Grab: Plantation Forestry in Uganda and Its Livelihood Impacts." *Journal of Rural Studies* 36: 13–21.

Maddison, Angus. 2001. *The World Economy: A Millennial Perspective*. Paris: OECD Development Centre Studies.

Makki, Fouad. 2014. "Development by Dispossession: *Terra Nullius* and the Social Ecology of New Enclosures in Ethiopia." *Rural Sociology* 79 (1): 79–103.

Malm, Andreas. 2015. "The Anthropocene Myth: Blaming All of Humanity for Climate Change Lets Capitalism off the Hook", *Jacobin*, March 30. Accessed September 1, 2015. https://www.jacobinmag.com/2015/03/anthropocene-capitalism-climate-change/.

Manzetti Luigi and Blake, Charles. 1996. "Market Reforms and Corruption in Latin America: New Means for Old Ways." *Review of International Political Economy* 3 (4): 662–97.

Marquette, Heather. 2004. "The Creeping Politicization of the World Bank: The Case of Corruption." *Political Studies* 52: 413–30.

May, Christopher. 2000. *The Global Political Economy of Intellectual Property Rights: The New Enclosures*. New York: Routledge.

May, Christopher. 1996. "Strange Fruit: Susan Strange's Theory of Structural Power in the International Political Economy." *Global Society* 10: 167–89.

McKibben, Bill. 2012. "Global Warming's Terrifying New Math." *Rolling Stone*, 19 July. Accessed September 1, 2015. http://www.rollingstone.com/politics/news/global-warmings-terrifying-new-math-20120719?page=3.

McMichael, Philip. 2010. "Agrofuels in the Food Regime." *Journal of Peasant Studies* 37 (4): 609–629.

McMichael, Philip. 2012a. *Development and Social Change*. 5th ed. London: Sage.

McMichael, Philip. 2012b. "The Land Grab and Corporate Food Regime Restructuring." *Journal of Peasant Studies* 39 (3–4): 681–701.

McMichael, Philip. 2013a. *Food Regimes and Agrarian Questions*. Halifax and Winnipeg: Fernwood Publishing.

McMichael, Philip. 2013b. "Land Grabbing as Security Mercantilism in International Relations." *Globalizations* 10 (1): 47–64.

Medhora, Shalailah. 2014. "Ebola Outbreak Shocked Unprepared Developed Countries, says CDC Health Agency." *The Guardian*, September 23.

Milanovic, Branko. 2012. *Global Income Inequality by the Numbers: In History and Now*. Washington, DC: World Bank Policy Research Working Paper 6259.

Milanovic, Branko. 2013. Author's Personal Communication with Professor Thomas Pogge, Yale University, 4 January, citing unpublished data provided by Branko Milanovic, Lead Economist at the World Bank.

Millar, Richard, Barbara Stocking, Jenny Borden, Alvaro Bermejo, Mike Mandelbaum, John Hilary, Ros Davies et al. "Currency Trading Tax to Help the Poor". 2009. Letters to the Editor, *The Guardian*, July 7. Accessed September 28, 2014. http://www.theguardian.com/world/2009/jul/07/letters-g8-italy.

Mintz, Sidney. 1985. *Sweetness and Power: The Place of Sugar in Modern History*. New York: Viking.

Moncau, Luiz F., and Pedro Nicoletti Mizukami. 2014. "Brazilian Chamber of Deputies Approves Marco Civil Bill." *Infojustice.org*, March 25. Accessed May 11, 2014. http://infojustice.org/archives/32527.

Moody, Glyn. 2014. "Brazil's 'Marco Civil' Internet Civil Rights Law Finally Passes, with Key Protections Largely Intact." *Techdirt.com*, March 27. Accessed May 11, 2014. http://www.techdirt.com/articles/20140326/09012226690/

brazils-marco-civil-internet-civil-rights-law-finally-passes-with-key-protections-largely-intact.shtml.
Mullings, Beverley. 2012. "Governmentality, Diaspora Assemblages and the Ongoing Challenge of 'Development'." *Antipode* 44: 406–27.
Murphy, Craig. 1984. *Emergence of the NIEO Ideology*. Boulder: Westview.
Myslivchenko, Aleksandr, ed. 1998. *Zapadnaja Social-Demokratija: Poisk Obnovlenija v Uslovijah Krizisa* [Western Social Democracy: Looking for a Renewal in an Age of Crisis]. Moscow: IFRAN.
Myslivchenko, Aleksandr. 2001. "Zapadnaja Social-Demokratija: Tendencii Obnovlenija i Modernizacii" [Western Social Democracy: Modernization Trends]. *Voprosy filosofii* [*Problems of Philosophy*] 11: 3–14.
Myslivchenko, Aleksandr. 2004. "Perspektivy Evropejskoj Modeli Social'nogo Gosudarstva" [Prospects for the European Model of Welfare State]. *Voprosy filosofii* [*Problems of Philosophy*] 6: 3–12.
NASA. 2015. "NASA, NOAA Find 2014 Warmest Year in Modern Record." Accessed September 1, 2015. http://www.giss.nasa.gov/research/news/20150116/.
Naumann, Friedrich. 1917. *Central Europe*. New York: Knopf.
Nissanke, Machiko and Erik Thorbecke, eds. 2007. *The Impact of Globalization on the World's Poor: Transmission Mechanisms*. Basingstoke: Palgrave Macmillan.
Nkrumah, Kwame. 1965. *Neo-Colonialism: The Last Stage of Imperialism*. London: Nelson.
North, Douglas. 1994. "A Framework for Analyzing the State in Economic History." In *The State, Critical Concepts, Vol. I*, edited by John A. Hall, 325–34. London: Routledge.
Nurse, Keith. 2006. "Diaspora, Migration and Development in the Caribbean". *FOCAL Policy Paper-FPP-04-6*. Accessed May 26, 2014. http://focal.ca/pdf/migration_Nurse_diaspora%20migration%20development%20Caribbean_September%202004_FPP-04-6.pdf.
Nyong'o, Peter A., Aseghedech Ghirmazion and Davinder Lamba, eds. 2002. *NEPAD: A New Path?* Nairobi: Heinrich Böll Foundation.
Ocampo, Jose Antonio. 2007. "The Instability and Inequities of the Global Reserve System." *International Journal of Political Economy* 36 (4): 71–96.
OECD. 2006. "Presentation of the OECD Economic Survey of Turkey, 2006 edition." Accessed September 28, 2014. http://www.oecd.org/newsroom/presentation-oftheoecdeconomicsurveyofturkey2006edition.htm.
OECD DAC Statistics. 2014. Accessed July 17, 2014. http://www.oecd.org/dac/stats/data.htm/.
Okonjo-Iweala, Ngozi and Dilip Ratha. 2011. "Homeward Bond." *New York Times*, March 11. Accessed May 26, 2013. http://www.nytimes.com/2011/03/12/opinion/12ratha.html.
Orlov, Boris, ed. 1998. *Evropejskaja Social-Demokratija nakanune XXI Stoletija* [European Social Democracy on the Eve of the Twenty-First Century]. Moscow: Pamjatniki istoricheskoj mysli.
Orlov, Aleksandr. 2012. "Evropejskaja Social-Demokratija: Trudnyj put' k Vozrozhdeniju." [European Social Democracy: Uneasy Recovery]. In *Ezhegodnik IMI – 2012* [IIS Yearbook - 2012], edited by Aleksandr Orlov, 12–32. Moscow: MGIMO-Universitet.

Ostrom, Elinor. 1990. *Governing the Commons: The Evolution of Institutions for Collective Action.* New York: Cambridge University Press.

Ostry, Jonathan, Andrew Berg and Charalambos G. Tsangaridis. 2014. *Redistribution, Inequality, and Growth.* Washington, DC: International Monetary Fund Staff, Discussion Note 14/2.

Öztürk, Özgür. 2010. *Türkiye'de Büyük Sermaye Grupları, Finans Kapitalin Oluşumu ve Gelişimi* [Big Capital Groups in Turkey: The Formation and Development of Finance Capital]. İstanbul: Sosyal Araştırmalar Vakfı.

Patel, Raj. 2007. *Stuffed and Starved: Markets, Power and the Hidden Battle for the World's Food System.* London: Portobello.

PBC (中国人民银行, The People's Bank of China). 2013. 关于防范比特币风险的通知 ['Notice on the Risk of Bitcoin']. Accessed September 2, 2015. http://www.pbc.gov.cn/publish/goutongjiaoliu/524/2013/20131205153156832222251/20131205153156832222251_.html.

People's Climate. 2015. "People's Climate March Wrap Up." Accessed September 1, 2015. http://www.peoplesclimate.org.

Peregudov, Sergej. 2000. "Zapadnaja Social-Demokratija na Rubezhe Vekov." [Western Social Democracy at the Turn of the Century] *Mirovaja jekonomika i mezhdunarodnye otnoshenija* [World Economy and International Relations] 6–7: 40–46.

Pesek, William. 2015. "U.S. Following 'Mahathir Doctrine' on IMF." *Bloomberg*, 12 January. Accessed September 2, 2015. http://www.bloomberg.com/apps/news?pid=newsarchive&sid=a6KthtLcUm54.

Piketty, Thomas. 2014. *Capital in the Twenty-First Century.* Cambridge, MA: Harvard University Press.

Pimentel, David, Paul Hepperly, James Hanson, David Douds and Rita Seidel. 2005. "Environmental, Energetic and Economic Comparisons of Organic and Conventional Farming Systems." *BioScience* 55 (7): 537–82.

Pogge, Thomas. 2008. *World Poverty and Human Rights: Cosmopolitan Responsibilities and Reforms.* 2nd ed. Cambridge: Polity.

Pogge, Thomas and Darrel Moellendorf, eds. 2008. *Global Justice: Seminal Essays.* New York: Paragon.

Powers, Shawn and Michael Jablonski. 2015. *The Real Cyber War: The Political Economy of Internet Freedom.* Urbana: University of Illinois Press.

PR Newswire. 2013. "Super Typhoon Haiyan Leads November Catastrophe Losses with $6bn Economic Impact, According to Impact Forecasting Report." *PR Newswire*, December 6. Accessed September 1, 2015. http://www.prnewswire.com/news-releases/super-typhoon-haiyan-leads-november-catastrophe-losses-with-6bn-economic-impact-according-to-impact-forecasting-report-234751561.html.

Pye, Oliver. 2010. "The Biofuel Connection – Transnational Activism and the Palm Oil Book." *Journal of Peasant Studies* 37 (4): 851–74.

Rabotjazhev, Nikolaj. 2012. "Evropejskaja Social-Demokratija v Poiskah Adaptacii k Menjajushhemusja Miru." [European Social Democracy Adapting to a Changing World]. *Politija* [Politeia] 3: 146–67.

Rabotjazhev, Nikolaj. 2013. "'Novaja' i 'Staraja' Social-Demokratija v Zapadnoj Evrope" ['New' and 'Old' Social Democracy in Western Europe]. *Politicheskaja nauka* [Political Science] 4: 106–133.

Rancière, Jacques. 2006. *Hatred of Democracy*. London: Verso.
Ritzer, George. 2000. *The McDonaldization of Society*. Newbury Park: Pine Forge Press.
Ritzer, George. 2004. *The Globalization of Nothing*. Thousand Oaks: Pine Forge Press.
Ritzer, George. 2011. *Globalization: The Essentials*. Oxford: Wiley-Blackwell.
Ritzer, George and Zeynep Atalay, eds. 2010. *Readings in Globalization: Key Concepts and Major Debates*. Oxford: Wiley-Blackwell.
Robin Hood Tax. 2014. "Everything You Need to Know." Accessed September 6, 2014. http://www.robinhoodtax.org/how-it-works/everything-you-need-to-know.
Robertson, Roland. 1995. "Glocalization: Time-Space and Homogeneity-Heterogeneity." In *Global Modernities*, edited by Mike Featherstone, Scott Lash, and Roland Robertson, 25–44. London: Sage.
Roden, John. 2010. "The International Anti-corruption Crusade: Neo-liberal Institutional Structures, Moralization, and Social Capital." *Undercurrent Journal* 7 (1): 12–22.
Roine, Jesper and Daniel Waldenström. 2014. *Long Run Trends in the Distribution of Income and Wealth*. Uppsala: Uppsala Center for Fiscal Studies.
Rose, Charlie. 2013. "Charlie Rose Talks to ExxonMobil's Rex Tillerson." *Bloomberg Business*, March 7. Accessed September 1, 2015. http://www.bloomberg.com/bw/articles/2013-03-07/charlie-rose-talks-to-exxonmobils-rex-tillerson.
Rose, Mark. 1993. *Authors and Owners: The Invention of Copyright*. Cambridge: Harvard University Press.
Rose-Ackerman, Susan. 1999. *Corruption and Government: Causes, Consequences, and Reform*. Cambridge: Cambridge University Press.
Rosenau, James N. 1990. *Turbulence in World Politics: A Theory of Change and Continuity*. Princeton: Princeton University Press.
Rosenau, James N. 1999. "Toward an Ontology for Global Governance." In *Approaches to Global Governance Theory*, edited by Martin Hewson and Timothy J. Sinclair, 287–302. Albany, NY: State University of New York.
Ryan, Lisa, Nora Selmet and André Aasrud. 2012. *Plugging the Energy Efficiency Gap with Climate Finance*. Paris: OECD/IEA.
Sahlins, Marshall. 1974. *Stone Age Economics*. London: Tavistock.
Sassen, Saskia. 2013. "Land Grabs Today: Feeding the Disassembling of National Territory." *Globalizations* 10 (1): 25–46.
Saurin, Julian. 1997. "Organizing Hunger: The Global Organization of Famines and Feasts". In *Globalization and the South*, edited by Caroline Thomas and Peter Wilkin, 106–123. Basingstoke: Macmillan.
Scholte, Jan Aart. 1997. "Global Capitalism and the State." *International Affairs* 73 (3): 427–452.
Scholte, Jan Aart. 2000. "Can Globality Bring a Good Society?" In *Rethinking Globalization(s): From Corporate Transnationalism to Local Interventions*, edited by Preet S. Aulakh and Michael G. Schechter, 13–31. New York: St. Martin's Press.
Scholte, Jan Aart. 2002. "Civil Society and Democracy in Global Governance." *Global Governance* 8 (3): 281–304.
Scholte, Jan Aart. 2005. *Globalization: A Critical Introduction*. 2nd ed. Basingstoke: Palgrave Macmillan.

Scholte, Jan Aart. ed. Forthcoming. *Global Democracy, Global Voices*.
Schulmeister, Stephan. 2011. *Implementation of a General Financial Transactions Tax*. WIFO Study Commissioned by the Austrian Chamber of Labour. Austrian Institute of Economic Affairs, June. Accessed September 6, 2014. http://stephan.schulmeister.wifo.ac.at/fileadmin/homepage_schulmeister/files/Implement_FTT_short_06_11.pdf
ScienceDaily. 2014. "A More Potent Greenhouse Gas than Carbon Dioxide, Methane Emissions Will Leap as Earth Warms." *ScienceDaily*, March 27. Accessed September 1, 2015. http://www.sciencedaily.com/releases/2014/03/140327111724.htm.
SELA. 2013. *Debt Burden and Fiscal Sustainability in the Caribbean Region. Meeting of Experts on Debt Burden in Middle Income Countries in Latin America and the Caribbean Caracas, Venezuela 30 July 2013 SP/RECD-pim-ALC/DT N° 2–13*. Caracas: Latin America and Caribbean Economic System.
Sell, Susan K. 2003. *Private Power, Public Law: The Globalization of Intellectual Property Rights*. Cambridge: Cambridge University Press.
Sell, Susan K. 2010. "The Rise and Rule of a Trade-Based Strategy: Historical Institutionalism and the Regulation of Intellectual Property." *Review of International Political Economy* 17: 762–90.
Sell, Susan K. 2013. "Revenge of the 'Nerds': Collective Action against Intellectual Property Maximalism in the Global Information Age." *International Studies Review* 15: 67–85.
Sen, Amartya. 1983. "The Food Problem: Theory and Policy". In *South-South Strategy*, edited by Althaf Gauhar, 91–103. London: Third World Foundation.
Sen, Jai and Peter Waterman, eds. 2012. *World Social Forum: Critical Explorations*. Delhi: Open Books.
Şener, Nedim. 2001. *Tepeden Tırnağa Yolsuzluk*. Siyahbeyaz [Corruption from Top to Bottom]. İstanbul: Metis Güncel.
Shilliam, Robbie. 2012. "Redemption from Development: Amartya Sen, Rastafari and Promises of Freedom." *Postcolonial Studies* 15 (3): 331–350.
Shvejcer, Vladimir, ed. 2005. *Evropejskie levye na rubezhe Tysjacheletij* [European Left at the Turn of the Millennium]. Moscow: Ogni TD.
Simmons, Alan, Dwaine Plaza and Victor Piché. 2005. "The Remittance Sending Practices of Haitians and Jamaicans in Canada." Paper presented at Expert Group Meeting on International Migration and Development in Latin America and the Caribbean, Mexico City, November 14.
Sitrin, Marina and Dario Azzellini. 2014. *They Can't Represent Us! Reinventing Democracy from Greece to Occupy*. London: Verso.
Solon, Pablo. 2014a. "Notes for the Debate: Vivir Bien/Buen Vivir." *Systemic Alternatives*, July 30. Accessed September 1, 2015. http://systemicalternatives.org/2014/07/30/1099/.
Solon, Pablo. 2014b. "The Systemic Crisis & Reconfiguration of Capitalism." *Systemic Alternatives*, February 10. Accessed September 1, 2015. http://systemicalternatives.org/2014/02/10/the-systemic-crisis-reconfiguration-of-capitalism/.
Standing, Guy. 2011. *The Precariat: The New Dangerous Class*. London: Bloomsbury Academic.

Starr, Amory. 2001. *Naming the Enemy: Anti-Corporate Movements Confront Globalization*. London: Zed.

Stiglitz, Joseph. 2003. "Democratizing the International Monetary Fund and the World Bank: Governance and Accountability." *Governance: An International Journal of Policy* 16 (1): 111–39.

Stilwell, Matthew. 2012. "Climate Debt: A Primer." In *Development Dialogue No. 61: Climate, Development and Equity*. Uppsala: Dag Hammarskjöld Foundation, 41–46. Accessed September 1, 2015. http://www.daghammarskjold.se/publication/development-dialogue-61-climate-development-equity/.

Story, Alan. 2003. "Burn Berne: Why the Leading International Copyright Convention Must Be Repealed." *Houston Law Review* 40: 763–801. Accessed August 27, 2015. http://core.ac.uk/download/pdf/89948.pdf.

Strange, Susan. 1987. "The Persistent Myth of Lost Hegemony." *International Organization* 41: 551–74. Accessed August 27, 2015. http://www.jstor.org/stable/2706758.

Strange, Susan. 1994. *States and Markets*, 2nd ed. New York: Continuum.

Sun Tzu. 1991. *The Art of War*. Translated by Thomas Cleary. Boston, MA: Shambhala.

Tandon, Yash, 2009. *Development and Globalisation: Daring to Think Differently*. Geneva: South Centre.

Tandon, Yash. 2015. *Trade is War: The West's War against the World*. New York: OR Books.

Tanzi, Vito. 1998. "Corruption around the World: Causes, Consequences, Scope, and Cures." *IMF Staff Papers* 45 (4): 559–94.

Therborn, Göran, ed. 2006. *Inequalities of the World*. London: Verso.

Therbon, Göran. 2013. *The Killing Fields of Inequality*. Cambridge: Polity.

Thomas-Hope, Elizabeth, Claremont Kirton, Pauline Knight, Natasha Mortley, Mikhail-Ann Urquhart, Claudel Noel, Hilary Robertson-Hickling and Easton Williams. 2009. "Development on the Move: Measuring and Optimising Migration's Economic and Social Impacts: A Study of Migration's Impacts on Development in Jamaica and How Policy Might Respond". London, Institute for Public Policy Research and Global Development Network. Accessed August 24, 2015. https://www.google.ca/search?client=safari&rls=en&q=Development%02+on+%02the%02+Move:%02+Measuring+and%02+Optimising+%02Migration%E2%80%99s%02+Economic%02+and+Social+%02Impacts:+A%02+Study+%02of+%02Migration%E2%80%99s+%02Impacts+%02on%02+Development+%02in+Jamaica%02+and+%02How%02+Policy+%02Might%02+Respond&ie=UTF-8&oe=UTF-8&gfe_rd=cr&ei=ro3cVfaQHuLK8gf91qw4.

Tooze, Roger. 2000. "Ideology, Knowledge and Power in International Relations and International Political Economy." In *Strange Power: Shaping the Parameters of International Relations and International Political Economy*, edited by Thomas C. Lawton, James N. Rosenau, and Amy C. Verdun, 175–94. Aldershot: Ashgate.

Towse, Ruth and Rudi Holzhauer. 2002. "Introduction." In *The Economics of Intellectual Property*, Vol. 1, edited by Ruth Towse and Rudi Holzhauer, ix-xxxii. Cheltenham: Edward Elgar Publishing Ltd.

Transparency International. 2000. *TI Source Book. Confronting Corruption: The Elements of a National Integrity System*. Berlin: Transparency International.

Trotz, D. Alissa. 2013a. "'Far from Home but Close at Heart': Preliminary Considerations on Regional Integration, Deterritorialization and the Caribbean Diaspora." Paper presented at Rethinking Regionalism: Beyond the CARICOM Integration Project, SALISES Regional Integration Conference, University of the West Indies, Kingston, Jamaica, October 7–9.

Trotz, D. Alissa. 2013b. "Challenging the Constitutional Tribunal Ruling in the Dominican Republic: Where is CARICOM Leadership?" Accessed August 25, 2015. http://www.stabroeknews.com/2013/features/daily/11/25/challenging-constitutional-tribunal-ruling-dominican-republic-caricom-leadership/.

Trotz, D. Alissa and Beverley Mullings. 2013. "Transnational Migration, the State, and Development: Reflecting on the 'Diaspora' Option." *Small Axe* 17: 154–171.

Tusikov, Natasha. 2014. *Chokepoints: Internet Intermediaries and the Private Regulation of Counterfeit Goods on the Internet*. PhD dissertation, Australian National University.

UN. 2008. "High-level Event on the Millennium Development Goals 25 September 2008. Committing to Action: Achieving the Millennium Development Goals. Compilation of Initiatives and Commitments Relating to the High-Level Event on the Millennium Development Goals." Accessed December 7, 2014. http://www.un.org/millenniumgoals/2008highlevel/pdf/commitments/Commitments%20compilation%20ENGLISH.pdf .

UN. 2009. *The State of the World's Indigenous Peoples*. New York: United Nations Department of Economic and Social Affairs.

UN. 2010. "Report of the Special Rapporteur on the Right to Food, Olivier De Schutter." United Nations General Assembly Document A/65/281. Accessed December 7, 2014. https://docs.escr-net.org/usr_doc/SRFood_access-to-land-report_en.pdf.

UNDP. 2007. *Human Development Report 2007/2008. Fighting Climate Change: Human Solidarity in a Divided World*. New York: United Nations Development Programme. Accessed September 1, 2015. http://hdr.undp.org/sites/default/files/reports/268/hdr_20072008_en_complete.pdf.

UNDP. 2014. *Human Development Report 2014, Sustaining Human Progress: Reducing Vulnerability and Building Resilience*. New York: United Nations Development Programme.

UNECA. 2013. *Economic Report on Africa 2013*. Addis Ababa: United Nations Economic Commission for Africa. Accessed September 2, 2015. http://www.uneca.org/publications/economic-report-africa-2013.

UNEP. 2011. *Towards a Green Economy: Pathways to Sustainable Development and Poverty Eradication*. Geneva: United Nations Environment Programme. Accessed September 1, 2015. http://www.unep.org/greeneconomy/Portals/88/documents/ger/ger_final_dec_2011/Green%20EconomyReport_Final_Dec2011.pdf.

UNEP. 2013. *The Emissions Gap Report 2013: A UNEP Synthesis Report*. Geneva: United Nations Environment Programme. Accessed September 1, 2015. http://www.unep.org/pdf/UNEPEmissionsGapReport2013.pdf.

UNFCCC. 1992. "United Nations Framework Convention on Climate Change." Accessed September 1, 2015. http://unfccc.int/resource/docs/convkp/conveng.pdf.

UNFCCC. 1997. "Kyoto Protocol." Accessed September 1, 2015. http://unfccc.int/kyoto_protocol/items/2830.php.
UNITAID. n.d. "Innovative Financing." Accessed September 5, 2014. http://www.unitaid.eu/en/how/innovative-financing.
UN Millennium Project. 2005. "Investing in Development: A Practical Plan to Achieve the Millennium Development Goals." Accessed December 7, 2014. http://www.unmillenniumproject.org/documents/MainReportComplete-lowres.pdf.
USAID. 2014. "Budget." Accessed September 1, 2014. http://www.usaid.gov/results-and-data/budget-spending.
Velikaja, Natal'ja. 2013. "Global'naja Social-Demokratija kak vyzov vremeni." [Global Social Democracy as a Challenge]. In *Levoe izmerenie. Po stranicam Internet-zhurnala 'Socialist'* [Left Dimension. Pages of the Online Magazine 'Socialist'], edited by Vadim Belov, 76–84. Moscow: Kljuch-S.
Vermeulen, Sonja and Lorenzo Cotula. 2010. *Making the Most of Agricultural Investment: A Survey of Business Models that Provide Opportunities to Smallholders.* London/Rome/Bern: IIED/FAO/IFAD/SDC.
Vestergaard, Jakob and Robert Wade. 2013. "Protecting Power: How Western States Retain the Dominant Voice in the World Bank's Governance." *World Development* 46: 153–64.
Vigna, Paul and Michael J. Casey. 2015. The Age of Cryptocurrency: How Bitcoin and Digital Money Are Challenging the Global Economic Order. New York: St Martin's Press.
Voigt-Graf, Carmen. 2004. "Towards a Geography of Transnational Spaces: Indian Transnational Communities in Australia." *Global Networks* 4: 25–49.
Weber, Heloise. 2014. "When Goals Collide: Politics of the MDGs and the Post-2015 Sustainable Development Goals Agenda." *SAIS Review* 34 (2): 129–39.
Weber, Heloise. 2015. "Reproducing Inequalities through Development: The MDGs and the Politics of Method." *Globalizations* 12 (4): 660–76.
WEF. 2013. *The Global Gender Gap Report 2013.* Geneva: World Economic Forum.
WEF. 2014. *Global Risks 2014.* 9th Edition Geneva: World Economic Forum. Accessed September 2, 2015. http://www3.weforum.org/docs/WEF_GlobalRisks_Report_2014.pdf.
Weiss, Anja. 2005. "The Transnationalization of Social Inequality: Conceptualizing Social Positions on a World Scale." *Current Sociology* 53 (4): 707–28.
WHO. 2011. *World Report on Disability.* Geneva: World Health Organization.
Wikipedia. 2015a. "Bitcoin". Accessed September 2, 2015. http://en.wikipedia.org/wiki/Bitcoin.
Wikipedia. 2015b. "Ripple." Accessed September 2, 2015. https://en.wikipedia.org/wiki/Ripple_(payment_protocol).
Wilkinson, Richard and Kate Pickett. 2010. *The Spirit Level: Why Equality is Better for Everyone.* London: Penguin.
WIPO. 2007. "The 45 Adopted Recommendations under the WIPO Development Agenda". Accessed on September 15, 2015. http://www.wipo.int/ip-development/en/agenda/recommendations.html.

Wolford, Wendy, Santurnino M. Boras Jr., Ruth Hall, Ian Scoones and Ben White. 2013. "Governing Global Land Deals: The Role of the State in the Rush for Land." *Development and Change* 44 (2): 189–210.
Woo-Cumings, Meredith. 2003. *South Korean Anti-Americanism*. Working Paper No. 93, Japan Policy Research Institute, Korea.
Woods, Ngaire. 2000. "The Challenge of Good Governance for the IMF and the World Bank Themselves." *World Development* 28 (5): 823–41.
Wolf, Martin. 2004. *Why Globalization Works*. New Haven: Yale University Press.
World Bank. 1997. *Helping Countries Combat Corruption, The Role of the World Bank*. Washington DC: World Bank, Poverty Reduction and Economic Management.
World Bank. 2000a. *Anticorruption in Transition: A Contribution to the Policy Debate*. Washington DC: World Bank.
World Bank. 2000b. *Helping Countries Combat Corruption, Progress at the World Bank since 1997*. Washington DC: World Bank, Operational Core Services and Poverty Reduction and Economic Management
World Bank. 2009. *Water and Climate Change: Understanding the Risks and Making Climate Smart Investment Decisions*. Washington, DC: World Bank. Accessed September 1, 2015. http://documents.worldbank.org/curated/en/2009/11/11717870/water-climate-change-understanding-risks-making-climate-smart-investment-decisions.
World Bank. 2012. *Turn Down the Heat: Why a 4°C Warmer World Must Be Avoided*. Washington, DC: World Bank.
World Bank. 2015. "Charges for the Use of Intellectual Property, Receipts". Accessed September 15, 2015. http://data.worldbank.org/indicator/BX.GSR.ROYL.CD?order=wbapi_data_value_2012+wbapi_data_value&sort=desc.
WRM. 2014. "Open Letter to the Food and Agriculture Organization." Accessed September 1, 2015. http://wrm.org.uy/all-campaigns/open-letter-to-fao-on-the-occasion-of-the-international-day-of-forests-2014.
Yermack, David. 2013. *Is Bitcoin a Real Currency? An Economic Appraisal*. Working Paper 19747, Cambridge, MA: National Bureau of Economic Research.
Yunus, Muhammad. 2007. *Creating a World without Poverty: Social Business and the Future of Capitalism*. New York: Public Affairs Press.
Zarlenga, Stephen A. 2002. *The Lost Science of Money: The Mythology of Money – The Story of Power*. New York: American Monetary Institute.
Zhou, Xiaochua (周小川). 2009. 关于改革国际货币体系的思考 [Thoughts on Reforming the International Monetary System]. Accessed September 2, 2015. http://www.pbc.gov.cn/publish/hanglingdao/2950/2010/20100914193900497315048/20100914193900497315048_.html.
Zürn, Michael. 1998. *Regieren jenseits des Nationalstaates: Denationalisierung und Globalisierung als Chance* [Governing beyond the Nation-State De-Nationalization and Globalization as Chance]. Frankfurt am Main: Suhrkamp.
Zürn, Michael. 2002. "Zu den Merkmalen Postnationaler Politik [On the Features of Post-National Politics]." In *Regieren in Internationalen Institutionen: Festschrift für Beate Kohler-Koch* [Governing in International Institutions: Festschrift for Beate Kohler-Koch], edited by Markus Jachtenfuchs and Michèle Knodt, 215–34. Opladen: Leske & Budrich.

Index

350.org, 134

aboriginal groups. *See* indigenous peoples
academics. *See* research
Access to Knowledge (A2K), 98
accountability, 57, 60, 87, 94, 102, 143, 148, 149
action research, 2, 4, 12, 15, 51, 58, 139
activism. *See* social movements
affect, 46, 48, 50, 68
Afghanistan, 127
Africa, 3, 7, 13, 19, 25, 28, 32, 34, 36–38, 41, 65, 87, 113, 115–18, 127, 146, 148
African Union (AU), 32
age, 1, 3–5
agriculture, 11, 12, 14, 19, 27, 36, 37, 39, 43, 109–22, 134–36, 141
aid. *See* development cooperation
air ticket tax, 91, 92
Alliance for a Green Revolution in Africa (AGRA), 37
alternative currency, 6, 41, 148, 149. *See also* digital currency; money
alternative development, 10, 32, 49, 50, 111, 118–22, 135, 136, 138. *See also* development
Antarctica, 128

anti-corruption. *See* corruption
Anti-Counterfeiting Trade Agreement (ACTA), 13, 93–95, 99–105
anti-globalization movement (AGM), 1, 6, 7, 11, 13, 21
Arctic, 128
Argentina, 59
Asia, 3, 19, 27, 38, 39, 61, 113, 116, 130, 146
ATTAC, 86
Australia, 1, 19
Azerbaijan, 66

bancor, 72
Bank for International Settlements (BIS), 77
banking. *See* finance
Barbados, 47
Basic Income Earth Network, 146
Berne Convention, 98
Bhutan, 133
biofuels, 110–14, 116, 117, 135
Bitcoin, 71, 72, 76, 78–80, 82, 148, 149. *See also* digital currency
Black Economic Empowerment (BEE), 12
Bolivia, 24, 133, 136, 147
Brazil, 5, 12, 42, 59, 81, 97, 104–6, 116, 134, 138

Bretton Woods Conference, 72
BRICS (Brazil, Russia, India, China, South Africa), 12–14, 42, 114, 146, 149
Britain. *See* United Kingdom
buen vivir, 136, 137
Building Global Democracy (BGD), vii, 2–4
Burundi, 37, 127
business, 27, 32, 35, 37, 39, 41, 44, 47, 48, 51, 60–62, 64–68, 82, 88, 93, 95, 97, 98, 100, 105, 107, 109, 110, 115–18, 125–27, 131, 132, 135–37, 142–44, 147, 149.
  See also global companies
Byzantium, 33

Cambodia, 127
Canada, 1, 44, 130, 147
capitalism, 1, 6–11, 17–22, 27, 28, 31, 32, 33–35, 41, 42, 46, 50, 58, 59–63, 65, 66, 68, 69, 94–96, 97–99, 101, 112, 115, 119, 121, 127, 129, 131–34, 136–38, 140, 141, 147
Caribbean, 1, 3, 10, 34, 36, 43–55, 147
Caribbean Community (CARICOM), 53, 54
caste, 5
Catalonia, 34, 39
Centre for the Study of Governance Innovation (GovInn), vii
Chad, 127
children, 41
China, 1, 12, 13, 17, 19, 25, 28, 35, 40–42, 47, 74, 80, 81, 114, 129, 138
Christianity, 20, 33
citizens, citizenship, 3, 14, 15, 23, 47, 49, 52, 54, 55, 87, 95, 102, 106, 107, 120, 140, 142, 148, 149
civil society, 4, 13, 22, 50, 54, 57, 58, 60, 63, 64, 69, 82, 85, 125, 139, 143, 146, 149.
  See also nongovernmental organizations; social movements

class, 3–7, 10, 12, 13, 18, 20, 21, 24, 26–29, 33, 38–41, 43, 47, 49, 51, 52, 59, 65, 66, 68, 69, 114, 126, 132, 138, 147
Clean Development Mechanism (CDM), 113, 127, 130, 131, 135
climate change, 1, 4, 9, 11, 25, 85–91, 93, 112, 113, 125–39, 141, 146, 147
climate debt, 133, 137, 146
climate justice, 13, 14, 117, 125, 127, 132–35, 137, 138
Climate Smart Agriculture (CSA), 127, 130, 131, 135
Climate Vulnerability Forum, 129
Cold War, 38, 62
collective action, 87, 139–43, 145, 148, 149
collectivism, 8, 28
colonialism, 9, 26, 28, 33–35, 40, 43, 44, 49, 54, 110, 112.
  See also imperialism
commodification. *See* capitalism
communism, 18–22, 62
conformism, 9, 10, 31
Continuous Linked Settlement Bank (CLS), 89–92
copyright. *See* intellectual property
country (as domain of social relations), 5–8, 11, 15, 17–29, 31, 36, 38–42, 45, 48, 49, 52, 53, 74, 75
core-periphery. *See* North-South relations
corporate social responsibility, 22, 27, 91.
  See also philanthropy
corporation. *See* business
corruption, 4, 9, 11, 38, 57–69, 139, 141, 147
Council of Europe, 60
Creative Commons, 102, 106
Crusades, 33
Cuba, 37
culture, 2–5, 18, 23, 24, 26, 45, 47, 49, 53, 62, 65, 93–95, 97, 99, 100, 103, 104, 106, 111, 135, 138, 147
currency transaction levy (CTL), 9, 10, 25, 85–92, 141, 147, 148

debt, 6, 39, 44, 46, 48, 73, 77, 115, 146.
    See also climate debt; finance
de-globalization. *See* delinkage
delinkage, 11, 26, 40, 41, 42, 135, 137, 138
democracy, 2–4, 6, 10, 11, 13, 22–24, 28, 38, 43, 49–51, 53, 54, 58, 69, 71–73, 75–79, 81–83, 94, 100, 102, 104, 105, 107, 109–11, 120, 121, 127, 132, 134, 138, 140, 147, 148.
    See also global democracy
Denmark, 125, 140
developed countries. *See* global north
developing countries. *See* global south
development, 14, 22, 25, 26, 31–33, 36, 37, 39, 40, 43, 45–47, 50, 58, 63, 73, 85, 88, 98, 99, 101, 109–23, 125, 127, 131–33, 135, 137, 141, 146, 147.
    See also alternative development; sustainable development
development cooperation, 6, 26, 40, 44, 46, 73, 86–88, 113, 117, 126, 130
diaspora, 9, 10, 43, 45–55, 141, 147.
    See also migration
digital currency, 72, 76, 78–83, 148, 149
digital divide, 94, 99, 102, 104
digital economy. *See* Internet
disability, 5
disciplines (academic), vii, 3, 4, 52.
    See also research
discourse, 14, 49, 62, 65, 103, 104, 132, 134, 141
distribution, 1–4, 6–15, 17, 18, 21, 24–28, 31, 32, 40, 43, 44, 45, 49, 58, 63, 69, 71–73, 75, 79, 83, 106, 110–12, 116, 125, 138–42, 145–49.
    See also inequality
diversity, vii, 1, 3, 4, 43, 49–51, 111, 136, 139, 147
Dominican Republic, 53–55

East African Community (EAC), 37
ecology, 2, 6, 11, 12, 20, 22, 25, 26, 31, 37, 38, 44, 88, 109–15, 118–22, 127, 130–38, 146, 147.
    See also climate change; environmental movements; sustainable development
Economic Partnership Agreement (EPA), 36, 37
Economics, 3, 9, 32, 38, 39, 51, 73, 74, 76, 89, 119
eco-socialism, 134, 138.
    See also socialism
Ecuador, 136, 147
education, 2, 3, 25, 27, 45, 50, 54, 69, 119, 137, 138
efficiency, 7, 9, 14, 43, 68, 72, 75–79, 81, 85, 86, 141–43, 147
elites. *See* class
emerging markets/powers, 78, 81, 138.
    See also BRICS
employment. *See* labour conditions
enclosures, 33, 110, 112, 114, 116, 117
England, 33–35, 38, 39, 112.
    See also United Kingdom
environment. *See* ecology
environmental movements, 13, 116, 125–27, 133, 135, 137.
    See also ecology; eco-socialism
epistemology. *See* knowledge
equality. *See* inequality
equity. *See* justice
Ethiopia, 117, 127
ethnicity. *See* race
euro, 8, 72–74, 77, 89
Eurocentrism, 33, 58, 59, 62, 65, 68
Europe, 3, 7, 13, 17, 19–24, 33–38, 42, 43, 54, 61, 65, 69, 73, 86, 93, 112, 116, 146–48
European Union (EU), vii, 12, 18, 20, 21, 36–39, 60, 73, 82, 86, 89, 93, 94, 113, 117, 146
extractivism, 134, 136

fair trade, 6, 86, 141
faith, 3, 5, 13, 18, 33, 50.
    See also Christianity; Islam; Judaism
family, 7, 44, 50, 51, 132, 133, 138
feminism, 52.
    See also gender; women

finance, financial markets, 1, 2, 4, 6, 10, 15, 27, 32–36, 39, 46–48, 51, 61, 62, 69, 71–75, 78, 79, 81, 82, 85–93, 103, 112, 115, 118, 130, 134, 139–41, 147–49.
  See also currency transaction levy; financial crisis
financial crisis, 9, 19, 21, 38, 39, 61, 65, 74, 77, 86, 88, 110, 112, 115, 140, 149
financial transaction tax (FTT), 86
Focus on the Global South, 135
Food and Agriculture Organization (FAO), 25, 114, 118, 130
food security, 37, 88, 109, 110, 112–15, 117–19, 122
food sovereignty, 9, 11, 14, 93, 109, 111, 118–23, 134, 135, 137, 141, 147
Ford Foundation, vii
foreign direct investment (FDI), 2, 13, 25, 32, 36–40, 44, 46–49, 67, 141, 145.
  See also global companies; investment
foundations. See philanthropy
France, 23, 34, 91, 92, 122
Friends of the Earth (FOE), 114

gender, 1, 3–7, 10, 41, 43, 52, 111, 132.
  See also men; women
geopolitics, 38
Germany, 1, 22, 88, 113, 116
Ghana, 38, 40
Gini coefficient, 5, 7, 15
global (as domain of social relations), 1–3, 5–8, 11, 17–19, 21–24, 38, 39, 41, 52, 74, 89, 109, 142, 143, 146, 149
global city, 45
global companies, 12, 27, 35, 37, 63, 65, 96, 97, 103, 107, 112, 131, 132, 143.
  See also business; foreign direct investment

Global Congress on Intellectual Property in the Public Interest, 105
global democracy, 2–4, 12, 15, 23, 24, 43, 58, 71, 75, 86, 92, 123, 147, 148
global financial crisis (GFC). See financial crisis
global governance, 2, 8, 9, 11, 14, 18, 24–28, 36, 44, 46, 47, 50, 67, 71, 75–77, 80, 82, 83, 86, 87, 90–92, 94, 96, 97, 107, 110, 114, 115, 118, 122, 125, 132, 135, 139, 142, 143, 145, 148, 149
global justice. See justice
Global Justice Ecology Project, 137
global money, 2, 9, 10, 25, 34, 71–83, 141, 147, 148.
  See also money
global north, 4, 32, 33, 44, 47, 51, 58, 62, 63, 77, 87, 91, 94, 98, 100, 101, 104, 106, 113, 116, 117, 127, 130, 131, 134, 137, 147.
  See also North-South relations
global public goods, 10, 74, 75, 85–92, 141
global social democracy, 7, 10, 17, 18, 20–29, 141, 146.
  See also global third way; social democracy
global south, 6, 10, 32, 33, 36–38, 40–42, 51, 58, 59, 61, 62, 69, 72, 73, 77, 85, 90, 94, 97–101, 104, 106, 110, 113–15, 117, 126, 129, 130, 133, 134, 137, 138, 146, 147.
  See also North-South relations
global taxes, 9, 25, 26, 31.
  See also air ticket tax; currency transaction levy; taxation
global third way, 17, 21–23, 28
global value chain, 36–40, 42
global warming. See climate change
globalization, 1, 5, 10, 17–22, 24, 28, 36, 37, 39, 40, 58, 86, 90, 92, 132
Google, 100, 105
good governance, 57, 60, 147.

governance, 1, 4, 8–14, 18, 20, 23, 26, 32, 38, 40, 44, 49, 58, 71–73, 75, 78–83, 87, 94, 95, 97, 100, 101, 105–7, 116, 119, 121, 126, 127, 130, 132, 135, 139–45, 148, 149.
  See also global governance; local government; regional governance; state
government. *See* state
Gramscianism, 66
Greece, 1, 21, 140
greenhouse gas (GHG), 113, 117, 125–28, 130, 133, 134.
  See also climate change
Greenland, 128
Grenada, 45, 47, 54
Group of Eight (G8), 86
Group of Seven (G7), 12
growth, 1, 10, 12, 14, 31, 37, 38, 42, 46, 117, 133, 135, 136, 138, 140, 142
Guyana, 45, 47, 54

Haiti, 46, 53–55
health, 2, 6, 8, 9, 13, 26, 32, 36, 44, 69, 85–87, 90–92, 98, 126, 129, 135
hegemony, 39, 40, 42, 45, 66, 72, 104, 111, 132
history, 5, 7, 15, 19, 21, 25, 31–35, 38, 41, 43, 44, 54, 62, 66, 74, 87, 95, 98, 107, 110, 112, 123, 133, 136, 142
Hong Kong, 35, 38
human rights, 13, 51, 53, 94, 111, 117, 121, 132, 137, 146, 147
humanitarianism, 15, 20, 26

ideology, vii, 3, 4, 14, 39, 40, 42, 58, 64, 66, 67, 103
imperialism, 10, 13, 27, 33–35, 38–42.
  See also colonialism
India, 12, 35, 42, 47, 73, 81, 97, 114, 129, 138
indigenous peoples, 5, 13, 24, 34, 54, 102, 106, 110, 112, 114, 127, 128, 131, 135–37, 147

individualism, 7, 8, 10, 14, 95, 96
Indonesia, 39, 82, 116
industry, industrialization, 19, 20, 25, 26, 33, 36, 38–40, 67, 110, 115, 118, 119, 128, 134, 137, 145
industrialized countries. *See* global north
inequality, vii, 1, 2, 4–8, 10, 13, 17, 19, 20, 22, 24–28, 31, 35, 40, 43, 44, 49, 52, 53, 58, 72, 73, 79, 81, 85, 93, 98, 99, 106, 109–11, 114, 115, 119, 121, 123, 126, 127, 134, 140–42, 146
injustice. *See* justice
intellectual property (IP), 8, 10, 25, 86, 93–107, 141, 147.
  See also Creative Commons
Intergovernmental Panel on Climate Change (IPCC), 126–28, 130
International Energy Agency (IEA), 128
International Institute for Environment and Development (IIED), 114
International Monetary Fund (IMF), 13, 39, 40, 44, 57, 59–61, 66, 74, 76, 77, 81, 135
international organization. *See* global governance, regional governance
International Organization for Migration (IOM), 47
international public goods. *See* global public goods
International Rivers, 130
Internet, 1, 2, 9, 14, 48–55, 78, 79, 81, 93, 94, 99–102, 104–7, 139, 140, 147
intersectionality, 5–6, 43
investment, 4, 9, 31, 32, 36, 38, 46, 47, 50, 51, 81, 109, 111–13, 115–18, 132–34, 139, 141, 145, 146, 148, 149.
  See also capitalism; finance; foreign direct investment
Ireland, 33
Islam, 33, 64, 65
Italy, 21, 34, 140

Jamaica, 44–47, 51
Japan, 39, 42, 73, 98, 112, 130
Judaism, 33
justice, 1, 3, 4, 6, 9–14, 20–22, 25, 28, 31, 43, 49–52, 54, 57, 59, 65–69, 71–73, 75–78, 81, 83, 106, 107, 109, 111, 118, 121, 127, 131, 132, 134, 137–41, 146, 147.
    See also climate justice
Justice and Development Party (AKP), 64, 65

Kenya, 37, 112
knowledge, vii, 4, 18, 47, 49, 51, 53, 93–103, 106, 107, 123, 137, 138, 141, 147
Knowledge Ecology International, 99
Korea, People's Republic of (North), 37
Korea, Republic of (South), 38, 39, 112
kwacha, 8
Kyoto Protocol, 129, 130

labour conditions, 8, 13, 19, 20, 22, 44, 64, 67–69, 74, 134, 141
labour movement, 6, 13, 20, 21, 69
land, 4, 32, 33, 69, 114–16, 119, 121, 134, 135, 139, 141, 147
land grabs, 11, 109, 110, 112–19, 122, 146
language, vii, 3, 19, 54
Laos, 127
Latin America, 3, 19, 28, 62, 63, 117, 136
law. See governance
least/less developed countries. See global south
legitimacy, 58, 59, 63, 65–68, 91, 100, 104, 145
liberalism, liberalization, 8, 19, 22, 27, 58, 62, 64, 66, 98, 135.
    See also neo-liberalism
Litecoin (LTC), 80, 82
local (as domain of social relations), 8, 11, 18, 19, 38, 41, 42, 49, 52, 53, 63, 69, 110, 113, 114, 118–20, 122, 131, 133, 135–37, 141, 143, 147–49
local government, 14
low-income countries (LICs). See global south

Madagascar, 113
Malaysia, 24, 39, 133
maldistribution. See distribution
Mali, 127
Marco Civil da Internet, 104
marginalization, 3, 4, 11, 13, 43, 49, 53, 99, 106, 148
markets, market forces, 8, 9, 14, 19, 20, 27, 35, 39, 41, 43, 45, 47–49, 59–61, 63, 64, 67–69, 78, 91, 105, 112, 119, 120, 126, 127, 130, 135, 138, 141–43, 147–49
Marxism, 20, 33, 40
media, 2, 12, 27, 54, 94, 123, 138, 147.
    See also social media
men, 41, 51, 121.
    See also gender
Mexico, 94, 98, 101, 104, 105
Micronesia, 133
Middle East, 3
migrants, migration, 1, 2, 4, 8, 9, 17–19, 26–29, 41, 44–47, 139
military affairs, 9, 35, 88
Millennium Development Goals (MDGs), 113
modernity, modernization, 18, 19, 23, 62, 96, 110, 113
money, 4, 8, 33, 35, 40, 41, 45, 46, 65, 71, 73–75, 80, 82, 83, 139, 141, 147–49.
    See also alternative currency; digital currency; global money
Morocco, 94
Mozambique, 116
multilateralism. See global governance
multistakeholder. See stakeholder
multitude, 13
music, 45, 95, 96
Muslims. See Islam

narrative. *See* discourse
NASA (National Aeronautics and Space Administration), 126
nation, nationalism, 15, 23, 28, 39, 46, 48, 49, 52, 65
nation-state. *See* state
nature. *See* ecology
neo-liberalism, 6, 9, 14, 22, 43, 44, 48–50, 52, 53, 57–69, 110, 120, 132, 133, 135, 137, 141, 142, 147
Netherlands, 34
network, 45–47, 52, 78, 82, 100, 140, 142, 149
New International Economic Order (NIEO), 6, 7, 9, 11, 13
New Partnership for Africa's Development (NEPAD), 32
New Rules for Global Finance, viii
New Zealand, 1, 130, 147
Nigeria, 34
nongovernmental organizations (NGOs), 13, 36, 62, 69, 85, 86, 99, 118, 125, 127, 133, 135, 140–43.
 See also civil society; social movements
North America, 3, 19, 43, 54, 146, 147
North-South relations, 18, 25, 26, 28, 29, 35, 40, 44, 45, 59, 63, 72, 73, 76, 79, 105, 113, 116, 133, 134, 138, 145, 146, 149

Occupy, 1, 6, 7, 13, 140
official development assistance (ODA). *See* development cooperation
open source, 103
Organisation for Economic Cooperation and Development (OECD), 59, 60, 67, 135
Ottoman Empire, 33

Pacific, 3, 128
Paraguay, 133
peace, 13
peasantry, 13, 33, 37, 38, 110, 112–14, 118–21, 127, 128, 135, 137
periphery. *See* global south
Peru, 136

philanthropy, 9, 22, 37, 47, 64, 140, 141
Philippines, 129, 132
Poland, 63
political economy, 1–3, 7–9, 13, 17, 33, 38, 39, 42, 43, 68, 71, 74, 83, 94, 95, 97, 109, 110, 112, 119, 126, 135, 139
Portugal, 21, 34
pound sterling, 74, 77, 89
poverty, 1, 5–7, 9, 19, 20, 25, 26, 44, 64, 85, 87, 88, 90, 92, 110, 118, 119, 126, 129, 131–33, 137, 138, 146
precariat, 19
private sector. *See* business
privatization, 57, 59, 62–69, 135
Protect Intellectual Property Act (PIPA), 99
protests. *See* anti-globalization movement; Occupy; resistance; social movements

Qatar, 117

race, 1, 3–7, 10, 12, 24, 43, 47, 52, 132, 133
Rastafarian Co-operative Movement for Food Sufficiency, 122
redistribution. *See* distribution
Reducing Emissions from Deforestation and Forest Degradation (REDD), 127, 130, 131
reform, reformism, 3, 9–11, 20, 22, 25, 31, 63, 72, 76–78, 81, 83, 102, 105, 117, 139, 141
refugees, 129.
 See also migrants
regime. *See* governance
region (as domain of social relations), vii, 1, 3, 4, 11, 21, 36, 38–55, 76, 81, 113, 126, 145, 146
regional governance, 11, 14, 21, 24, 25, 27, 36, 53, 64, 89, 142, 145, 146
regulation. *See* governance
religion. *See* faith
remittances, 10, 46, 48, 50, 51, 141
renminbi (RMB), 74, 80

research, researchers, 13, 21, 36, 48, 52, 54, 74, 85, 86, 90, 93, 96, 99, 105, 112, 114, 118–20, 122, 126, 128, 130, 139, 143.
  See also action research; disciplines (academic)
resistance, 4, 6, 11, 13, 14, 21, 27, 31, 32, 35, 38–41, 68, 69, 114, 116, 117, 132, 137, 138.
  See also social movements
risk, 75–77, 79, 80, 83, 91
Robin Hood Tax, 86
rules. *See* governance
rupee, 73
Russia, 1, 3, 12, 17, 19, 20, 22, 24, 42, 59, 62, 63, 81, 82, 130
Rwanda, 37

Saint Vincent and the Grenadines, 45, 54
Saudi Arabia, 66, 117
Scotland, 39
Senegal, 34, 38
sexuality, 4, 5, 10, 43, 52
Sierra Leone, 34
Singapore, 24, 32, 35, 38, 98
slavery, 33–36, 43, 54, 115
Slovakia, 5
smallholders. *See* peasantry
social capital, 22
social democracy, 6, 7, 15, 17, 20–24, 26–29.
  See also global social democracy
social media, 14, 52, 53, 94, 104, 105.
  See also media
social movements, 4, 13, 14, 21, 24, 57, 83, 93, 94, 103–6, 116, 121, 122, 127, 132, 133, 135, 137, 140, 146.
  See also civil society; environmental movements; food sovereignty; nongovernmental organizations
socialism, 17, 18, 20–24, 27, 61.
  See also eco-socialism
solidarity, 6, 15, 28, 51, 111, 119
South Africa, 1, 4, 5, 12, 19, 24, 42, 105, 138

sovereignty, 39, 40, 91, 92, 109, 120, 143.
  See also food sovereignty
Soviet Union, 19, 22
Spain, 21, 23, 34, 140
Special Drawing Right (SDR), 71, 72, 76–78, 81, 83
Sri Lanka, 133
stakeholder, 107, 109, 139, 140, 142, 145, 148
state, 11, 14, 18, 20, 22–25, 27, 38–41, 43–53, 55, 57, 59–66, 68, 69, 78, 80–82, 85–92, 95, 97, 102, 104–6, 110, 111, 113, 115, 116, 118, 120, 121, 125, 128, 131–33, 135, 137, 138, 142, 143, 147–49
Stop Online Piracy Act (SOPA), 93–95, 99, 101, 103–5
structure, 5, 6, 9–11, 13, 15, 27, 31, 38, 40, 44, 49, 52, 86, 93, 95, 119, 121, 123, 137, 139–42, 144–46, 149
Structural Redistribution for Global Democracy (SRGD), 3, 4, 12, 109
sustainable development, 14, 22, 37, 114, 137, 138, 146–48.
  See also ecology
Sustainable Development Goals (SDGs), 85, 91, 113, 146
Sweden, 1, 5, 34

Taiwan, 38
Tanzania, 37, 38
taxation, 8, 9, 47, 60, 86, 87, 90, 144.
  See also global taxes
technology, 14, 18, 25, 36, 37, 50, 78, 93, 97–99, 102, 105, 106, 118, 126, 130, 134, 137, 138, 143, 144, 149; in Foucauldian sense, 46
terrorism, 27–29
Thailand, 1, 39
Third World. *See* global south
Tobin tax, 9
trade, 2, 6, 9, 14, 18, 19, 32, 34–37, 41, 44, 47–49, 60, 61, 64, 69, 71–73, 75, 77, 78, 81, 90, 94, 97, 98,

101, 103, 105, 115, 116, 118, 122, 132, 135, 136.
  See also fair trade
trade unions. *See* labour movement
Trade-Related Aspects of Intellectual Property Rights, Agreement on (TRIPS), 97, 102
transformation, transformism, 3, 9–11, 21, 31, 48, 49, 59, 60, 63, 66, 83, 111, 112, 116, 120, 121, 126, 127, 131–33, 136–39, 141, 147, 148
transnational corporations. *See* foreign direct investment; global companies
transnational relations, 45, 46, 50–53, 55, 93, 105, 114, 116, 117, 122, 138
Trans-Pacific Partnership (TPP), 97, 99, 100, 102–104, 107
transparency, 32, 57, 60, 61, 66, 67, 90, 94, 100, 104, 122, 141, 148
Transparency International, 62, 69
transscalarity, 11, 42, 52, 58, 122, 140, 142, 144, 149
transterritoriality, 46
Trinidad and Tobago, 44, 48, 51, 54
Turkey, 1, 59, 62, 64–67, 140

Uganda, 37, 40
Ukraine, 24
United Arab Emirates (UAE), 112
United Kingdom (UK), 22, 39, 43, 44, 86, 115
United Nations (UN), 36, 47, 60, 90–92, 109, 117, 121, 122, 125, 126, 128, 131
United Nations Conference on Trade and Development (UNCTAD), 114
United Nations Development Programme (UNDP), 126
United Nations Environment Programme (UNEP), 126
United Nations Framework Convention on Climate Change (UNFCCC), 113, 125, 126, 128, 129, 131, 133, 137, 138

United States of America (USA), 5, 12, 19, 23, 24, 34, 35, 38, 39, 42, 60, 61, 72–74, 82, 86, 88, 93–100, 102–7, 112, 127, 130, 133, 147
United States dollar (USD), 72–77, 89
Universal Negro Improvement Association, 52
universities. *See* research
urban, urbanization, 5, 109, 111, 118

Venezuela, 59, 133
La Vía Campesina, 13, 111, 118–22, 135
Vietnam, 82
violence, 6, 41, 42, 44, 54, 60, 114, 117, 121, 132.
  See also war

war, 2, 18, 20, 33–35, 38, 138
water, 37, 69, 88, 119, 126, 129, 136
wealth, 1, 5–8, 12, 25, 27, 28, 31, 32, 86, 114, 115, 127, 138, 140, 146
welfare state. *See* social democracy
West, Western, 5, 17–22, 24, 25, 27, 28, 32–35, 38, 40–42, 58, 62, 83, 94, 95, 97, 138
Wikipedia, 93, 103
women, 4, 13, 41, 44, 50, 51, 54, 121, 128, 133, 137.
  See also gender
World Bank, 40, 57, 59, 60, 62, 69, 77, 98, 109, 112, 118, 126, 135
World Economic Forum (WEF), 91, 140
World Health Organization (WHO), 25, 92
World Intellectual Property Organization (WIPO), 97, 99, 105
World Social Forum (WSF), 12, 91, 134
World Trade Organization (WTO), 12–13, 32, 40, 97, 122, 135

yen, 72, 74, 77, 89
youth, 5, 13, 54, 133, 134.
  See also age

Zambia, 38
Zimbabwe, 1

List of Contributors

Pınar Bedirhanoğlu is Associate Professor in the Department of International Relations at Middle East Technical University in Ankara, Turkey. She got her PhD in International Relations from the University of Sussex. She has published in English and Turkish and also has articles translated into German and French, on neo-liberal state restructuring; state–capital relations and privatizations in Turkey; the political economy of corruption and neo-liberal anti-corruption policies; the politics of capitalist transformation in Russia; and the 2008 financial crisis. Her most recent research addresses the neo-liberal transformation of state security structures and critique of financialization.

Valentina Fedotova is Professor, Principal Research Scientist, and head of the programme 'Social Philosophy and Development of Civil Society in Russia' at the Institute of Philosophy, Russian Academy of Sciences, Moscow. She has also held visiting positions in the United States, Germany, China, and Turkey. Her research interests focus on modernization, global capitalism, democracy, and political culture. Her twelve monographs include *Modernization: From Equality to Freedom* (co-author, 1995); *Modernization of the 'Other' Europe* (1997); *Anarchy and Order* (Nauka, 2000); *Good Society* (2005); and *Global Capitalism: Three Great Transformations. Socio-Philosophical Analysis of Relations between Economy and Society* (co-author, 2008), *Modernization and Culture* (2015); and *Academic-Postacademic Sciences Relations as a Social Problem* (2015).

Lorenzo Fioramonti is Professor of Political Economy at the University of Pretoria (South Africa), where he directs the Centre for the Study of Governance Innovation. He holds the only Jean Monnet Chair in Africa as well as the UNESCO-UNU Chair in Regional Integration, Migration, and Free

Movement of People. He is Senior Fellow at the Centre for Social Investment, University of Heidelberg and at the Hertie School of Governance, and Associate Fellow at the United Nations University. His research covers alternative economic paradigms, governance of the commons, global political innovations, and new forms of supranational regionalism. His most recent books are *How Numbers Rule the World: The Use and Abuse of Statistics in Global Politics* (2014) and *Gross Domestic Problem: The Politics behind the World's Most Powerful Number* (2013).

Dorothy Grace Guerrero is a freelance author, analyst and consultant oriented to a transformative and system-change perspective with over twenty-five years experience in activism, research, and development work. She previously coordinated the Climate and Environmental Justice Programme at Focus on the Global South in Bangkok. She has published on climate justice, China and emerging economies/BRICS, deglobalization, transnational corporate capture, Asian regionalism and impacts of ASEAN investments on natural resources and local livelihoods, and democratization in Korea. She co-edited the volume *China's New Role in Africa and the South*. Originally from the Philippines, she is now based in London.

Blayne Haggart is an Assistant Professor of Political Science at Brock University in St. Catharines, Canada. He holds a PhD in Political Science from Carleton University. He has also worked as a journalist and as an economist with the Canadian Library of Parliament, serving on various parliamentary committees. His current work focuses on copyright politics, knowledge governance, and the long-term viability of online social movements. His book, *Copyfight: The Global Politics of Digital Copyright Reform*, was published in 2014.

Nina Hall is a Post-Doctoral Fellow at the Hertie School of Governance in Berlin. She researches performance and effectiveness of international organizations and has a forthcoming book on *How Migration, Refugee and Development Organizations Respond to Climate Change*. Her research on global governance been published in the *Australian Journal of Political Science*, *Global Governance* and *Global Environmental Politics*. Nina has also worked with the World Economic Forum on effective leadership of multilateral institutions and with the New Zealand Ministry of Foreign Affairs and Trade, UNICEF Nepal, and the United Nations Department of Political Affairs in New York. She completed her doctorate in International Relations at the University of Oxford.

Huang Mendang is a graduate student in theoretical economics at Tsinghua University in Beijing. She has been involved in several research projects, which mainly focus on the financial and monetary system in China. After graduation, she will join an investment bank as an adviser to Chinese companies on mergers and acquisitions.

Inge Kaul is Adjunct Professor at the Hertie School of Governance, Berlin, and former Director of the Offices of the Human Development Report and Development Studies of the United Nations Development Programme (UNDP) in New York. She has published widely on issues of global governance and the financing of international cooperation and is the lead editor of *Providing Global Public Goods: Managing Globalization* and *The New Public Finance: Responding to Global Challenges* (2003 and 2006) and co-author of the *Governance Report 2013* (2013). Her current research focuses on global public policy and economics.

Liu Taoxiong is Professor of Economics in the School of Social Sciences at Tsinghua University and Executive Director of the Center for Strategy and Policy Study. He received his PhD from Tsinghua University. His research covers monetary theory, economics of growth, and political economy. He has authored three books and dozens of articles in both Chinese and English, including in influential Chinese journals such as *China Economic Quarterly, Strategy and Management* and *Comparative Economic & Social Systems*. He has worked at Tohoku University in Japan and Harvard University in the United States as a visiting professor. He has also served as policy adviser for several cities in China.

Beverley Mullings is Associate Professor of Geography at Queen's University, Canada. Her research covers feminist political economy and urban studies, addressing questions of social transformation, neo-liberalism, and the politics of gender, race, and class in the Caribbean and its diaspora. Her articles have appeared in *Annals of the Association of American Geographers*; *Gender, Place & Culture*; *Journal of Economic Geography*; *Antipode*; *Review of International Political Economy*; and *Small Axe*. Her current research examines the relationship between diaspora and development within neo-liberal modes of governance, with a particular interest to explore how complex circuits of Caribbean individuals, families, and communities might be engaged to challenge ethno-racial, gender and class inequalities.

Alfred G. Nhema is a Senior Lecturer in the Department of Political and Administrative Studies at the University of Zimbabwe. He has also taught at universities in Canada and the United States. He has served on a number of international advisory boards and has also worked at senior levels in the NGO sector. His publications include *Democracy in Zimbabwe: From Liberation to*

Liberalization (2002); *The Quest for Peace in Africa: Transformation, Democracy and Public Policy* (editor, 2004); and *Managing and Resolving African Conflicts* (co-editor, 2 volumes, 2008).

Jan Aart Scholte is Faculty Professor in Peace and Development at the University of Gothenburg. Previously, he held appointments at the University of Sussex, the Institute of Social Studies, and the University of Warwick. His research covers globalization, global governance, civil society in global politics, and global democracy. His publications include *Globalization: A Critical Introduction* (2005), *Building Global Democracy? Civil Society and Accountable Global Governance* (editor, 2011), and 'Reinventing Global Democracy', *European Journal of International Relations* (2014). He is a former lead editor for the journal *Global Governance* and lead convener of the Building Global Democracy programme. He works with many movements and policymakers on changing global governance.

Yash Tandon is former Executive Director of the South Centre, an intergovernmental think tank for developing countries based in Geneva, and Founding Director of the Southern and Eastern African Trade Information and Negotiations Institute (SEATINI), an African regional NGO. He has a long career in national and international development and independence struggles as a policymaker, activist, professor, and public intellectual. Yash has degrees in economics and international relations from the London School of Economics and has taught at Makerere University, Uganda, University of Dar-es-Salaam, Tanzania, the LSE in the United Kingdom, and Columbia University in the United States. He is currently undertaking research on alternative development theories and war and violence.

Alissa Trotz is Associate Professor of Women and Gender Studies and Caribbean Studies at New College, University of Toronto. She is also Associate Faculty at the Dame Nita Barrow Institute of Gender and Development Studies, University of the West Indies (Barbados). Her published work addresses such topics as Caribbean migration and diaspora; the gendered politics of neo-liberalism, social reproduction, and women's activism; and transnational feminism and the Caribbean. Her current research interests include transnational call centres in the Caribbean and history, memory and violence in colonial and contemporary Guyana. She edits a weekly newspaper column, 'In the Diaspora', in the *Stabroek News*, Guyana.

Heloise Weber is Senior Lecturer in International Relations and Development Studies at the School of Political Science and International Studies, University of Queensland, Australia. She has published widely on the global politics of development, inequalities, and poverty reduction strategies, as well as on theoretical and methodological concerns in the global politics of development. She is the co-editor (with M.T. Berger) of *Recognition and Redistribution: Beyond International Development* (2013) and editor of *Politics of Development* (2014). She is co-author (with M.T. Berger) of *Rethinking the Third World: International Development and World Politics* (2014). She is currently working on a book about the global politics of microcredit and poverty.